What's News:
The Media
in American Society

WHAT'S NEWS:
THE MEDIA
IN AMERICAN SOCIETY

Elie Abel, *Editor*
Robert L. Bartley
George Comstock
Edward Jay Epstein
William A. Henry III
John L. Hulteng
Theodore Peterson
Ithiel de Sola Pool
William E. Porter
Michael Jay Robinson
James N. Rosse
Benno C. Schmidt, Jr.

Institute for Contemporary Studies
San Francisco, California

Inquiries, book orders, and catalog requests should be addressed to the Institute for Contemporary Studies, Suite 811, 260 California Street, San Francisco, California 94111—415—398—3010.

Library of Congress Catalog Number 81—81414
Cloth available through Transaction Books, Rutgers—The State University, New Brunswick, NJ 08903

Library of Congress Cataloging in Publication Data
Main entry under title:

WHAT'S NEWS.

    Includes bibliographical references and index.
    1. Press—Uninted States—Addresses, essays,
    lectures. 2. Mass media—United States—Addresses.
    essays, lectures. 1. Abel, Elie.
    PN4867.W49   302.2'3   81-81414
    ISBN 0—917616—41—3   AACR2
    ISBN 0—81855—448—3 (Transaction Books)

CONTENTS

CONTRIBUTORS

ELIE ABEL
Harry and Norman Chandler Professor of Communication,
Stanford University

ROBERT L. BARTLEY
Editor, The Wall Street Journal

GEORGE COMSTOCK
S. I. Newhouse Professor in Public Communications,
Syracuse University

EDWARD JAY EPSTEIN
President, E. J. E. Publications, Ltd.

WILLIAM A. HENRY III
Associate Editor, Time

JOHN L. HULTENG
Professor of Communication, Stanford University

THEODORE PETERSON
Professor of Journalism, University of Illinois

ITHIEL de SOLA POOL
Arthur and Ruth Sloan Professor of Political Science,
Director, Research Program on Communications Policy,
Massachusetts Institute of Technology

WILLIAM E. PORTER
Professor and Chairman, Department of Journalism,
University of Chicago

MICHAEL JAY ROBINSON
Research Professor, Director, Media Analysis Project,
George Washington University

JAMES N. ROSSE
Professor of Economics, Associate Dean of Humanities and
Sciences, Stanford University

BENNO C. SCHMIDT, JR.
Professor of Law, Columbia University

PREFACE

For much of American history the mass media have been the center of controversy—from the days of yellow newspaper journalism in the latter part of the last century to Vice-President Agnew's attack on the media a decade ago. But while controversy has been unrelenting over the years, its nature has changed a great deal since the advent of the electronic media—radio and television.

Electronic media have brought with them a greatly increased ability to influence people, so it was natural that concerns would arise about how that increased influence was being used. Such concerns reached their peak when critics such as Agnew charged that the media were undermining the war effort in Vietnam. It was a period when divisions in the country ran deep, and accusations of ideological bias were commonly directed against the media.

The highly charged, adversary climate has calmed considerably since the end of the 1960s, but important issues remain unsettled about the role and influence of the media in American society. These issues exist, however, within limits set by our strong tradition of a free press, backed by the First Amendment to the U.S. Constitution. This tradition against governmental interference places the concern about issues and the burden of reform on the media themselves or on other private, nongovernmental institutions.

Developing plans for a study of the mass media, we decided it was important to find an editor who had experience both as a working journalist and as an academic, and that contributors to the study also come as much as possible from both worlds. For this purpose, no one was better qualified than Elie Abel, a former *New York Times* reporter and NBC television correspondent before becoming Dean of the Graduate School of Journalism at Columbia University. He is now a full-time academic, teaching communications at Stanford University.

The book includes a broad range of media authorities and commentators and makes it clear that many in the media are very much concerned with how the media wield their very considerable influence.

H. Monroe Browne
President
Institute for Contemporary Studies

San Francisco, California
June 1981

I

Introduction

1

ELIE ABEL

The First Word

**Radio, television, and print media. News coverage in
Europe and the United States. Economic factors. The
use of segmentation. Government regulation of broadcasting. The electronic future in information systems.
A lack of perspective.**

The media, to begin with, are plural. Television is a medium,
singular. So is radio, the newspaper, the magazine, the motion picture. Looked at together, as in the chapters that
follow, they are the media, plural.[1] A trifling point, some will
say, but it is made without apology. To understand media, we
need to differentiate their separate structures and their
effects upon individuals and society in the mass.

W. Phillips Davison, the Columbia University sociologist,
sought to delineate certain of these differences in an offhand

remark some years ago. "Radio," Davison said, "is the *alert-ing* medium. It tends to be the first medium that tells us something noteworthy has happened, although the account will be sketchy. Television is the *involving* medium. It engages the emotions more completely than the others. Print is the *informing* medium. It alone is capable of handling complexity."

Davison's set of distinctions is useful, though not, of course, exhaustive. Nor does it apply with equal force in all countries. In much of Europe, for example, radio does not shrink from complexity, and television producers frequently filter out or dilute action film that might startle or alarm the audience.

But we are concerned in this volume with the United States media and, as Theodore Peterson points out in the lead essay, our media are distinctively American, products of American soil and climate.

MEDIA CHARACTERISTICS IN THE UNITED STATES

Certain characteristics of our media that set them apart from those of many other countries can be readily identified: ours are private —not state —enterprises, operated for prof-it. Both print and electronic media, in fact, are highly profit-able by present-day corporate standards. Unlike other mass production industries, they give away their product, or sell it for less than the cost of production. It is through the sale of advertising that they earn their profits. Pay TV, an industry still in its infancy, could set a new pattern. For those who can afford the asking price, it offers motion pictures on the home screen, free of commercial interruptions. The potential is there for a new medium that will offer high-culture and other special-interest programs to fairly affluent specialized audiences. The key to other successful media is the tactical shrewdness of their managers in assembling audiences for sale to the advertiser by designing a product that will appeal to particular segments of the population. These may be defined by geography (newspapers, city magazines, local TV stations) or by shared special interests (*Car and Driver* magazine, for example, or the *Atlantic* or *Rolling Stone*, each with its special constituency). Much the same process of segmentation is seen in the proliferation of some 7,000 radio stations across the land which offer country and Western music, rock, jazz, soul, or classical formats—and, less commonly, all-news—in accordance with the tastes and interests of particular ethnic, age, and income groups. It would seem that American media consumers increasingly define themselves as belonging to this or that special segment of the population, instead of sharing the broader attitudes and interests of the larger community. This process of segmentation, skillfully exploited, led to the emergence of literally hundreds of successful special-interest magazines at a time when broad-spectrum publications such as *Life, Look,* and the *Saturday Evening Post* were forced (chiefly by the competition of TV for national advertising) to cut their losses and suspend publication. Television had proved to be a more cost-effective means of reaching a heterogeneous national audience with consumer advertising. The marketplace of ideas, in short, must accommodate itself to the economic forces of the market.

The crucial distinction between the United States and many other countries, so far as the print media are concerned, has to do with the political/philosophical climate in which they operate. It is marked by the total absence here of government control, licensing, or regulation. We have no Official Secrets Act, as in Britain, no statutory Right of Correction, as in France, no state news agency or government newspapers, as in the Soviet Union. It is only a slight exaggeration to describe publishing as the only branch of Ameri can industry or commerce that is guaranteed by the Constitution a sturdy immunity from government interference. Although the First Amendment guarantee is less than explicit ("Congress shall make no law abridging ... the freedom of speech or of the press"), the federal government has—with rare exceptions—taken a hands-off attitude toward the industry, respecting above all its immunity against interference in the editorial process. Broadcasting, on the other hand, continues to be regulated by the Federal Communications Commission, originally for technical reasons of spectrum scarcity, now thoroughly obsolete. The awkward fact that most American cities have fewer newspapers than broadcasting stations is ignored by the rulemakers.[2] From time to time, broadcasters have campaigned for an end of regulation on the ground that the First Amendment ought to apply equally to all information technologies, electronic no less than print. It is a sleeping issue for the moment, but one that is likely to draw more attention in the next several years as the Reagan administration presses its drive to eliminate—or at least reduce—excessive federal regulation in other fields.

THE IMPACT OF TELEVISION

Whatever the outcome, the debate is bound to be complicated by the advent of new communication technologies just over the horizon (they are discussed by Ithiel de Sola Pool in his chapter). We are told, for example, that before long newspapers will be delivered to our homes electronically, rather than being hurled in the general direction of the front walk by a boy on a bicycle. If the electronic newspaper is not yet an operating reality, an intermediate development—the delivery of news and advertising on the home TV screen, along with entertainment guides and other consumer information prepared by a newspaper staff—is already being tested in Coral Gables, Florida.

The clear, sharp line separating print from electronic technologies can be expected to blur as home information systems are introduced on a commercial scale. If and when newspapers routinely distribute their product through an electronic technology, their exclusive claim to First Amendment protections could become moot. Free expression in the United States would, I believe, be better served by an unambiguous determination that electronic media (which could not have been foreseen by the drafters of the Bill of Rights) are fully entitled to the same protections enjoyed by newspapers, magazines, and books. The public interest is not advanced by perpetuating the fiction that spectrum scarcity exists, demanding in turn the regulation of broadcast content; nor by turning a blind eye to the fact that a majority of Americans today, for better or worse, depend primarily upon the electronic media to keep them informed, a function the press alone performed in pre-electronic times.

I do not argue that television can ever supplant the printed word in dealing with complicated issues, foreign or domestic. TV remains, in the words of Felix Rohatyn, "a very difficult medium for a politician [seeking] to explain a very complicated problem to lots of people." Without the work of the newspapers, Rohatyn contends, New York City would have gone bankrupt in the late 1970s. To understand the city's plight, one had to look at the numbers—and TV is not at its best in dealing with numbers. Nor (as William A. Henry III suggests) is TV as we know it the ideal medium for presenting the day's events in historical perspective. "We are assaulted by facts and events which are presented as though they had no real connection to the facts of yesterday and the day before," according to Hodding Carter, assistant secretary of state for public affairs in the Jimmy Carter administration. (His comment, incidentally, was directed at all media.)

Americans, nevertheless, appear to be transfixed by television. A. C. Nielsen Company estimates that children in the age group from two to eleven spend thirty-one hours watching TV in an average winter week. (See George Comstock's chapter for the implications of such findings as these.) We blame television for the decline in reading skills among our children and for the surging rate of violent crime. Yet popular attitudes toward the medium are decidedly ambiguous. To some, among them members of the so-called Moral Majority, the industry represents a monstrous power center—reaching into every home—that must be curbed, reformed, or or somehow purified. Intellectuals have all along sniffed at TV for catering to the lowest common denominator of public taste. Yet *TV Guide* has far and away the largest circulation of any magazine published in the United States, an interesting example of synergism between one medium and another.

PROBLEMS FOR DISCUSSION

We have chosen to address in this book a number of media issues that continue to perplex many Americans in this troubled time—such issues as the role of the marketplace in shaping our media, for example; how they came to depend so heavily upon advertising revenues; their obligations toward the community; the effects of chain ownership; why the family-owned newspaper is vanishing from the American scene; how the proliferation of new communication technologies may be changing our society; why the press does not do a better job of reporting economic and business news; how it is that most presidential candidates come off like buffoons on television; whether, in the computer age, the individual's right to privacy is endangered; monopoly aspects of publishing and broadcasting.

All of these questions, and a great many more we cannot enumerate here, led the Institute for Contemporary Studies to commission this book. We have called upon a distinguished group of scholars and journalists to contribute the essays that follow. If the product of our collaborative effort does not settle many barroom arguments, we hope it will help to clear away certain popular misconceptions and to stimulate informed discussion about the media's role in American society.

II

Background and History

2

THEODORE PETERSON

Mass Media and Their Environments: A Journey into the Past

The early American press. Demography, democracy, education, and industry. The advertising business. Technological changes. Audience action and reaction. Standardization, expansion, and ownership. Media responsibility.

In 1895, when magazines were turning from an elite to a mass audience, the editor of the *Independent*, a major Protestant weekly, took up his pen to deplore the change. What, he wondered, would happen to such highly regarded magazines as *Century* and *Harper's* which, speaking quietly to genteel readers, were among the leaders in publishing? They could not enlarge their constituencies beyond the educated class that appreciated them. "The fit audience in an educated country like ours is not few, but it is not yet unlimited; nevertheless it is the only audience worth addressing, for it contains the thinking people," he wrote. "The rest may or may not be sturdy citizens, may count in the militia and the population and the lower schools; but they are not the ones who delight to seek the instruction they most need."

He had good cause to worry, for the world he knew was vanishing. Change was everywhere in the last two decades of the nineteenth century, as the nation tipped from an agricultural economy to an industrial one; as factories sprang up to produce goods not just for their own regions but for the entire nation; as inventors devised one new marvel after another; as railroads, which had long since equaled all the rest of the world in track mileage, continued to push their lines across the land; as ship after ship set down its load of immigrants to help swell the populations of already growing cities.

Besides altering the American landscape, those changes were bringing into being today's mammoth, omnipresent system of mass communications. In the 1890s book publishers, feeling pressures from the banks and investment trusts to which they had turned for capital, were casting off their leisurely, gentlemanly ways of doing business and beginning to manufacture products for markets. By 1890 the editorial staffs of the large metropolitan dailies had evolved from the one-man operations of a half-century earlier into the large, specialized ones of today. In the early 1890s S. S. McClure, Frank Munsey, and Cyrus Curtis reinvented the magazine, which had been around since 1741, and sold it to the expanding but previously neglected middle class. By charging the reader far less than production costs, by filling magazines with stories and articles appealing to popular

tastes, they amassed the huge national audiences that advertisers paid handsomely to reach. In 1895, in the basement of
a Paris café, the two Lumières showed the first motion picture to a paying audience and thus foreshadowed the Hollywood film industry which, at its peak, drew 90 million Americans into theaters every week and spread its version of the
American way of life around the globe. In 1896 Marconi applied for a British patent on his wireless; a decade later, from
Massachusetts, R. A. Fessenden sent out the first radio
broadcast of voices and music and demonstrated the ultimate feasibility of the broadcast industry.

From its beginnings, the press of America has been influenced by the soil and the climate of the land in which it
has had its roots. On the one hand, it has been shaped by the
social and economic conditions of American life—by the
nature of the economy; by the state of invention, technology,
and manufacture; by the size, geographic distribution, and
demographic characteristics of the population. On the other
hand, it has been shaped by ideas—by society's beliefs in the
nature of man, the nature of society, the nature of the relationship of man to government, the nature of knowledge and
truth. In brief, the American press has been conditioned by
the way Americans live and think.

The first printing press arrived in Boston, along with a
band of Puritans fleeing England, in 1638. Its use was conditioned by its milieu. It at once was put to printing a freeman's
oath that set forth the conditions of citizenship, an almanac,
and a book of hymns. The output of the few presses that soon
followed was heavy on theological works and sermons, on
government laws and proclamations. The press then was an
instrument of religion and government. The authorities controlling it had small interest in using it to print creative
literature and *belles lettres*. The colonial newspapers appeared first in seaports which, as centers of population,
trade, politics, culture, and news, had the conditions to nur-
ture them. Their early publishers were often postmasters,

who were likely to hold the prevailing ideas of the ruling groups, who might easily be removed from their appointive positions if they offended, who were well placed to keep abreast of what was going on, and who might pick up additional revenue from public printing.

The press was no less affected by the profound changes that touched virtually all aspects of American life after the Civil War. Those changes revolutionized the media, much as they made possible the birth and growth of the automobile industry by providing the technology, the manufacturing techniques, the raw materials, and the expanding market for Fords and Chevrolets. Under their impact, the press was transformed from a personal craft of relatively easy access to an impersonal industry of restricted entry. The press became a mass-production, market-oriented industry, and it adopted the techniques and took on the characteristics of other mass-production industries.

Let us look at some of the forces that revolutionized American life in the latter years of the nineteenth century and see how they affected the media. Although they were interrelated, let us take them up singly for the sake of clarity and convenience.

POST–CIVIL WAR CHANGE AND INDUSTRIALIZATION

One force having an impact on the nation and on the media was the growth in sheer numbers of people, who comprised the markets for the media themselves and for the goods and services their advertisers sold. For every person in the nation in 1790, there were about nineteen in 1900. Between 1870 and 1900 alone, swollen by 11.5 million immigrants, the population almost doubled—to 76.1 million. Where those people lived was important to the media, and increasingly that came to be in the cities. When federal census-takers took count in 1790, just five towns had populations of more than 8,000—Boston, New York, Philadelphia, Baltimore, and Charleston—and together they accounted for about 135,000 people. But the growth of just one of those towns illustrates what was happening throughout the nation as a trickle of immigrants swelled to a tide and as factories attracted workers to their benches. The population of Boston grew from about 15,000 in 1750 to nearly 25,000 in 1800, nearly 137,000 in 1850, and nearly 561,000 in 1900. So it was elsewhere. Chicago had a population of around 300,000 when the great fire of 1871 made 90,000 of its people homeless. By 1890, when the movement to the suburbs had already begun, the population was 1 million. Urbanization intensified in the last two decades of the nineteenth century. The number of centers with populations of more than 8,000 doubled, as did their total population. Some 40 percent of the nation's people were no longer counted as living in rural areas by 1900.

Two other influences on the development of the media were the spread of popular democracy and the spread of free public education. The spread of democracy, by eroding class distinctions, helped to create the great middle class whose tastes, interests, and demands the media have assiduously cultivated. Even after the American Revolution, some states allowed only adult property owners or taxpayers to vote and set high property requirements for officeholders. When the Constitution was drafted, only an estimated six out of every hundred males were entitled to the ballot; by the mid-1900s most white adult males could vote without owning property. But eliminating such barriers to the franchise as race, sex, religion, literacy tests, and the poll tax was a struggle that lasted well into the second half of the present century.

Along with the movements for a universal franchise were movements for free universal education. In the early 1830s some states began to organize systems of free public schools. Massachusetts installed the first state board of education in

1839; fifteen years later it passed the first law making school attendance compulsory. Eighteen other states had similar laws by 1880. Meanwhile, the courts had held that general taxes could be levied to support public high schools as well as elementary schools and state colleges. The number of high schools jumped from fewer than 800 in 1870 to 5,500 twenty years later, when nearly three out of every four American children were attending school. Despite the huge influx of immigrants, illiteracy declined from 17 percent of the population in 1800 to 13 percent in 1900.

But it was the industrial and technological revolution, gaining momentum after mid-century and bursting forth in the 1880s and 1890s, that perhaps had the greatest direct impact on the press. Although artisans had carried on most of their manufacture in shop and household and their markets had been mainly local, by 1850 the farmer had begun to feel a challenge to his supremacy in the nation's economy. He would nevertheless remain the greatest source of the nation's wealth for the next three decades or so. The value of manufactured products, however, increased sixfold between mid-century and the century's close, and in 1900 it was double that of agriculture. Industrialization had become supreme.

Underlying that shift in economic balance was the practical application of a long list of inventions and discoveries. Underlying it, too, was the introduction of mass production and the growth of the factory system. When Eli Whitney took on a large government order for muskets in 1800, he met it by using standardized interchangeable parts. The technique was refined and extended in the latter half of the century to the manufacture of such diverse items as clocks, typewriters, and farm machinery. Henry Ford extended it even further in the early twentieth century by introducing the assembly line.

In that burst of industrialization, old industries expanded and new industries were born. All of them reached out for raw materials and converted them into a profusion of products, not only for their neighbors but for buyers anywhere. For the market had changed. It was no longer just a specific locality, but individuals scattered across the land. The people were there now, and a web of railroad lines could carry the goods to them. Boring as statistics may be, a few will dramatize what was taking place. Between 1850 and 1910 the average manufacturing plant increased its capital more than thirty-nine times, its work force nearly seven times, the value of its output nineteen times. The number of industries of all types jumped from 140,000 in 1860 to 250,000 in 1880; between then and 1900 it more than doubled again. The labor force engaged in nonagricultural work went up from 41 percent in 1860 to 50 percent in 1880 to 62 percent in 1900. Between 1880 and 1890 steel and cement production increased eightfold, coal and pig iron production quadrupled, and petroleum output more than doubled. Mileage of railroad track increased by about 170 percent. Bank deposits quadrupled, and the national wealth doubled.

THE PRESS AND THE ADVERTISER: A DEMOCRACY OF CONSUMPTION

With the adolescence of mass production, modern advertising was born. From something that the press merely accepted, advertising came to pay all of the medium's bills—or at least a large share of them. The media have not always treated advertising with the reverence they do today. One nineteenth-century advertising agent had to importune a publisher to reveal the circulation of his magazine. Reluctantly, furtively, the publisher scribbled a number on a scrap of paper and handed it to the agent.

The new mass-production industries found advertising an almost necessary marketing tool, especially as they tried to imprint the brand names of their merchandise on the

public's consciousness. Signs, handbills, notices in local
newspapers were no longer adequate after markets had been
transformed from contained areas into widely scattered
populations. Some means was needed to carry messages
about products—old ones expanding their markets, new
ones seeking acceptance—to potential customers wherever
they might be. The magazine emerged as the first national
advertising medium. More than 150 companies were advertising some 2,500 products nationally by 1897. Department
stores, which flourished in the last three quarters of the century, and other retail outlets stepped up their local advertising to bring in customers, and newspapers were the beneficiaries. Periodicals and newspapers took in $39 million in ad-
vertising revenues in 1880, perhaps double the amount of a
decade earlier. The amount had grown to $71 million by
1900.

When the press courted and won the patronage of the advertiser, it became different from other industries in an important way. It became the only industry that normally gives
away its wares or sells them for less than production costs.
Financial support underwent a fundamental shift as the
press became an adjunct of the marketing system. Newspapers and magazines, instead of drawing their revenues
largely from readers, subsidies, or both, relied chiefly on the
advertiser. The subscription charge became essentially a fee
to qualify the reader for the advertiser's interest. Radio and
television, coming along after the new form of support was
well established, dispensed with even the qualifying fee.
Almost from the start, their major product has been an audience that advertisers want to speak to. (In radio's infancy,
though, David Sarnoff thought revenues would come from
the sale of sets. Even one advertising trade magazine
editorially recoiled from the prospect of advertising's con-
taminating the airwaves.) Books continued to depend on
readers for their revenue. Eventually the bulk of them
became brightly packaged, short-lived consumer goods,

marketed much like other convenience items. Movies, too, relied on audience support.

The accelerated industrialization also affected the advertising business, which had been dominated after the Civil War by brokers who bought large blocks of space in newspapers and magazines, then sold them in smaller pieces to advertisers for whatever they could get. The numerous advertising agencies of the 1890s, however, undertook such functions as media selection, copy preparation, and even some rudimentary market analysis for their clients. Advertising men themselves, starting about that time, worked to gain social acceptance and to brighten their public image by insisting that they were professionals. They formed national professional organizations and local clubs, drew up codes of ethics, tried to lay down a base of scientific principles of advertising, and strove to get their formal programs of advertising education into schools and colleges. As the population flowed westward, Chicago emerged as a major advertising center; its renaissance after the great fire had given the city an aggressive commercial spirit. One trade magazine estimated that just before World War I between 60 and 70 percent of all national advertising campaigns originated there. One writer credited Chicago's agencies with placing 45 percent of all advertising carried by the nation's magazines.

Just as universal suffrage was seen as the means to political democracy, advertising came to be seen as the means to a democracy of consumption. In the eyes of its practitioners at the turn of the century, advertising could help to spread the bounty that the factories were turning out, could help to bring all classes of people the "right methods of living." *Agricultural Advertising* thus extolled the egalitarianism of advertising in 1912: "Advertising is no respecter of persons; it is the great leveler of class distinctions—the one platform on which we may truly say 'all men are created equal.'" Because advertising helped to make mass production possible by facilitating consumption, its champions regarded it as having a key role in the economy. To the media was ascribed the task of servicing the economic system by promoting the sale of goods and services.

To understand the mass media today, it is essential to understand that nineteenth-century legacy of the press. The significant point is that, as a result of it, the press took on the characteristics of the other mass-production industries its advertising served. It took advantage of new technology in gathering its raw materials and in manufacturing its final product. It specialized and standardized the tasks of its workers. It standardized not only the steps in the manufacture of its product, but also the product itself. By doing so, it was about to turn out, with great efficiency, a low-cost product that found ready acceptance in the mass market. Like many other industries, it underwent consolidation and concentration of ownership.

ADVANCES IN PRODUCTION AND COMMUNICATION

Throughout the nineteenth century newspapers were gradually adopting the division of labor techniques that were a part of mass production. When James Gordon Bennett started his *New York Herald* in 1835, he arose at 5:00 A.M., scribbled some copy before breakfast, worked on business affairs in the morning, spent the afternoon gathering news, and returned in the evening to his office (where he dealt with customers over a desk made of two barrels with planks on top). When Lincoln Steffens reported on the industry in 1897, he could tick off the budgets for the various departments of a large daily—$290,000 for local news, $220,000 for editorial and literary matter, $180,000 for illustration, $125,000 for correspondents, $410,500 for mechanical production, and so on. By then, when the *New York World* had

1,300 employees, today's organization of a newspaper was fairly well set. There were people to supervise the editorial, business, and mechanical departments. There were people to gather, write, and process the news and features in their various categories.

The other media today depend on a similar division of labor. The magazines that one picks up at the supermarket are the result of the specialized labors of editors, writers, copy-checkers, a graphic designer, production coordinators, advertising salesmen, printers, circulation managers, and distributors. The images that one sees on the TV picture tube are the result of a system involving independent packagers, producers, directors, writers, performers, cameramen, engineers, editors, composers, arrangers, and musicians. The editor of a magazine of multimillion circulation once remarked to a friend that his staff was so large and so compartmentalized that he had no significant influence on content unless a subject particularly interested him.

By enabling the media to conquer time and distance, to reach wide audiences swiftly and often instantaneously, the wonders of technology have given stunning speed and efficiency to the mass media. One new development after another during the nineteenth century narrowed the time span between event and reader and pushed back limitations on the reach of the press. Domestic news in the early century moved at the pace of a man or horse; news from England was thirty-six days away by sailing ship. The telegraph after the 1840s sped transmission of domestic news. The steamboat made England two weeks closer at first, then three weeks, and the transatlantic cable after the Civil War joined England to New York. The telephone, the teletype, the wirephoto all shortened transmission time. For the broadcast media of the twentieth century, electronics completely eliminated space and time. Wars, revolutions, assassinations, presidential inaugurations, football games, and horse races could all take place in the family living room.

Technological advances also heightened the speed and capacity of production. Mechanical typesetting largely did away with the need for hand compositors, of whom the *New York World* employed 210 before the linotype came along. The steam press that replaced the hand press could turn out 2,000 copies an hour; the electrically driven rotary press increased that capacity tenfold. Photoengraving supplanted wood or copper engravings, painstakingly etched by hand, sometimes in several parts by several craftsmen. Color printing put an end to such expedients as employing 150 women to tint illustrations by hand, as done by *Godey's Lady's Book*. In recent years, electronics have made even the high-speed letterpress outmoded. The linotype has been replaced by phototypesetting and computer composition, video display terminals and optical character recognition. The letterpress itself has been pushed aside by offset printing. Some dailies in traffic-clogged urban centers have set up satellite printing plants to speed distribution. Many magazines also have turned to automated composition and gravure printing.

Without those technological improvements in production, the print media would never have been able to reach the vast audiences of today, for press capacity was a very real limitation. The broadcast media, from the birth of the networks, had the capability of becoming the most pervasive of the mass media. It is easy to forget how recently, in an historical sense, the media have made possible instantaneous nationwide communication. Only sixty years ago, in 1919, President Woodrow Wilson faced tremendous difficulties when he tried to rally public support for the League of Nations. For twenty-two days he journeyed by train through seventeen states in which he made forty formal speeches, only one with the aid of a public address system. Even so, he directly reached only a few thousand people. By contrast, a peak audience of 69.5 million persons watched the 1980 election returns on television.

All of that efficiency brought with it a countervailing

danger—that the media have become *too* efficient, that they dispense too much information and opinion too rapidly. For one thing, the fear is that they have preempted much of the discussion that people once carried on among themselves face to face. Somewhere in the media most people can find opinions and interpretations of events coinciding at least approximately with their own, and they generally suffice. People may still do some serious talking about public issues, but for the most part they seem to let the media do the discussing for them. And the opinions received by the media, some fear, are less likely to be held with meaning and strength than those reached as a result of face-to-face debate and sober judgment. For another thing, the media may churn out more information than the individual can absorb and respond to. The flood of words and pictures in the media may have what Paul Lazarsfeld and Robert Merton call a "narcotizing dysfunction." A conscientious citizen may learn from the media about some serious problem of the day, talk with friends about ways of resolving it, yet do nothing about it. He mistakes knowing about the problem for doing something about it. The *New Yorker* once put it this way in commenting on one of the starving Biafran children pictured in *Life*: "Unless we are stirred to action by his photograph, his expression of deprivation and hope will within a few weeks be buried beneath the weight of other news and other issues of *Life*. The real child, too, will probably be buried." No person in a complex society can hold thoughtfully developed opinions on all matters or act upon but a small fraction, of course. But some issues are so important that responsible citizens should be stirred to action regarding them.

STANDARDIZATION OF PRODUCT

Another feature of mass production that the media adopted was standardization of product. Today a newspaper editor or reporter transferring from an East Coast daily to a West Coast daily has no problem applying his peculiar skills, for newspapers across the United States are more alike than different in their techniques, format, content, and news values. One issue of a given magazine is much like every other, for once an editor has hit upon the editorial balance that pleases his readers, he changes it gradually or not at all. And the spin-off of television series is testimony to the inherent sameness of broadcast fare.

Efficiency demanded that the mass media, operating under time pressures, standardize their ways of gathering, writing, editing, and packaging their content. The drive for saturation of their markets compelled them to common denominators of content. They had to carry material that would interest and be understood by the vast majority of their audiences. For newspapers, the traditional inverted news form was efficient. It was easy to write, it could be chopped from the bottom to meet space needs, and it gave the reader the basic facts in a paragraph. The spare, objective news account evolved as much from commercial considerations as philosophical ones. The rise of press associations serving papers of disparate political complexions, the desire of newspapers to maximize readership—they dictated it. As Lincoln Steffens observed in 1897, "The commercial ideal contains distinct appreciation of the power of opinion, but it prizes just as highly the authoritative statement of all the news." Even the width of newspaper columns seemed forever determined by the amount of handset type that would not fly apart on a press. Today's advertising layouts and advertising rates are tied to standardized column widths.

Over the years a vastly increasing number of Americans used the products of the mass media, as they did other mass-produced goods. A few comparisons can help to stake out the changing dimensions of the media market. The largest daily newspaper in the United States in 1835 was the *New York Sun* with a circulatiion of 15,000. The largest in 1887 was the

New York World with a circulation of 250,000. In the late 1970s the *New York Daily News* was selling more than 1.6 million copies a day. The *Ladies' Home Journal,* after fifteen years under Edward Bok's editorship, in 1904 became the first magazine to hit the incredible circulation of a million. Today nearly sixty magazines have circulations of at least a million, and several have sales far beyond that; *TV Guide* and *Reader's Digest* both have more than 18 million. In 1980, according to one study, 94 percent of American adults read an average of 11.6 different magazine copies each month. Book sales have jumped sharply in the past half-century. Movies had moved by 1905 from the vaudeville stage, where they were just part of the bill, to small storefront theaters, where they especially attracted the working class and immigrants whose deficiencies in reading were no hindrance to their enjoyment. Weekly movie attendance leaped from 10 million in 1908 to a peak of 90 million in 1946–1948, after which it dropped drastically. Even so, movies still pulled a weekly audience of 20 million in the mid-1970s.

Along with a rising level of education, two developments in the twentieth century—especially after its mid-point—fostered extensive use of the media. One was a redistribution of income that, flattening extremes, gave enormous purchasing power to the great mass of Americans. What had once been luxuries—automobiles, air-conditioning, dishwashers—became necessities. What had once been pleasures of the wealthy—foreign travel, wine with dinner—fell within reach of the many. Another was an increase in leisure time as the work week shortened and as appliances lightened household chores. The twin themes of most specialized magazines born after World War II were, at bottom, how to spend one's disposable income and how to spend one's disposable leisure.

As those audiences were expanding, the base of media ownership was contracting. The concentrations of ownership and economic power that industrialization brought to other fields came to the mass media as well. Since another chapter in this book discusses the media baronies, a few sentences about the trend toward bigness and fewness seem sufficient. From their peak just before World War I, the numbers of newspapers and of cities with competing papers have steadily declined. As the number of chain newspapers has grown more than twentyfold, their share of total circulation has risen from 10 percent to more than 70 percent. Book publishing is dominated by a handful of giants and conditioned by the marketing needs of a few retail bookstore chains. Magazine publishing, although perhaps the media industry still most easy of entry, has become just one more target for conglomerates in recent years. Cable television systems, which promised diversity in broadcasting, have already become the property of a shrinking number of companies.

SOCIETY AND THE RESPONSIBILITY OF THE PRESS

But the communications system was shaped not just by inventions and technology, trade and commerce, population growth and urbanization. It was shaped as well by society's ideas of what the press should be and do. When the colonists came to America they brought from their homeland not only the models for their newspapers but also the government's methods of keeping the press under control. When they fought for freedom of the press, they invoked the arguments used back home. And when as Americans they drafted their Constitution, they drew heavily on British thinkers for their ideas of just what freedom of the press meant.

Their concept of press freedom, taking generously from the ideas of eighteenth-century Enlightenment, rested on the assumptions underlying the democratic form of government. Fundamental to their reasoning was a faith in natural rights, natural reason, and natural law. Put simply, their belief was this: Blessed with natural rights and natural reason, man had come into a harmonious universe, one governed in all its reaches by the unchanging laws of nature. Man voluntarily formed governments, the chief end of which was to protect and preserve his innate rights; hence, the ideal government was that which governed least. Because man desired to seek truth and because his reason empowered him to find it, man was capable not only of governing himself but also of discovering the immutable laws of nature and bringing his institutions into harmony with them.

In both self-government and discovery, the press became a powerful instrument, for it was a major carrier of information and a forum of ideas. But if the press were to serve man well, it had to be kept free from all outside control. History demonstrated that government was the perpetual enemy of freedom. Freedom of expression, then, meant freedom from government restraint. It was a negative liberty, as reflected in the negative cast to the First Amendment: "Congress shall make no law ... " It made no provision for the man without a press of his own. Nor did it provide means of opening the lips of those who chose to remain mute, for it assumed that men would speak if free to do so.

The theory invested great faith in the power of truth to emerge victorious in the free clash of ideas. It therefore gave the press a virtually unlimited freedom. The supreme safeguard was man's reason, but another was the laissez-faire marketplace. If some men chose to lie or distort, other men would find it profitable to expose them. If some elements of the press failed to serve the public, they would falter or die as citizens cast their votes with their coins. Prepublication censorship and government subsidy to the press were especially abhorrent, for each in its way would jam the delicate mechanism through which truth ultimately emerged.

As that theory evolved, the press became endowed with a special public purpose and trust. Society has charged it with a half-dozen special duties. One is contributing to the enlightenment that a free people need to govern themselves wisely. A second is to serve the political system by furnishing a wide range of information, discussion, and debate about public affairs. Another is to protect the rights of the individual by keeping a keen eye on government and by shouting a warning whenever those rights are in jeopardy. Since the press should be free from any influence that government subsidy might carry with it, another obligation is to earn its way in the marketplace. An accepted function from the earliest days has been to provide entertainment. And as we have seen, industrialization gave it a sixth one—to service the economic system by bringing together buyers and sellers of goods and services.

Although no other theory has replaced that one in practice, its basic assumptions have been seriously challenged. The discoveries of Darwin in evolution, of Einstein in relativity, have cast doubt not only on the doctrine of natural rights but on the static nature of the universe itself. The supremacy of reason was questioned by Marx, who contended that the material conditions of life shape man's ways of thinking, and by Freud, who saw man as motivated less by rational thought than by dark subconscious forces. A great deal of modern social psychology pictures man as viewing the world through a filter of rigid attitudes and stereotypes, as seeking out information and points of view that he agrees with while avoiding those that he disagrees with, and as acting largely in accord with peer norms. From the turn of the century onward, observer after observer has contended that a free marketplace of information and ideas does not exist, if indeed it ever did; they cite, among other things, the concentration of press ownership and network domination of broadcasting. And William Ernest Hocking, for one, has rejected the idea that truth will necessarily triumph in the constant clashing of ideas; with no umpire to pronounce victory or defeat, debate becomes merely inconclusive or endless.

In the mid-1940s the Commission on Freedom of the Press, chaired by Robert Maynard Hutchins, spent many months trying to find a prescription for a free and responsible press that was compatible with modern thought and the complexities of modern society. It sought ways to satisfy the public's need for information and opinion despite the presence of a concentrated, profit-motivated media system on the one hand and a powerful government on the other. The social responsibility theory that it came up with broke with the basic philosophical assumptions of classical liberalism. It saw freedom of expression as grounded in acceptance of moral duties rather than in natural rights, for instance; and stressing the positive rather than the negative aspects of liberty, it saw the government as promoter as well as protector of freedom. Although the report enraged the press generally, it did find sympathetic readers among some professionals and was instrumental in acquainting several generations of journalism students with the idea of social responsibility. But now, thirty-five years later, it is difficult to discern any direct effects that the commission had on the mass media.

In retrospect, perhaps its greatest importance was as a symbolic turning point in thinking about the media. It represented a common feeling that many institutions, the media among them, had failed to serve the best interests of society and that traditional liberalism was inadequate to promote the individual's goals. If only in sentiment, it foreshadowed or paralleled such features of the media landscape as laws for access to meetings and records, staff participation in editorial policy, newspaper ombudsmen, and surveillance of media performance by journalism reviews and citizens' groups. In some ways, it also foreshadowed current problems arising from interpretations of what the First Amendment really means, which Benno Schmidt discusses in a later chapter.

Here this chapter ends, but its story does not. The media will continue to be affected by their environments, although perhaps not as massively as when the editor of the *Independent* decried the headlong rush toward mass audience. Who the people are, where and how they live, what tools and resources they have and how they use them—all those things will help to fashion the media in the future as they have in the past. And so will how people think. What should be the role of government, what should be the relationship of press to government and of government to press, what should be the relationship of the press to the people it serves? How those perpetual questions are answered will also determine what the press will be.

3

JAMES N. ROSSE[1]

Mass Media:
The Economic Setting

The consumer costs of communication. "First copy" costs in print and broadcast media. Economies of scale. Public goods. Advertising, in print and on the air. Monopolistic competition, perfect competition, monopoly, and market segmentation. The FCC. The effect of economics on public policy.

The mass media include newspapers, television, radio, magazines, cable television, sound recordings, and motion pictures. Their defining characteristic is that each involves a single source producing messages that are received by many individuals.

The largest broadcast media industries are the daily newspapers and over-the-air television. In newspapers, an editor
selects and bundles together a group of messages into a
package, which is then reproduced and distributed to a mass
audience of readers. The principle is the same for television,
even though the package must be sequential, with only one
program transmitted at a time.

Most mass media carry a mix of paid (advertising) and unpaid (news, comment, entertainment) messages, with some
mass media specializing in one or the other. Billboards, for
instance, are an important paid medium, specializing in advertising. So are direct mail advertisers. Neither is a small
business; for instance, about half as many advertising dollars flow into direct mail as into *all* newspapers. Books and
movies are among the principal media specializing in unpaid
messages. However, the defining characteristic—a single
source with multiple recipients—also includes phonograph
records and tapes and videotapes as mass media.

The mass media are more diverse than the above comments suggest. For instance, subcategories of paperbacks,
hardcovers, and educational publications exist within books,
and each of these has many interesting subdivisions. Similar
subcategories and subdivisions could be identified in many of
the other media. Yet because of their broadcast nature, all
these industries share important economic features which
require special methods of analysis. This chapter will examine the distinctive economic attributes of the various
mass media industries and consider their implications for
public policy.

IMPORTANCE OF THE MEDIA

Mass media industries are not large relative to other sectors
of American business. If they were combined into a single en-

terprise, it would rank around sixth on the *Fortune* 500 list; its revenues would be smaller than the Ford Motor Company's and just larger than IBM's.

Of course, most of the mass media industries have a social importance far beyond their simple economic value—a fact widely recognized by scholars, critics, commentators, politicians, the courts, and the media themselves.

A less obvious fact is that conventional measures almost always understate their real economic importance. For instance, TV will probably have revenues of less than $10 billion this year, considerably less than 1 percent of the gross national product; revenues of the entire TV industry will probably be less than one-fifth those of General Motors. That comparison is deceptive, however, because it omits the expenses borne by viewers. Here I have in mind not only the cost of the receiver, but also the value of time spent watching television.

It is true that most consumer goods require a fair amount of time in their use, but the mass media are exceptional. For instance, a typical car owner may spend $6 to $8 in automotive services for every hour he spends using his car. Again, family vacations cost from $3 to $4 per hour per person. In contrast, the total direct cost of an hour's TV watching breaks down as follows: programming and transmission costs are between two and five cents, and it costs another two to four cents to own a television set. So the total direct cost of over-the-air television is between four and nine cents per hour. By far the most expensive input is the viewer's time. A less-flattering way of putting this is that TV advertisers not only buy an hour of your time for pennies, they also induce you to spend nearly as much to buy your set!

Television is the most dramatic example. The direct cost of newspapers is probably about fifty cents per hour of reading time; of paperback books, probably close to a dollar per hour; and of movies, slightly more. In short, conventional measures of economic importance understate the economic value of mass media products in comparison with other, more conventional products because mass media products typically require more investment of consumers' time than other products. Lest we take the point too seriously, however, it is important to note that the criterion used here would make the mattress industry the most important of all.

In considering the distinguishing features of mass media industries in general, the reader should keep in mind that traditionally (and for good reasons) newspapers and television are at the center of public concern. The contents of the other chapters in this volume attest to this fact, which is reinforced by our understanding of the important role these media play in our political and commercial life.

PUBLIC GOODS AND ECONOMIES OF SCALE

Mass media industries use technologies that have pronounced economies of scale which occur in two distinct processes, production and distribution.

The economies of scale in production are apparent. The cost of creating a message is independent of the number of times it is reproduced for consumption. In newspapers, this phenomenon is called the "first copy" cost. It covers acquiring and editing material, assembling advertising copy, typesetting, and creating printing plates. This cost must be incurred before even one copy of the paper can be produced, but it need not be repeated for subsequent copies. Any number of further copies can be made for the bare cost of reproduction.

Similarly, in television, the cost of creating a given program is independent of the number of viewers; once the commodity has been created, the cost of adding one more viewer is zero.

In distribution as well, economies of scale are common among mass media industries. The clearest example is television. From the standpoint of a broadcasting station, the cost of distributing the product to an additional viewer within the station's broadcasting area is zero.

In the case of newspapers, the phenomenon is present in a slightly more complicated form. In the first place, the cost of reproducing a copy of the paper—in addition to the phenomenon of first-copy cost discussed above—appears to decline as the number of copies increases. Secondly, if one were to hold constant the number of reproductions, the cost per unit of published space appears to decline as the quantity of published space increases. This phenomenon appears to be independent of whether the space published is advertising or nonadvertising copy. Finally, as the density of distribution increases in a circulation area, the cost of distribution per subscriber declines; this means that a single distribution system (or newspaper) can distribute its product to readers more cheaply than can two independent distributors serving the same market. Hence, there are substantial economies of scale in newspaper distribution.

Many of these costs of production and distribution are such that mass media products have important "public good" characteristics. (The term "public good" is used by economists to designate products where an increase of consumption creates no additional cost to the producer or to society. The message component of all mass media products has this property. For some, the distribution component also has elements of a public good.)

In the case of over-the-air television and radio, both the program content and its mode of transmission are public goods; in both cases, the technological cost of adding an additional viewer is zero. In the case of the print media, the content is a public good but it is embodied in the printed page; a private good is thus used to distribute and market the public good.[2]

Among the many consequences of this public good component in mass media products, two stand out as particularly
important. First is the growth of all types of networks. The
cost of transporting an already created message to a new
geographic area to increase its distribution is typically small
compared to the cost of creating that message anew. From
this fact follows the existence (although not the precise
form) of television networks, including both the "big three"
and the less well-known syndication services. From this fact
also flows the existence of news services such as AP and UPI,
newspaper syndication services, cable-TV "superstations"
distributed nationwide via satellite, and a worldwide motion
picture distribution system. Each of these networks takes advantage of the fact that media messages can be reused by
new audiences without incurring any new creation costs.

A second, although less evident, consequence is that the
"normal" economic rules for efficient pricing do not apply to
markets for mass media messages. This is a fact of fundamental importance in the public-policy analysis of media industries. In most industries, the public-good element of production is small or negligible, and setting prices equal to the
additional cost of producing the last unit of output normally
yields enough revenue to cover costs and yield a return to investors; thus, for most industries, a rule that asserts that
price should equal marginal cost is both possible and, usually,
desirable.

However, when an important fraction of an industry's
costs consists of a public-good component, marginal cost pricing will not make the industry profitable. The clearest example is broadcast television where the marginal cost of
adding a viewer is zero. If television stations were forced to
rely on selling their product to viewers at marginal cost, their
revenues would be zero.

The economist's usual efficiency rule thus creates a dilemma in mass media industries. If price is set equal to marginal
cost to induce efficient use, then the industry cannot cover

the costs of creating the content. On the other hand, if price is set larger than marginal cost so that the industry can at least break even, then the usual criterion of efficiency cannot be satisfied.

One possible answer to this dilemma is subsidy: price the product at marginal cost and make up the industry's deficit with a lump-sum transfer from government, foundation, or whatever. At least as a first approximation, this is the way in which we run our educational system. At one level, this "solution" does not answer the problem at all, since every subsidy imposes a cost somewhere else in the economy— typically, through taxes. More immediate to the case at hand, the idea of government subsidy is at odds with the historical desire for an independent mass communications system. Its only appreciable application in mass communication industries—and that a small one—is the Corporation for Public Broadcasting.

A second answer to the dilemma has been to permit monopolistic competition to exist.[3] This allows prices to exceed marginal cost by enough to permit the profitability needed for survival. This solution has the defect of denying the product to some consumers who would be willing to pay the cost of distributing the product to them, but who would be unwilling to pay the higher price needed to permit the producer to recover the costs of content creation as well. Those industries where the public-good problem is solved by this method—book publishing, sound recordings, and motion pictures—are marked by instability and low (on average) profitability. The recent development of cable and over-the-air subscription television (pay TV) is another example of this solution. Prices are set high enough to cover costs, and those prices ration the product to those who are willing to pay for it. It is too early to tell whether pay TV will be subject to the same kinds of instability that have marked book publishing, sound recordings, and motion pictures. Whatever the case, it seems likely that pay TV will greatly increase the variety television offers by making it possible to cater to specialized audiences. Just as small print runs of specialized books can be made profitable by charging higher prices, so pay TV opens up the possibility of making programs for much smaller audiences than at present, to be paid for directly rather than through advertising revenues. Note that advertising plays little or no role among these media.

A third response to the public-good pricing problem has been to transform the public good into a private good by relying on advertising as the main source of revenue. This strategy has enabled radio, television, magazines, and newspapers to survive.

ADVERTISING

Advertising mitigates the problems of marketing public goods by converting them into private goods. In over-the-air TV, for example, the program and its transmission are both public goods, but they can be thought of as being used to attract audiences. Audiences are then "private goods" to be sold to advertisers. Audiences are private goods since their attention for an interval of time, once sold and used, cannot be resold or reused.

This describes the basic way television markets operate, and it does not far miss the mark in the case of newspapers and magazines. In the latter cases, subscription charges do exist, but the price paid by the reader is far less than the reproduction and distribution cost of producing the paper or magazine; without advertising revenues, newspapers and magazines would be both smaller in volume and more expensive to purchase.

Over-the-air commercial TV and radio are wholly supported by advertising, of course. Daily newspapers generally receive about 60 to 80 percent of publishing revenue from the sale of advertising; commercial magazines, from almost zero to 100 percent, depending on the relative attractiveness of their audience to advertisers. Occasionally advertising finds its way into mass market paperback books, and some movie theaters earn significant advertising revenues.

The importance of advertising revenue fundamentally changes the nature of competition for most mass media industries. Broadcasters, newspapers, and the like do not compete for consumer dollars; they compete for consumer attention. The principal reason why daily newspapers are sold, for example, rather than given away, appears to be so that paid circulation can serve as evidence to advertisers that the newspaper's subscriber base consists of people who actually read the paper; free distribution often would be less costly than paid distribution. The growing commercial success of free weekly newspapers and "throwaway" shoppers suggests further the unimportance of circulation revenues. Similarly, magazines which depend on advertising often lose money on new subscribers when the cost of acquiring the subscription is counted. At the same time, magazine circulation audit rules restrict the number of issues that can be sent free after a subscription expires; otherwise, advertisers could not be sure that the product was being valued by all of the circulation that the publisher claimed.

Packaging a desirable audience to sell to advertisers is complex. Aside from developing an optimum editorial/ program package to attract desirable readers/viewers, the media firm must take into account the effects on readership/viewing of the advertising itself. In general, the view that consumers see advertising as an irritant appears valid for some but not all media. The irritant effect seems most powerful on television, perhaps because the timing of the advertising is outside viewers' control and because advertisements disrupt programs. In contrast, readers apparently value newspaper advertising; research has consistently found that increased advertising promotes circulation, other things being equal. This difference may stem from a higher information content in newspaper advertising or from the reader's ability to select which ads to read and when to read them.

PRODUCT DIFFERENTIATION AND MONOPOLISTIC COMPETITION

The combination of economies of scale and the importance of advertising revenue shapes the product development strategies of mass media firms. The economies-of-scale effect means that any given, homogeneous demand can be served more economically by one than by several suppliers. For multiple firms to prosper, they must serve different or segmented markets. An obvious and common form of market segmentation is geographic. Readers' interest in local news and advertising makes local rather than national newspapers the main daily American press, and all but the largest cities have only a single newspaper. Regional magazines (such as *Sunset* and *New York*) are a growing magazine specialty.

But differentiation can and does take place along other dimensions as well. Consumers have differing demands for information and entertainment; *Scientific American* and *Penthouse* are not substitutable. Similarly, in New York City, the *Times*, the *Daily News*, and the *Wall Street Journal* (no longer regarded as primarily a New York publication) have radically different editorial packages appealing to the respective tastes and interests of their various segmented audiences. Serial products (newspapers, magazines, and some television shows) can develop loyal audiences by developing a distinctive content mix.

The fact that advertising, too, is targeted at specific groups makes this possible. Broadly speaking, daily newspapers are more attractive vehicles for local advertising, while television and national magazines are more suited to national advertising; but finer distinctions are equally important. Magazines tend to seek a well-defined demographic profile in their readership so as to attract an advertising clientele interested in marketing to a particular age-income-education-sex-race-occupation group. It is not simply editorial content that differentiates the *New Yorker* from *Popular Mechanics*; the products advertised in them vary radically as well.

This strategy has been fairly successful for advertising-oriented media but has, until recently, been pursued only weakly by such sales-oriented media as books. Book publishers tended broadly to specialize in a market type (educational, popular trade, mass market, professional, etc.), but the unique nature of each title limited a publisher's ability to sell reliably to a definable group. This uniqueness, combined with the fact that publishers compete—at least, within their specialties—for most titles, simultaneously limits the forces leading to monopolization due to economies of scale.

In recent years, however, the entertainment book industry has begun to develop successful "serializing" strategies. The prime example is Harlequin Books, a once-small Canadian publisher that is now among the top five mass market paperback houses. Its strategy was to develop a highly standardized product—the 196-page romance, set in an "exotic" locale with a formula plot line, with little individuality among its authors. The success of this strategy is indicated by Harlequin's growth from obscurity to the $65 million mark in a decade and by the efforts of all major mass market houses to imitate it, either through direct competition (e.g., Pocket Books' Silhouette Romances and Fawcett's Coventry Romances) or through similar efforts with other types of books (e.g., Warner's Man of Action Books).

IMPLICATIONS FOR COMPETITION

In analyzing segmented markets, economists should employ models that are appropriate to differentiated rather than homogeneous products. Differentiated products are those among which purchasers can clearly distinguish brands in a way that is significant to them. Thus, wheat and sugar are undifferentiated products, while automobiles are highly differentiated. Mass media products are all differentiated, some of them highly so. The distinction almost always matters to the audience and to advertisers.

Where differentiated products are present, the economic theory appropriate to market analysis is that of monopolistic competition, which must be distinguished from the neoclassical theories of monopoly and perfect competition.[4]

The neoclassical theory of *perfect competition* assumes that each producer is small relative to the product market. With undifferentiated products, each firm thus takes the market price as given and unaffected by its own decisions. Similarly, the character of the product is taken as both given and the same for each firm.

In contrast, the theory of *monopolistic competition* begins with the presumption that each firm is large relative to the size of the markets for its products. In fact, each firm produces distinguishable products; so, in a limited sense at least, it can be said that markets are coextensive with the firm's products. Another way of saying this is that each firm has at least some pricing discretion because each product is unique in the minds of buyers. More important, competition between products occurs at the level of the firm rather than that of the industry; the constraint on an individual firm's ability to increase price arbitrarily comes from the availability of substitute products. The theory of monopolistic competition generally — but not always — presumes the presence of many producers of close substitutes for any given product.

Monopoly theory, on the other hand, generally ignores the availability of substitute products. The firm is presumed capable of setting price, constrained only by what buyers are willing to pay and unconstrained by the competitive reactions of other actual or potential suppliers of substitute products to the market.

A key difference between neoclassical monopoly and perfect competition, on one hand, and monopolistic competition, on the other, has to do with how an array of products is chosen for production. In the former cases, it is assumed that firms choose which products to produce; they cannot or do not consciously change the character of their products. The operation of markets simply determines which of a fixed array of products actually is produced.

In the theory of monopolistic competition, on the other hand, firms are presumed consciously to modify old products and to develop new ones in response to market activity. It is thus presumed that markets directly affect the characters of those products.

Monopolistic competition ought not to be viewed as an "intermediate case" between perfect competition and monopoly. It is built upon quite different presumptions about what markets can and should do by way of product development. Also, it should be clear that "monopoly" and "monopolistic" are not synonymous, although it is hard even for professional economists to maintain the verbal distinction.

Market adjustments in monopolistic competition are generated by the entrance or exit of firms attracted or repelled by profitability considerations, and by the pricing and product choices of individual firms. If firms behave independently, then a stable market occurs when no inducement to entrance or exit exists (firms earn a competitive rate of return on investment) and when no individual firm can improve its profitability by changing price or product.

While these distinctions may seem arcane to non-

economists, they are important in analyzing media industries. Many of today's antitrust and regulatory policies had
their roots in an era when the role of markets in determining
which products get produced and how they compete with one
another was less well understood than it is today. For instance, it is often taken as axiomatic that any price deviating
from marginal cost is clear evidence of deviation from a hy-
pothetical social optimum. Given the presumptions of
neoclassical theory, that is a true proposition. However, in a
monopolistic competitive market it is false; no such
equilibrium is attainable, since price must always be greater
than marginal cost to permit firms to break even.

As a second example, neoclassical theory leads more or
less automatically to the presumption that if a firm has any
pricing discretion at all, then it must be earning monopoly
profits. In the case of monopolistic competition, no such
presumption can be made; demand curves are always down-
ward sloping, but entry and new-product development can
generally be presumed to eliminate excess profits in the
longer run.[5]

As a third example, the identification of a "relevant
market" for purposes of antitrust litigation or other policy
analysis is heavily influenced by considerations of
monopolistic competition. For instance, applying neoclassical
theory to the newspaper industry in a simple-minded fashion
would lead to the conclusion that virtually all newspaper
firms are monopolies; after all, newspapers are primarily
differentiated from one another by city of location, and there
are few cities with more than one general circulation daily
newspaper firm. However, this application of neoclassical
theory would neglect the fact that newspapers compete for
reader attention and advertising dollars with a whole range
of other media products.

As another "relevant market" example, neoclassical theory might suggest that book publishing, with its thousands of
independent firms, is a highly competitive industry.

Monopolistic competition theory, with its focus on product characteristics, could lead the policymaker to examine the fabric of competition more closely. He might find, then, that the mass marketing of paperbacks, for example, effectively restricts access to that marketplace to a much smaller number of competing producers.

The presumptions of monopolistic competition often lead to different kinds of policy questions. For instance, instead of just asking the price-quantity-profitability questions, they lead analysts to question the number and character of products generated by market operation. Further, neoclassical theory leads to a more or less blind prohibition of vertical integration or other vertical constraints on competition; in contrast, although monopolistic competition analysis is not fully developed here, it is easy to find cases where such vertical constraints actually improve social welfare.

It is the defining characteristic of mass media—a single source creating messages for distribution to a large audience—that gives mass media the quality of public goods. It is this that makes media markets monopolistically competitive. Since additional consumers can be served at the bare cost of reproducing and distributing the product once it has been created, competitive firms producing *identical* products seldom can survive in competition with one another. Competition forces prices below a level that covers the cost of creating the message. In this sense, the effects of the essential public-good character of media products are indistinguishable from those of pervasive economies of scale. Thus, it is an essential characteristic of media products that they are differentiated. Interproduct competition takes place at the level of the firm, and the basic presumptions of monopolistic competition, rather than those of neoclassical competition and monopoly, are relevant.

INTERMEDIA COMPETITION

An important implication of the preceding discussion is that patterns of competition within and among mass media industries are more complex than a simple application of competitive market theory would suggest. In particular, advertising serves to link the advertising-dependent media rather closely.

The relative importance of the various advertising categories is rather surprising to most people. One finds, for example, that more dollars are spent on newspaper advertising than on all the electronic media combined. Pure advertising media are substantial; in particular, direct-mail advertising revenues are over 14 percent of the total. Despite the existence of thousands of stations, radio controls under 7 percent of the broadly defined advertising market.[6] Magazines have under 6 percent of total advertising expenditure.

Of particular interest is the influence of television, which entered the marketplace in 1949 and now captures over 20 percent of all advertising expenditure. In the last ten years, local TV advertising has displayed exceptional growth, partially reflecting the increased viability of UHF and stations in smaller metropolitan areas. Not surprisingly, there have been significant declines in the shares of other media as a result.

A close examination of these declines reveals a differential impact, as well as the central role played by market segmentation. The share of advertising going to television has increased in every year since 1949 except for rather precipitous declines during 1970 and 1971, which probably resulted from the regulatory ban on cigarette commercials. Newspapers' share dropped from nearly 37 percent in 1947 to 29 percent in 1963, and has remained fairly stable since then. The fall was most severe in those national markets where television is most effective. Local display and classified advertising now provide 85 percent of newspapers' revenue, up from 75 percent when TV was just coming on the scene. Faced with the new competition, newspapers were forced to rely on their comparative advantage in regional submarkets. In absolute terms, however, the newspaper industry has managed to exploit this advantage through successful product differentiation. In fact, until the more general declines of the late 1960s and early 1970s, newspaper advertising as a percentage of personal consumption expenditures was stable and actually rose slightly—even as television grew in importance.

The magazine industry has also suffered a steady decline in its share of total advertising dollars—from 12.1 percent in 1945 to 5.2 percent in 1975. Until the early 1960s, revenues were steady relative to consumers' personal expenditures, with rapid declines occurring thereafter. This decrease adversely affected such national, general-interest weeklies as *Life, Look,* and the *Saturday Evening Post.* This was predictable, given their close substitutability with television. Specialty publications, which have successfully identified and segmented audiences by interests, have managed at the same time to double their share of total magazine-advertising revenues; by exploiting the demand for a highly differentiated product, they have weathered the increased competition.

Many influences operated on the radio industry during this period, especially wartime newsprint restrictions and the growth of FM. But the most dramatic impact was made by TV. Radio networks were particularly affected, since television could deliver a superior product to similar audiences. Thus, while radio networks sold advertising amounting to about 4.0 percent of U.S. totals in 1949, their share is now a meager 0.3 percent. In response to television competition, radio has sought to serve local markets, which today supply about 73.0 percent of radio's advertising revenue.

Competition for audiences among media is considerably less direct than competition for advertising revenue. Its principal manifestation is shifts between media in response to the development of new media. The growth of broadcast television provides the best recent evidence of this adjustment process. Combining visual stimulus with action and timeliness, television has become the main source of light entertainment and "visual impact" news. Among the responses by other media are the following:

The rapid decline in radio drama, which now is marketed mainly as a novelty. Radio has shifted almost totally to music, though recently such specialties as all-news programming have developed, probably to serve the automobile commuter.

The death of general-interest magazines and their replacement with special-interest magazines, serving audiences that are large but too geographically diffuse to be suited to television.

The decline of newspapers as the primary source of national and local news.

Emerging new mass media—videodisc, computer-based "information utilities," and pay TV—will no doubt continue these trends, forcing the older media companies to again rethink their product differentiation strategies.

REGULATION

An important additional factor in shaping the strategies of the media industries has been government regulation. The principal regulated media have been radio and television, through federal licensing rules administered by the Federal Communications Commission (FCC). However, other administrative law and antitrust law policies, such as those determining eligibility for preferential postal rates and those permitting the combination of non-editorial newspaper functions, have also influenced the structure of media markets and the content of media products. Space prohibits extensive treatment of the role of regulation in media markets at this time, but a single example can illustrate the potential for unintended consequences.

The "localism" policy of the FCC failed to achieve its objectives precisely because of the commission's failure to recognize the essential public-good character of over-the-air television. In the late 1940s and during the 1950s the FCC had the task of licensing TV stations. There are many trade-offs to be considered, and the FCC spent a long time thinking about them. It finally decided that an important criterion should be "localism"—that is, the available UHF and VHF spectra should be allocated so as to maximize the number of communities that had local TV outlets. This meant that broadcast power should be limited in order to permit more local stations, and that urban centers should have proportionally fewer licenses than rural areas.

The egalitarian intent of the policy is clear. The FCC wanted to spread the benefits of the new medium as widely as possible across the country, putting the source of programming as close to the grass roots as possible.[7]

The FCC's policy has not been successful, even on its own terms. Local programs are scarce. Further, to the extent that programs do originate locally, they do so more in the larger markets than in the smaller markets favored by the federal policy. Why is this? Precisely because of the public-good character of the product. Aside from transmission costs, a large audience can be served by a given program as cheaply as a small one; the program content is a pure public good. Further, if you are going to broadcast a program to the whole country anyway, it is cheaper to do so simultaneously in large sections of the country. Consequently, the cheapest and most effective way to organize the production of over-the-air television is through networks. As a result, virtually all popular TV programs originate in one of three networks. Local stations serve as relay stations rather than as local voices.

In fact, a case can be made that the FCC's policy of localism has actually *reduced* the number of independent voices. It goes as follows: the reason we have only three networks is that there are enough three-license cities to permit each of those networks to reach nearly the whole population. Had the FCC allowed more power for larger transmission areas, and had it concentrated more licenses in fewer cities, the same statement could have been made about four, five, or possibly even six networks instead of three. This would have meant "regional" rather than "local" origination.

Therefore, the FCC's failure to perceive the essential public-good nature of TV led it, in the 1940s and 1950s, to follow what has turned out in retrospect to be a misguided policy which has limited the number of viable networks to three. This, in turn, has concentrated considerable economic wealth and political power in the three networks and their affiliates who, needless to say, are stalwart defenders of the existing state of affairs.

The above analysis has been carried out with the benefit of 20–20 hindsight, of course. At the time that decisions were being made, vision was not so clear; it is at least arguable that the FCC made the best set of decisions, given the state of knowledge and congressional directives at that time.

CONCLUSION

The preceding example highlights the futility of attempting to make policy for an industry without understanding its economics. My purpose in this chapter has been to help equip the reader to critically examine public policies in the mass media in the light of that economics.

The key facts can be summarized in four buzzwords:

public goods: The public-good nature of mass media content, arising from the fundamental "broadcast" nature of media, leads to substantial economies of scale which, in turn, shape the economic structure of media markets.

advertising: Mass media firms privatize their public goods by turning audiences into commodities that can be sold to advertisers; advertising markets are the principle arena of economic competition.

monopolistic competition: Successful mass media firms differentiate their products to hold an audience that is attractive to a sufficient number of advertisers to permit profitability.

regulation: Government regulatory policies have shaped mass media industries in significant but often unintended ways.

Understanding the economics summarized by these buzzwords can help us understand why media markets operate the way they do. It can also provide a better base for developing and analyzing policy proposals, for independent and effective media are those that earn their independence in the economic marketplace.

III

Institutional Problems

4

BENNO C. SCHMIDT, JR.

The First Amendment and the Press

Free expression versus social questions. The CIA and censorship. Prior restraint. Seditious libel and the clear and present danger rule. The *Sullivan* case. Print and broadcast media in conflict. The Fairness Doctrine. Newsgathering. The Burger Court. The approaching challenge.

Freedom of the press in the United States is rooted in the First Amendment to the Constitution:

Congress shall make no law respecting an establishment of religion, or prohibiting the free exercise thereof; or abridging the freedom of speech, or the press; or the right of the people peaceably to assemble, and to petition the Government for a redress of grievances.

57

The amendment suggests different senses of rights. It opens with guarantees of religious liberty and closes with the rights to assemble peaceably and to petition the government. In between are the free expression guarantees, embodying both these different—and occasionally opposing—conceptions of rights: principles of personal (and perhaps group) autonomy, and policies which encourage diversity of expression and political participation. Reflecting its eighteenth century heritage, the amendment is couched in negative terms. It imposes no governmental obligation to promote free expression or to guarantee equality of access to the marketplace of ideas. Like the rest of the Bill of Rights, the First Amendment conceives of individual liberty as being let alone.[1]

"We are under a Constitution, but the Constitution is what the judges say it is," Charles Evans Hughes once observed. Freedom of speech and of the press in the United States finds its form in an ongoing process of constitutional adjudication as the Supreme Court evolves general principles out of particular judgments, responding pragmatically and provisionally to such problems as radical dissent, incitement to illegal conduct, libel, pornography, commercial advertising, parades and public demonstrations, the licensing and regulation of radio and television, to mention only a few. There is little wonder that no simple, unified theory of the First Amendment has managed to embrace such a motley array.

AVOIDANCE AND OBSCURITY

The law of freedom of the press does not radiate from any central premise, but consists rather of a group of separate doctrines. They share some common themes, but each takes its form primarily from a particular function and from the legal terrain on which it rests. Indeed, different areas of First

Amendment law often are not on speaking terms with one another.

Within the various clusters of First Amendment law, obscurity surrounds most basic questions. When the Court must mediate between the values of free expression and social policies calling for control, it tends to avoid broad constitutional pronouncements by resorting to narrow decisions. Avoidance is easy in many cases because First Amendment law is enmeshed with common law, legislation, and administrative law. Constitutional questions thus tend to slide into nonconstitutional answers in such areas as libel and privacy, national security restrictions on press disclosures, subversive advocacy, journalists' claims of privilege not to disclose confidential sources, and the entire field of broadcast regulation; cases are decided on the basis of construction of statutes, traditional principles of criminal responsibility, or common law rules. Basic questions are thereby avoided. No one has the slightest idea, for example, how far the First Amendment protects the press from criminal liability for disclosing national security secrets. Nor can we know whether the First Amendment guarantees access to the public forum of the streets and parks for parades or demonstrations as opposed to merely protecting against official bias or reliance on vague standards. The list of unanswered but central questions could be multiplied.

MODERN SIGNIFICANCE

Not until the 1960s did the law of freedom of expression really begin to live up to its billing as preeminent among constitutional rights. As the civil rights movement surged into the streets, First Amendment protection for parades, demonstrations, and other expressive activities in public places became enmeshed in the most critical issue of domestic policies: the struggle for racial justice. The First Amendment also found itself injected into fundamental social questions in a rush of cases involving the legal status of mass communications media. Beginning in 1964 with *New York Times* v. *Sullivan*—in which the Supreme Court found in the First Amendment a barrier to the traditional law of libel as applied to newspaper criticism of public officials—numerous cases involving the constitutional rights of the press, including radio and television, have shifted the First Amendment's focus from how our society treats dissidents and nonconformists to the mass communications media, raising issues of enormously greater complexity and significance.

As now conceived, the First Amendment narrows drastically our law's options in dealing with print media. It ordains a *laissez-faire* conception of the government's role. Publications may not be regulated broadly to advance the general good. And even narrow controls must overcome intense constitutional resistance. For print media, the First Amendment has erected an all but irrebuttable presumption that, as Learned Hand put it, "right conclusions are more likely to be gathered out of a multitude of tongues, than through any kind of authoritative selection."

At the same time, our law regarding radio and television has rested on virtually an opposite premise: broadcasters are considered "public trustees," and every aspect of their operations, including what they put on the air, is subject to the question of whether it is in "the public interest." Created by statute in 1927 in response to the explosive growth of radio, broadcast regulation contradicts the First Amendment's most secure historical principle—that government may not condition the right to publish on prior office approval. No one may broadcast without a license, and the government licenses only those broadcasters it believes will serve the public interest. Beyond licensing, we permit controls on broadcasting that would fly in the face of constitutional tradition if applied to newspapers, magazines, or books.

Set against the extraordinary freedom we grant to print media, our law's treatment of broadcasting seems fundamentally different; and so it is. But there is also much common ground. As with print media, the United States has turned away from government ownership and operation of radio and television, a common arrangement in many other democracies. Nor do we treat broadcasters as common carriers like the Post Office or the telephone company, obliged to carry all messages. Moreover, despite the contradiction of licensing, First Amendment values cling to radio and television with extraordinary persistence. Concern for free expression and editorial autonomy sharply limits official control over broadcasting content—even more so in recent years. Compared to other nations, the U.S. law's regulation of broadcasting is striking in its faith in private decision-making and in a marketplace of public expression substantially free of government intervention.

PRIOR RESTRAINT: THE MOMENTUM OF HISTORY

The two principal themes of the American law of freedom of the press rest on insights drawn from the main features of English law: the wholesale system of licensing and censorship of all publications and the draconian criminal law of seditious libel, the theory of which was that virtually any criticism of government was deemed to contain the seeds of disorder and, indeed, of incipient rebellion.

History has rooted in our constitutional tradition the strongest aversion to official censorship. We have learned from the English rejection of press licensing and from our own experiences that the psychology of censors drives them to excess, that censors have a stake in finding things to suppress, and that—in systems of wholesale review before publication—doubt tends to produce suppression. American law tolerated movie censorship for a time, but only because movies were not thought to be "the press" in First Amendment terms. Censorship of the movies is now dead, killed by stringent procedural requirements imposed by unsympathetic courts, by the voluntary rating system, and most of all, by public distaste for the absurdities of censorship in operation.

U.S. law has tolerated requirements of prior official approval of expression in several important areas, however. As mentioned above, no one may broadcast without a license, and even though the Communications Act explicitly prohibits the Federal Communications Commission (FCC) from exercising any "power of censorship," the licensing system inevitably produces pressures for regulation of program content. Licensing is also grudgingly tolerated—because of the desirability of giving notice and of avoiding conflicts or other disruptions of the normal functions of public places—in the regulation of parades, demonstrations, leafletting, and other expressive activities in public places. But the courts have taken pains to eliminate administrative discretion that would allow officials to censor public forum expression because they do not approve its message. A more controversial system of censorship operates in the Central Intelligence Agency (CIA), where employees contract to submit for clearance anything gained in the course of employment which they propose to publish about the agency. Although the courts permit the CIA only to bar publication of properly classified information, the Supreme Court recently held that all information—classified or not—must be submitted for prepublication review, and that failure to abide by this system is a breach of trust giving rise to very substantial money damages. The "secrecy agreement" on which CIA censorship rests will doubtless appeal to other government departments; the system will probably spread at least through the state and defense departments. Arrangements

of such significance to public debate about government—
and of such incongruity with central First Amendment no-
tions—should not be permitted to rest on contracts forced on
public employees. Whether wholesale censorship is necessary to protect legitimate secrecy ought to be determined by
Congress and, without legislative authorization, should not
be tolerated by the courts.

Notwithstanding these areas where censorship has been
permitted, the clearest principle of First Amendment law is
that the least tolerable form of official regulation of expression is prior official approval for publication. It is easy to see
the suffocating tendency of prior restraints where all expression—whether or not ultimately deemed protected by the
First Amendment for publication—must be submitted for
clearance before it may be disseminated. The harder question of First Amendment theory has been whether advance
prohibitions on expression that do not require wholesale sub-
mission of all expression should be tarred with our historical
aversion to censorship. The question has arisen most frequently in the context of judicial injunctions against publication, and even though injunctions do not involve many of the
worst vices of wholesale licensing and censorship, the
Supreme Court answer has been a resounding "Yes."

The seminal case was *Near* v. *Minnesota*, handed down in
1931 by a closely divided Court but never questioned since. A
state statute provided for injunctions against any "malicious,
scandalous, and defamatory newspaper," and a state judge
had enjoined a scandal sheet from publishing anything scandalous in the future. Despite the fact that the Minnesota
scheme did not require advance approval of all publications
but came into play only after a publication had been found
scandalous, and then only to prevent further similar publications, the majority of the justices likened the injunction to
English censorship. To enjoin future editions under an essentially vague standard was thought, in effect, to put the newspaper under judicial censorship. Chief Justice Charles Evans

Hughes's historic opinion made clear, however, that the First Amendment's bar against prior restraint was not absolute. Various exceptional instances would justify prior restraints, including this pregnant one: "No one would question but that a government might prevent actual obstruction to its recruiting service or the publication of the sailing dates of transports or the number and location of troops."

It was forty years before the scope of the "troop-ship" exception was tested. The *Pentagon Papers* decision of 1971 reaffirmed the principle that judicial injunctions are considered prior restraints and are tolerated only in the most compelling circumstances. This principle barred the injunction sought against publication of a classified history of our government's decisions in the Vietnam war, although—unlike *Near*—the government had sought to enjoin only readily identifiable material, not unidentified "similar" publications in the future. Ten different opinions discussed the problem of injunctions in national security cases, and the only proposition commanding a majority was the unexplained conclusion that the government had not justified injunctive relief. But chilling that victory for freedom of the press were admonitions, loosely endorsed by four justices, that the Espionage Statutes might support criminal sanctions against the *New York Times* and its reporters. No journalists were indicted, but the prosecutions of Daniel Ellsberg and Anthony Russo rested on a view of several statutes that would reach the press by punishing newsgathering activities necessarily incident to publication. Since the dismissal of these cases for reasons irrelevant to these issues, the extent of possible criminal liability for publishing national security secrets remains unclear.

Aside from these speculations about possible criminal liability, the central theme in the *Pentagon Papers* case was the Court's reluctance to start issuing secrecy orders without legislative guidance. That lost the case for the government, which had argued that—without regard to legislation—the president should be able to get injunctive relief to prevent "grave and irreparable danger" to the public interest. The government could not, in any event, prove that publishing the *Pentagon Papers* would cause such harm, but even apart from that, the Court was well advised to avoid fashioning rules on publication of defense secrets. Courts are ill-suited to assess the risks of disclosing particular secrets. Nor do the First Amendment or decisions under it offer clear standards once one rejects the absolutist construction that anything can be published, no matter what the damage to national security. The best hope in a nuclear age for accommodating the needs of secrecy and the public's right to know lies in the legislative process where, removed from pressures of adjudicating particular cases, general rules can be fashioned. The courts' role in this area is to review legislation, not to make rules of secrecy in the first instance.

The *Pentagon Papers* case underlines how little the United States has relied on law to control press coverage of national defense and foreign policy matters. For most of our history the press has rarely tested the limits of its rights to publish. Secrets were kept because people in and out of government with access to military and diplomatic secrets shared basic assumptions about national aims. The Vietnam war changed all that. The *Pentagon Papers* dispute marked the passing of an era in which journalists could be counted on to work within understood limits of discretion in handling secret information. The future will tell whether the United States can afford obscurity and a bare minimum of secrecy laws that prohibit press revelations of classified defense information.[2]

The third major decision striking down a judicial order not to publish involved neither national security nor scandal, but the right of a criminal defendant to a fair trial. A state court enjoined publication of an accused's confession and some other incriminating material on grounds that if prospective jurors learned about it they might be incapable of impartiality. In the *Nebraska Press Association* decision, the

Supreme Court decided that the potential prejudice was speculative and it rejected enjoining publication on speculation. The Court also thought that, even if prejudice occurred, it could be dealt with in such other ways as closing pretrial proceedings to the public and the press, ordering witnesses, parties, lawyers, police, and others not to reveal prejudicial information to the press, and carefully choosing and instructing jurors.

These decisions and others have firmly established the doctrine that the First Amendment tolerates no—or virtually no—prior restraints. It is one of the central principles of our law of freedom of the press. On the surface, the doctrine concerns only the form of controls on expression. It bars controls prior to publication, even if criminal or civil liability following publication would be constitutional. But as with most limitations of form, the prior restraint doctrine has important substantive consequences. Most important, it precludes wholesale administrative licensing or censorship of the press. The doctrine also prevents control by injunction of those types of expression for which general legislative prohibitions are extremely difficult to formulate, or are necessarily overbroad, or are politically impractical. The doctrine means that if expression cannot be controlled by general legislation, it will not be controlled *ad hoc* by judicial injunctions.

Although the Supreme Court has stretched history in subjecting judicial injunctions to the full burden of our law's traditional aversion to prior restraints, there are sound reasons for viewing all prior controls—not only wholesale licensing and censorship—as dangerous to free expression. It tends to be administratively easier to prevent expression in advance than to punish it after the fact. The inertia of public officials in responding to a *fait accompli*, the chance to look at whether expression has actually caused harm rather than speculating about the matter, public support for the speaker, the interposition of juries and other procedural safeguards of the usual criminal or civil process, all tend to reinforce tolerance when expression can only be dealt with by subsequent punishment. Moreover, all prior restraint systems, including injunctions, tend to divert attention from the central question of whether expression is protected to the subsidiary problems of whether the efficacy of the prior restraint system is protected. Thus, before a prior restraint system has decided whether some particular expression can be disseminated, the expression must be held back. The time it takes a prior restraint process to decide, in other words, works against free expression. On the other hand, where law must wait to move against expression after it has been published, time is on the side of freedom. Once a prior restraint is issued, the authority and prestige of the restraining agent are at stake. If it is disobeyed, the legality of the expression takes a back seat to upholding the obligation of obedience to the prior restraint process. All in all, even such prior restraints as judicial injunctions—which are more discriminating than wholesale censorship—tend toward irresponsible administration and an exaggerated assessment of the danger of free expression.

This is not to say that prior restraints may not sometimes be preferable to other ways of controlling expression. A prior restraint can give notice to a potential publisher that a particular publication will be unlawful, while a criminal statute that might or might not apply to a particular publication may not afford any reasonable notice at all. There are times also when the prior restraint system, as such, will be in a better position than an individual publisher to tell whether information is lawful to publish. The CIA censorship system may be of this sort. In other words, there are exceptions to the rule that prior restraints should be viewed as the least tolerable types of official interference with free expression.

SEDITIOUS LIBEL AND THE
FIRST AMENDMENT

When the First Amendment was passed, the great unanswered question was whether it did away with the law of seditious libel. The Supreme Court first confronted this question after World War I, when it reviewed a number of convictions for expressions against the war effort. Following the lead of Justice Holmes, the Supreme Court looked not to the law of seditious libel for justification in punishing speech, but rather to traditional principles of legal responsibility for attempted crimes. In English and American common law, an unsuccessful attempt to commit a crime could be punished if the attempt came dangerously close to success, while preparations for crime—in themselves harmless—could not be punished. With his gift of great utterance, Holmes distilled these doctrinal nuances into the rule that expression could be punished only if it created a "clear and present danger" of bringing about illegal action, such as draft resistance or curtailment of weapons production. Given his corrosive skepticism and his Darwinian sense of flux, the clear and present danger rule became in Holmes's hands a fair protection for expression. But in the hands of judges and juries more passionate or anxious, measuring protection for expression by the likelihood of illegal action proved evanescent and unpredictable.

There were other problems with the clear and present danger rule. It took no account of the value of particular expression, only of its tendency to cause harmful acts. Since the test was circumstantial, legislative declarations that certain types of speech were dangerous put the courts in the awkward position of having to second-guess the legislature's factual assessments of risk in order to protect the expression. Nor was the clear and present danger rule helpful in situations where expression was punished not because of its tendency to produce illegal action, but because it was deemed harmful in itself—as with libel or obscenity—or because it was noisy, produced litter, or had other collateral effects that needed regulation.

Despite these shortcomings, the clear and present danger rule was a major advance over the law of seditious libel, which presumed the harmful tendency of virtually any criticism of government. The clear and present danger rule, on the other hand, opened the question of harm to argument and to the emergence of a higher standard of risk. For these reasons, among others, Holmes concluded that the First Amendment had invalidated the law of seditious libel. But a majority of the Supreme Court did not take this step until 1964, and then not in a criminal prosecution but in a civil action for defamation.

The *Sullivan* case

During the 1960s, the furious sectional resentments of the civil rights struggle revealed the chilling potential of the traditional law of defamation. Under this law, false statements of fact that damaged a person's reputation could lead to recovery of damages regardless of whether the publisher was at fault, unless one of a confusing myriad of exceptions and privileges excused the publisher from liability. An advertisement in March 1960, placed by supporters of Martin Luther King in the *New York Times*, recited the repressive activities of Alabama police with several minor inaccuracies and exaggerations. L. B. Sullivan, commissioner of public affairs in Montgomery, brought suit for defamation against the *Times* and the sponsors of the ad, and an Alabama jury thought $500,000 was about right to repair his damage. Similar suits against the *Times* and CBS in Alabama sought damages totaling millions of dollars.

The Supreme Court reacted to this intolerable situation in 1964 with sweeping changes in the constitutional status of defamation law (*New York Times* v. *Sullivan*). Libel would no longer be viewed as a category of expression beneath First Amendment protection. But what standards would apply? The Court found the answer in history, conceiving the political repudiation of the notorious Sedition Act of 1798 as revealing the "central meaning" of the First Amendment: a right to criticize government and public officials.

In this perspective, Alabama's altogether typical law of libel looked rather like the discredited Sedition Act (which had also allowed for a defense of truth). As the Court put it,

A rule compelling the critic of official conduct to guarantee the truth of all his factual assertions . . . leads to . . . "self-censorship." . . . [W]ould-be critics of official conduct may be deterred from voicing their criticism, even though it is believed to be true and even though it is in fact true, because of doubt whether it can be proved in court or fear of the expenses of having to do so.

Sullivan did not protect all expression about government, but it limited recoveries for defamatory falsehoods about official conduct to those made with "knowledge that [a statement] was false or with reckless disregard of whether it was false or not." The Court did not regard falsehoods as worthy of protection in their own right; rather it protected non-deliberate falsehoods about public officials as a tactic necessary to give truthful statements adequate breathing room. Even as to public officials, therefore, *Sullivan* falls well short of unrestricted freedom of the press and our law's tradition of protecting reputation from false and damaging statements.

On the level of substantive doctrine, both in relation to the First Amendment and to defamation law, *Sullivan* was not a radical departure. The theory that certain broad categories of expression, such as libel, were simply beyond the First Amendment's reach had been eroded in several prior decisions and would continue its decline after *Sullivan*. With respect to defamation law, the *Sullivan* rule as applied to criticism of public officials was a common-sense extrapolation from the traditional privilege for reporting public affairs and from the fair-comment doctrine; it was patterned after rules applicable in a number of states to libels of public figures. On the level of constitutional dynamics, however, *Sullivan* was a major change, federalizing a diversity of local rules—that had been left to state courts—into a single national body of doctrine overseen by a Court peculiarly sensitive to First Amendment problems.

Later libel decisions have shown how far *Sullivan* fell short of absolute protection for speech about government or about matters of public interest. The Court has declared that a private person who is libeled need not meet the *Sullivan* standard of showing that defamation was malicious—in the *Sullivan* sense of its being virtually a deliberate lie—though it does require private persons to prove that a publisher was to some extent at fault or careless. A few people who are not government officials must meet the *Sullivan* test in order to recover for libel, but such "public figures" are limited to those who have voluntarily thrust themselves into public controversy.

Sullivan and the later libel decisions represent a somewhat uneasy accommodation between free expression and the values of protecting personal reputation from false and damaging assertions. *Sullivan* no doubt bars some deserving officials and public figures who are damaged by reckless falsehoods from recovering anything, but the lucky few who meet the stringent requirements are likely to recover astronomical damages that are out of line with any real injury they may have suffered. The Supreme Court should focus its attention on damages in libel cases. This would protect a free press from ruinous, punitive assessments, and would open the way to loosening the *Sullivan* standards so that officials and public figures can vindicate themselves when they are damaged by irresponsible falsehoods but cannot show those falsehoods to have been deliberate.

THE FIRST AMENDMENT AND
THE ELECTRONIC MEDIA

If law echoes intuitions of public policy, as Holmes taught us, American society's intuitions about the mass media are strikingly ambivalent. The First Amendment commands that government not interfere with the substance or process of publication; anyone with a printing press and the means of distribution can publish just about anything without legal interference. As mentioned before, however, the law of broadcast regulation requires broadcasters to have prior official approval in the form of an FCC license, and allows control over program content that the courts would not tolerate if applied to print media.

Most significant—and most dramatically at odds with the law as it applies to the print media—are the regulations that require balance in public affairs programming and provide access for persons or points of view the broadcaster might not choose to air. The most important of these is Section 315 of the Communications Act, requiring broadcasters to grant "equal opportunities" to opposing political candidates. Section 315 does not require broadcasters to put political candidates on the air; but if a broadcaster elects to give or sell a candidate air time (other than in the course of a newscast or coverage of a news event), he must then give other candidates for the same office a similar opportunity.

In theory, Section 315 seeks to guarantee fairness and to promote public awareness of election issues and candidates. But in practice, it probably inhibits so much worthwhile material that the gain in evenhandedness is not worth the cost. It has unquestionably constrained broadcasters' coverage of serious political candidates. If broadcasters give free time to major candidates in elections of popular interest, Section 315 gives candidates of minor and even frivolous parties a right of access—a boring and sometimes offensive exercise that broadcasters are understandably reluctant to subsidize and inflict on their (fleeting) viewers.

An even more controversial regulation of programming is the Fairness Doctrine. The FCC has long regarded broadcasters as "public trustees" obliged to cover important public issues, and this concept gradually has hardened into the Fairness Doctrine which imposes a two-part duty on broadcasters: to devote reasonable time to controversial issues of public importance and, when an issue has been raised, to provide reasonable opportunity for contrasting viewpoints to be heard. Although the Fairness Doctrine in principle would justify sweeping official supervision of broadcasting, its actual impact has been cushioned. Particular programs need not be balanced; the test of fairness is the broadcaster's overall programming. Moreover, the FCC does not insist on overall fairness in any precise sense, but relies initially on the editorial discretion of the broadcaster. Only if this is abused will the FCC overturn a licensee's judgment on such questions as whether an issue is so important and controversial that some programming must be devoted to it, whether such an issue has in fact been addressed in programming and, if so, what constitutes a "reasonable opportunity" for contrasting viewpoints. Recent court decisions, sensitive to the need to protect editorial autonomy and reduce official supervision of programming, have given wide scope to broadcaster discretion in Fairness Doctrine controversies, repudiating the FCC's second-guessing of broadcasters' judgments in some fairly extreme cases.

The result is substantial freedom for broadcasters under the Fairness Doctrine, though the threat of administrative sanctions remains in the background. Indeed, the first part of the Fairness Doctrine—the obligation to cover important issues—is left almost entirely to broadcasters' discretion. The second part—the obligation, once an issue has been raised, to be balanced in presenting contrasting views—has led to much more significant interference with programming. In the 1960s the FCC imposed explicit access obligations. "Personal attacks" during discussion of controversial public issues were judged to give the person attacked a right of reply; likewise, the commission ruled that editorials favoring one candidate gave competing candidates a right to respond, although this went beyond the requirements of Section 315.

In the *Red Lion* decision of 1969, the Supreme Court unanimously sustained these access requirements, relying on the notion that because the broadcast spectrum is "scarce" and because broadcasters are licensed to use a piece of it only as a temporary privilege, "[i]t is the right of the viewers and listeners, not the right of the broadcasters, which is paramount." The access requirements were viewed as enhancing public debate; not only were they not barred by the First Amendment, the Court held, they positively supported First Amendment values. This notion seemed capable of expanding into a broad government power to promote diversity of expression in mass communications media of all kinds, including print.

In its decision five years later in *Miami Herald* v. *Tornillo*, however, the Supreme Court declined to apply the expansive logic of *Red Lion* to the print media. The Court unanimously struck down a state statute granting political candidates a right of reply in newspapers that attacked them. It thought the statute would inhibit newspaper criticism of political candidates and thus limit rather than enhance public debate. This is a striking contrast to *Red Lion*'s conclusion that rights of reply enhance public debate. Yet *Miami Herald* did not even mention *Red Lion*, much less explain the contradiction. Perhaps because the Court was aware of the inconsistency with *Red Lion*, it was careful not to rest the *Miami Herald* decision on the chilling effect alone, but went on to contend that the statute would invade the autonomy of publishers as the sole judges of what is printed.

Miami Herald underlines the current Supreme Court's commitment to a divergent constitutional treatment for print and broadcast media. Just why this should be so is not so easy to understand. For many years the accepted wisdom has been that the electromagnetic spectrum is physically scarce in ways that the machinery of print publication is not, and even if this is absurd in an economic sense, it is deeply engrained in legal thinking. Moreover, many people think of the airwaves as a public resource—like navigable water-ways— that is not suitable for private exploitation, whereas printing presses, paper, and ink are private goods. Perhaps most significant, because the right to use the airwaves is valuable and is given away by the government, it seems only fitting to many that public duties should be imposed in return.

In the recent *Pacifica* decision, upholding the FCC's ban on a radio broadcast of a comic routine about dirty words—at least, at times when children may be tuned in—the Supreme Court went beyond these traditional arguments for regula-tion and emphasized that broadcasting, in relation to print, is an especially intrusive medium; its audience was deemed more captive, less selective, and less critical of messages received than audiences for other mass media. Children have free access to it, largely without effective parental control. The Court thought that the capacity to switch channels or turn the set off was insufficient to protect consumers from the nuisance of vulgar indecencies over the air.

Some people go even farther, and argue that because broadcasting (they suppose) has vastly more influence than have the print media over political and cultural attitudes, it must be subject to rather broad regulation if we are to con-trol our destiny. All these perceptions indicate strong resis-tance to applying to broadcasting the principle of noninter-ference which is at the heart of First Amendment thinking about print media.

Beyond the sense that there are basic differences between broadcast and print, it may be that a basic ambivalence about the idea of freedom of the press underlies the inconsistency in the way our law treats print and broadcasting. Doubts about the *laissez-faire* First Amendment tradition for print — as commercialism in publishing, the monopoly power of newspapers, and the sensationalism all around, erode some of the more naive premises of freedom of the press — tend to reinforce the tradition of regulating broadcasting. Learned Hand once said of the First Amendment: "To many this is, and always will be folly; but we have staked upon it our all." Our law's ambivalent approach to the mass media suggests that we have hedged our stake. If the First Amendment is indeed folly, at least the half loaf of legal control provided by the law of broadcasting may protect society from some of the damage that irresponsible mass media could inflict. At the same time, the constitutional status of print media can provide society with the insurance of a free press. The choice between freedom of the mass media and governmental regulation for the greater good may be one of those insoluble dilemmas for public policy to which our law is justified in responding by looking firmly in opposite directions.

THE "RIGHT" TO GATHER NEWS

To date, the United States Supreme Court has been extremely cautious in sketching the contours of a First Amendment right to gather news. In *Branzburg* v. *Hayes*, the majority, in the course of deciding that reporters have no privilege under the First Amendment to refuse to disclose confidential sources of information when questioned by a grand jury investigating crimes, stated that "newsgathering is not without its First Amendment protections." At present, the

heart of that right is only the modest protection that reporters must be treated equally with members of the public.
But since journalists would rarely be excluded anyway from
places or information sources open to the public, the right of
equal access does not count for much.

Some justices would go farther. Several argued that barring press access to prisons, even if nondiscriminatory, "may
so undermine the function of the First Amendment" that
government should be forced to justify such barriers. In
Branzburg, moreover, the majority stated: "Official harass-
ment of the press undertaken not for purposes of law enforcement but to disrupt a reporter's relationship with his
news sources would have no justification." This suggests that
restrictions and inhibitions on newsgathering may not be imposed for the impermissible purpose of restricting the free
flow of information that the public has a right to know, and
that courts might come to examine the motives behind official actions that interfere with newsgathering.

At present, the only instance in which the Court has
upheld a right of access for newsgathering is in the case of
access to criminal trials. The decision in *Richmond Newspapers, Inc.* v. *Virginia* rested on the traditional openness of
criminal trials, and found no real justification for their being
closed to the public and the press. At this point, it remains to
be seen whether the Court will recognize rights of access to
other governmental proceedings that have traditionally been
open, such as legislative debates.

THE BURGER COURT AND
FREEDOM OF THE PRESS

It is often said that the present Supreme Court is unsympathetic to freedom of the press. The charge is exaggerated.
On the central issue of freedom of expression—the right to

publish or communicate—the Burger Court has extended First Amendment protection to such types of expression as advertising and campaign spending, not previously protected. It has taken the first cautious steps to delineate a right of newsgathering. It has removed due process restrictions on cameras in the courtroom. With respect to prior restraints, the Burger Court has been highly protective. Moreover, it took the enormously important step of protecting the editorial autonomy of the print media from the sort of interference imposed on radio and television in the name of the public interest.

Where free expression collides with personal reputation and privacy, on the other hand, the Burger Court has cut back on the scope of First Amendment protection for the press. It has created an easier standard for libel recovery by private persons than for officials or public figures. Perhaps more troubling are the hints that in the right case the Burger Court would sustain press liability for publishing truthful information thought to invade personal privacy. The Court's enthusiasm for suppression of obscenity reflects its view that pornography inevitably assaults the privacy of unwilling persons, as well as degrading the urban environment. These views reveal a pained prudery.

Aside from the privacy and obscenity decisions, most of the petitions lost by the press in the past decade have involved restrictions on newsgathering, and indirect ones at that. The Court has been reluctant to rule that the First Amendment protects activities that are not directly a part of the communication process. Partly, the Court is concerned about how it could limit such rights, and partly, it does not want to create special constitutional privileges for the press which would allow it to engage in conduct not permitted to the rest of us or to be free of duties generally imposed. So long as freedom of the press is focused on the right to communicate, the First Amendment protects the press and the rest of us alike, a parallelism which numbers among its many victims the absence of any need to define just who is "the press." In this respect the Burger Court may well be a better friend of a free press than those who seek special press privileges. Legal privileges tend to breed legal responsibilities, as the law of broadcast regulation attests, responsibilities that might damage freedom of expression more than does the absence of privileges designed to protect it.

LOOKING AHEAD

The great question for the future of freedom of the press in the United States is how our law will cope with technological innovation, economic forces in the marketplace of ideas, and the ever-increasing social significance of the mass media. Technological change and economic forces have already scrambled the foundations of our law's fundamental differentiation of print and broadcast media. Cable television and direct-broadcast satellites, and the promise of even more abundant technologies in the near future, are making television a much more diverse medium of expression than newspapers or magazines. The "multiplicity of tongues" premise that underlies our *laissez-faire* approach to print media will soon come closer to describing electronic media than print, if it does not already, and yet our law of broadcast regulation is based on the premise of scarcity. The distinction between print and electronic media is breaking down in even more direct ways. Newspapers and books may soon be "delivered" via the television set. Should they be subject to the rules of broadcast regulation or protected by First Amendment principles applicable to print? The question suggests the growing absurdity of our law's divergent treatment of print and electronic media. But if convergence must be the fate of First Amendment doctrines for print and electronic media, whether the convergence will take us in the direction of *laissez-faire* or more stringent regulation is not so clear.

Economic forces pose a second set of challenges. Few developments could be more subversive to established doctrines of freedom of the press than the trend to monopoly, concentration, and centralization in the mass media, especially in print. In First Amendment theory and more generally, the premise of a system of government noninterference is competition and diversity. But most newspapers are now monopolies, more and more newspapers and broadcast stations are parts of chains, and the bulk of news in newspapers and on radio and television comes from the two national wire services. At the least, we may expect that these trends will accentuate pressures for an affirmative government role in promoting fairness, balance, and rights of access.

The trend toward centralization highlights a further challenge to traditional principles of freedom of the press: public concern about the vast economic and political power of the press. To some, at least, it seems a bizarre constitutional principle that puts enterprises of the most colossal power beyond the reach of effective regulation with respect to the most important things that they do. In the next century our successors may look back on our constitutional principles of freedom of the press in the rather patronizing way in which we tend to regard the heyday of *laissez-faire* constitutional protection for economic enterprise a half century ago.

But the power of the press is not necessarily an argument for lessening its constitutional protection. On the contrary, given the predictably self-interested quality of much government regulation of expression, the power of the press may reinforce rather than erode claims of independence from government. The press indeed may be the most powerful counterweight our society can muster to the growing weight and influence of the central government.

5

ITHIEL de SOLA POOL

The New Technologies: Promise of Abundant Channels at Lower Cost

Electronic developments in communication. Copiers, computers, and tapes. Old media and new. Group communications—CATV. Developing countries and the satellites. Program diversity—quantity or quality? Computers and copyright control. Information overload. The loss of individuality.

For half a century, from about 1920 till about 1970, the literature on the media redounded with critiques of conformity, uniformity, monopoly, and massism. The word used has in fact been "mass media," not just "media," as though size and universal coverage were of the essence. The alleged effects of the mass media included the enveloping of society in a pseudoculture of pop material, with common clichés, common stars, and common fads from border to border. Even today, the literature on trends in politics or culture stresses the growth of media influence, of media monopolies, of conglomerate ownership, of the destruction of authentic grassroots culture, and the dominance instead of groupthink. We are described as the products of the hidden persuaders.

In the last few years, however, a new alarm has been heard that perhaps the mass media are on the edge of destruction. The great TV networks and the press are seriously concerned about their future (cf. Smith 1980a; idem 1980b). Sociologists and humanists are beginning to worry about whether the new technologies of communication will destroy the cultural institutions of the present and, if so, what the results will be.

INDUSTRIAL CHANGES AND COMMUNICATION

The mass media revolution which created conformist mass society was but one aspect of the industrial revolution. Entrepreneurs found that they could drastically cut production costs by using a combination of power machinery, the factory system, and the assembly line. Competition from the standardized commodities that poured out of the new factories drove handcrafts and cottage industries from the market. This happened with textiles, pots and pans, automobiles—indeed, with virtually all manufactured products. Cheap goods, albeit uniform and prosaic ones, became available to all consumers.

Exactly the same thing happened in the production of

media. The craftsman's print shop that produced one sheet
at a time was displaced by the power press (adopted by *The
Times* of London in 1814) and the rotary press. With a
handpress a printer could turn out 2,000 sheets in a ten-hour
day; the press that made it possible to sell the *New York Sun*
at a penny a copy turned out 10,000 papers in an hour. Before
1835, 5,000 copies a day was a good circulation for a newspaper. By 1836, the *New York Herald*, the second penny
paper, had a circulation of 40,000.

In the twentieth century, at the same time that Henry
Ford was developing the assembly line, movies and broadcasting took mass production in the media to new heights.
Today, both in this country and abroad, great newspapers
may have circulations of more than a million (*Pravda*'s is 7
million), and cost but a few cents. Top TV shows will be seen
by over 20 million people, not to mention the 80 million who
saw "Roots" or the 77 million who watched Lyndon
Johnson's withdrawal from the presidential race. Audiences
of this size make each exposure cheap. In the early 1970s advertisers calculated that they had to pay only a couple of
cents per viewer/hour. Low costs like this are possible
because messages are produced centrally in great factories
called studios or publishing plants.

Plastics, electronics, copiers, and computers

But a second industrial revolution began recently, a change
which is affecting both ordinary commodities and messages.
This second industrial revolution is characterized not by the
more efficient production of standard products, but by the
development of new products which meet a variety of human
needs. In industry, the revolution began with the development of plastics for consumers' use. More recently, the most
revolutionary sector has been electronics; new gadgets of all
sorts, from hand-held calculators to lunar landing modules,
have been created.

Fundamental changes in manufacturing processes have permitted greater diversification of products. Instead of reducing costs by standardization, ways have been found to give the customer some of the variability of craft products at a reasonable cost. Today's automobile marketing strategies seek to catch consumers' tastes in color, style, size, and image. If one now takes all the variations of make, engine size, body model, color, optional features, and accessories that Detroit offers, there are more permutations than cars on the road.

If Detroit is in trouble today, this is partly because it has not yet fully adapted its productive processes to its changed marketing goals. Assembly-line production remains the norm, but ways are now being found to diversify output at reasonable cost. "Robotics" is the flag word of the moment. Computers allow for individualized production under factory conditions and at costs near those of a monolithic assembly line. Computers keep track of the complicated inventory and logistics involved in having alternative parts. Computer-controlled machines can maintain efficiency even while varying the product from item to item as it passes down the line.

The trends have been the same in the production of messages. Various methods of electrostatic reproduction and offset printing have reduced the competitive advantage of enormous runs on giant rotary presses. A key invention was the Xerox. Chester Carlson marketed the first commercial copier in 1960. On the storefront window of copying services is often a sign saying "instant printing." That is insightful sociology: copying machines eliminate the bureaucracy, professionalism, and planning required for traditional printing or even for mimeographing. In those older forms, once a memo or report was written, it was handed to a professional to type over again on a stencil or Monotype or Linotype. The professional was part of a bureaucratic hierarchy with its own union rules, priorities, and schedules. To engage that apparatus was a considered investment decision. The process imposed planning. But with a copying machine, whenever impulse tells one to distribute a manuscript, it will be done, whatever state it happens to be in.

Copiers and simple printers thus reduce the "massness" of communication by improving the economics of small print runs. With a copier, one can print a single copy of a book at a cost not very different from that charged by a publisher of 2,000 copies or more. A number of publishers these days never allow a book on which they own the copyright to go out of print; if an order comes in, they copy the master, bind it, and sell it in an edition of one. Other publishers announce a specialized title, but do not print until the orders are in and they know how many copies to produce.

Other new technologies favoring individualization of communication include audio and video tape recorders. These allow people to build personal libraries of what they are interested in. On the production side, cheap portapacks and minicams have led to a video revolution. "Video freaks" all over the world are producing imaginative material; just as for producing print, the overheads are going down.

At the moment of writing, television—the most massive medium that there has ever been—is at the edge of transformation. In country after country new channels are being added, despite the resistance of what were monopolies or oligopolies. In Italy, the national TV network, RAI, has had to allow the coming of numerous commercial channels. In Britain, a fourth channel is coming. On the European continent, plans are being made for additional channels broadcast direct by satellite into the home.

But these are modest advances. The massive change in video is coming by way of videodiscs, videocassettes, and by community antenna television (CATV) and optical fiber systems that deliver eighty, one hundred, or more channels. Such CATV systems are currently being created in several American cities.

CATV makes it economical for the first time to provide programming for the tastes of fairly small groups. This is being financed by pay cable. If a pay-TV system can collect $1.00 from each viewer for a two-hour film, it can earn as much with only one twenty-fifth of the audience a conventional system would need which collected two cents an hour per viewer from advertisers.

ELECTRONICS AND THE NEW MEDIA

The key to all these changes is the technology of microelectronics and computing. In newspapers and magazines, computers have transformed the composing room, billing and distributing, the morgue and the advertising organization. Reporters and editors sit at consoles, not at typewriters, saving hours in revising and producing text. Computer-controlled editing and composition allow newspapers and magazines to produce local and specialized editions of the same issue with different ads and different features in each.

All that, however, is only the first step. Systems for displaying information directly from computer memories on terminals in the home threaten to displace the press. Coming soon, besides display on cathode-ray tube (CRT) screens, will be synthesized voice output and input. Computerized query-answering systems will have an obvious advantage in giving each user a tailored response to his own particular question. A reader will be able to retrieve a set of facts or a report that matches his particular interest instead of reading a journal edited to meet the needs of a universe of readers.

But the notion that the old media will be displaced is probably wrong; few media have ever been completely replaced by new ones. Men did not stop speaking when they learned how to write; they did not stop writing by hand when they learned how to type; they did not stop reading when broadcasting came along. Sometimes a new medium may be so convenient that an old one declines; cinema attendance went down when television arrived. More often, however, all that a new medium does to an old one is to slow its rate of growth; more books are published than ever before, but less than would be if newspapers, magazines, and broadcasts had not preempted so much of readers' time. So when we talk loosely of a possible "decline" of one medium with the growth of another, we most likely refer to only a relative decline. The growth of computerized information retrieval can be expected to have its greatest impact on the printing of hard copy, reference books, but we cannot predict whether the number printed will actually decline.

Later in this chapter we will review some problems with the new individualized media, problems which the old media have solved. We will conclude that both mass communications and specialized communications will probably continue to grow, but that we are entering a period in which specialized communications will grow faster than mass communications.

This change in relative growth rates is only part of what is happening. Up to now there have been two distinct kinds of media with a large gap between them: mass media and person-to-person media, such as the telephone. Two things are happening now. We have just reviewed how individualized communication aided by computers is joining person-to-person communication at that end of the spectrum. The other change is that the gap between mass and individual communication is being filled with new kinds of communications which we will call "group communications."

A mass medium counts its audience in thousands or millions; the mere fact of the numbers requires that only a few people talk and the rest listen—mass media are almost necessarily one-way media. Person-to-person communication, on the other hand, is normally in pairs or very small groups in which each person talks in turn if not at once. In between those extremes are kinds of communications among groups numbering in the tens or hundreds; those are what we call here "group communications." In them—depending on the technology—there may be an opportunity for anyone to express himself; but if so, there has to be a protocol to handle the competition for the floor. A public meeting or a class in school are familiar examples; someone at the front is in control.

Despite the revolutionary developments of the past couple of centuries, relatively little had happened to change group communications until recently. Carbon paper and mimeograph machines allowed circulation of memoranda to small sets of people; multiple prints could be made from photographic negatives. But the major breakthroughs towards group communication came with xerography, CATV, satellite teleconferencing, and computer communications networks.

A CATV system with 100 or so channels is ideal for audiences in the tens or hundreds. It is not yet used that way very often, but the prospects are there. To activate an otherwise idle channel costs very little, so the lease of a channel to a modest-size group can be quite feasible whenever the system is not fully loaded. Cablecasters are not now set up to provide that kind of common carrier service; they can make more money as program providers. They have no motivation to lease channels to others, for that draws audience away from their own programs. But perhaps public policy will ultimately compel cablecasters not to treat their plant as a privileged monopoly. If they were compelled to act as carriers, they would be able to do so at a reasonable profit.

The main limitation of CATV for group service is that cables are laid in tree configuration. For that reason, the only groups that can be served well are ones that are geographically localized. That is very favorable for neighborhood activity, but it is not useful to such dispersed groups as associations of specialists.

What is promising for dispersed groups is direct satellite teleconferencing systems such as are being pioneered by Satellite Business Systems. For the next decade, rooftop antennae pointed at satellites will be so expensive that they will be used only by such affluent groups as business corporations. Early in the twenty-first century, however, we may anticipate switched broadband electronic transmissions reaching into the home—probably by using optical fibers coupled with satellite long-distance interconnections—making possible dispersed group teleconferencing at costs ordinary people can pay. That assumes that people will want to sit and watch full video as they assemble as groups—and sometimes thcy will. But nonvideo teleconferencing, either by voice or by electronic mail over the computer networks, is as well or better adapted to many needs, is much cheaper, and is already available.

IMPLICATIONS FOR COMMUNICATIONS

What are the likely effects of these changes in the technology of communications?

Some of the usual assertions about communications in a future computer-based system are probably wrong. The literature is full of worry about privacy. Laymen scared by two-way cables and computers have fantasies of Big Brother snooping on them. Granted, a government that chooses to use electronic technology to monitor its population can do so. Computers can keep records on people and can be attached to sensors that note where they are going and what they are doing. The same electronic technology, however, can also be extremely useful in protecting privacy. An electronic file can be made far more secure than a piece of paper in a filing cabinet. An electronic message can be encrypted at very little cost; the technology of encryption is gaining rapidly over the technology of code breaking. Nothing in the technology of computer communications is inherently less favorable to hiders than to seekers. Computers change the game between them; snoopers can collate more data faster, but it is also possible for hiders to protect themselves more efficiently. As the game changes, the parties on each side have to be alert to prevent their opponents from gaining an advantage, so the privacy advocates have reason for being active. We as analysts, however, should not fall into the trap of assuming that computers are somehow unfriendly to privacy; they can be as much of a help as a hindrance.

Another probably baseless fear is that electronic communication will widen the gap between the privileged and the powerless. It is always true that the early users of a new and initially expensive technology are the affluent. In Britain, early this century, the Laborites opposed the Post Office spending money on the rich man's instrument, the telephone, rather than on the poor man's instrument, the mails. In partial consequence, the British working class did not get telephones until later than their American counterparts. So, too, with electronic message systems, computer conferencing, and CATV: if they are treated as luxuries, they will long remain luxuries, but if they are allowed to diffuse, they will turn out to be far better adapted to the needs of poor people and poor countries than present communication systems.

Telephones, electronic message systems, and satellites are appropriate to villages in developing countries. If a peasant today has a medical problem or a pump that is not working, what can he do? He must take a day and pay the fare to travel by bus to the nearest town for help. What are the alternatives? One is to build local clinics or service institutions; that is good, but inevitably these facilities are suboptimal in size, underequipped, and poorly staffed. Another alternative is to support these local service efforts by improved communications, allowing aid to be given through direct liaison with expert service centers. A small earth station can connect the village with the whole country, using voice telephone communications that do not depend on literacy and message services that do not take a week through the mails. Ordinary TV displays or audio cassettes can present the messages. These are cheap and appropriate technologies for rural communications.

The same point can be made for the poor country as a whole. A poor developing country is not going to have a Library of Congress, a fully rounded university, or a set of major research institutions in all the scientific fields it needs. It can, however, have a few excellent specialists working on its problems—using the best information resources that exist anywhere in the world—if it is willing to tie itself by satellite and computer communications to centers where the knowledge resources exist. Rather than fading in isolation, the poor country's experts can productively use laboratories and libraries half the world away.

PROBLEMS WITH THE NEW MEDIA

So we should be skeptical of the frequent alarms that the new communications technologies are a threat to privacy or likely to freeze present privilege. But we should be equally skeptical of the enthusiasms of true believers in electronic communications. Let us consider what some of the problems may be like when there are hundreds of video channels available, and when electronic computer-based message systems are in every home and office.

First, can we produce enough good programs to fill all those TV channels and the thousand radio channels that could be provided in every city? The answer is clearly, "No." The talent does not exist. If all these channels are to be used, they will not be used for entertainment but for meetings, for chitchat, for amateur efforts, for the transaction of business, and for many other things we do not associate with the mass media.

Certainly, increased diversity will not necessarily improve overall quality. Growth in information output has different implications for the best than for the average quality of what is produced. Increased diversity (which is associated with increased output) may lead to a decline in average quality—by certain standards, at least. It takes oligopolists to produce elaborate products, be they newspapers, TV shows, or opera. Great opera companies or symphonies are typically one to a metropolis. Dozens of small competing companies could not put on comparable performances. So, too, great newspapers with many featured pages, foreign correspondents, and similar expensive services require lots of money. Tiny organs of opinion cannot do the same thing. So the fragmentation of an audience impacts those elements of quality that are costly.

On the other hand, diversity is to be prized. It allows fuller participation and more outlets for creativity. We face a conflict of values: do we prefer a society in which many inevitably mediocre local athletic teams compete and attract the public's attention to one where the whole nation watches a few superstars? Do we prefer to foster a multiplicity of musical performers or to focus on the best and most exquisite talent? A widespread bed of varied experiments may lead to a few products of great value; this fact adds to the difficulty of the trade-off.

On these value questions, different societies will make different choices. We note here that the technologies of information production—including the computer, electrostatic reproduction, portapacks, and various other devices—are making it economically possible to multiply centers of production and encourage do-it-yourself communication. All other things being equal, this will shift the social balance toward expanded production of what may occasionally be brilliant material but, on the average, will be fairly ordinary.

Likely problems can be better understood if we focus on a new medium with which we already have experience. Let us look at what happens on computer networks. Hundreds of these already exist; their rapid growth testifies to their efficiency and value. Many large companies have internal electronic mail systems. Special interest conferencing and mail groups have been built on such networks as ARPANET, Telenet, and Tymenet. Modern newspapers with their computer banks of stories are another example.

Using these systems in a fully developed form, it is possible for anyone with a terminal to input or receive text, edit it, revise it, and send it on to anyone else on the system. Gone is the fixed text that came off a printing press by the thousand. Computer files are like handwritten manuscripts; every copy is different, and the problem is to identify the veridical text. But there is an enormous difference. In the days of the scribes, the copies were few; with computer manipulation there can be thousands of variations. Diffusion of text comes to resemble conversation.

Copyright and control

In the past, an author or scientist worked carefully over an article, then sent it off to an editor who worked it over some more. Finally, it appeared in print. That canonical form was catalogued, indexed, copyrighted, and debated. Increasingly, an author now drafts a rough text on his word processor and allows others on the network to see it in early form. They may edit and revise it. Thus it appears in a myriad of forms and in changing generations. There is no canonical form to be indexed or copyrighted.

Market control, political control, and intellectual control of products become more difficult when production proliferates all over. Controllers depend on scarcity to monitor strategic bottlenecks. Compensation for intellectual products is secured by having a tap through which these products can be released or held back.

Historically, copyright was a byproduct of the printing press. In Anglo-Saxon common law, no right could be claimed except in a legible copy of the text. The print shop was a well-defined place where copies were made in substantial numbers; identifiable persons thus could be held liable. Judges saw no reasonable way of controlling who sang a song or who read out a text orally; no copyright could be enforced against them (cf. *White Smith* v. *Appollo*, 209 U.S. 1 [1908]). In recent times, producers of movies, records, tapes, and computer output have sought—and in various legal systems, won—some copyright protection. In many instances, however, the rights granted are unenforceable. Magnetic tapes, electrostatic copies, and computer output are virtually uncontrollable.

How societies should respond to this changed reality is a policy issue outside the domain of this paper. Suffice it here to note some dilemmas. On the one hand, it can be argued that unenforceable laws are bad laws. On the other hand, it can be argued that, without appropriate means to compensate the producers, the flow of intellectual artefacts will dry up. New means must be found to support knowledge and the arts.

THE NEED FOR GUIDANCE

There are other problems, too, with a totally fluid, conversational, communication system, whether oral or written at a terminal. It is unsatisfactory for many purposes. Meetings flounder without *Robert's Rules of Order* to structure the conversation. Companies with computer message systems rigidly constrain what is entered by use of forms. A bill or an order is not entered as a free-form letter; each position and code word has its special significance under a rigidly prescribed standard. Newspapers using CRT terminals have had to adopt elaborate rules as to who may change what file.

Illusory, also, is the notion that being able to use a retrieval system to make one's own newspaper or journal out of the whole data base of knowledge is always desirable. Computer processing provides us with powerful tools for managing information overload by scanning much larger amounts of material than we could research in any other way. Still, we also need human guidance to find things worth spending time on. We pick the books we read from reviews and recommendations more often than by searching a catalogue. When thousands of dramatic performances are on videodiscs, we will need reviews and recommendations to help us pick the ones we want to see. The unedited wire services and reporters' raw stories would make a poor newspaper. It is too much work to plow through such an unedited bulletin board, no matter how good the computer tools available. We rely on editors to scan the news and select important events of which we should be aware, even if the stories deal with topics about which we had no anticipation of being interested.

ELECTRONIC COMMUNICATION IN THE FUTURE

The media of the future thus will be a compromise between the tightly edited mass media of the past and the opposite extreme of a purely responsive on-line retrieval system. The technology allows increased amorphousness and individualization. It allows those who are dissatisfied with what the mass media give them to seek and find alternatives. But sheer amorphousness will please no one. Information users and providers, both, will constantly be seeking new systems, new controls, new structures which will put information into meaningful standardized forms that are easy to use.

The most successful of such systems will have audiences of millions. They will continue to be mass media, and will be dominant, even if in the system of information as a whole the balance has moved far towards individualization and diversity. The countervailing tendency to provide—or even to enforce—easy and widely known systems will always be there.

Those who see inefficiency and disorder in the growing free flow and diversity of communications may believe that only by regulation can some order be imposed. The search for a system to pay for intellectual creativity in computer communications is a case in point; there is a strong temptation to try to stop the flow of text from computer node to computer node without controls for royalties. Attempts to limit the flow of personal and proprietary data across national frontiers provide another example. Even more frightening is seeing newspapers and telephone companies debating, as they are today in the halls of Congress, about who should be allowed to publish what information on the electronic yellow pages of the future; the newspapers are afraid of the telephone monopoly taking away their want ads, and their answer is to try to deny to telephone companies the First Amendment right to publish information over the telephone.

Indeed, we find ourselves today in a curious and dangerous situation. While we have for print media a tradition of unregulated private endeavor under the First Amendment, the government still regulates electronic communications. What will happen as our total system of communication becomes electronic? We could find ourselves inadvertently abandoning the First Amendment tradition if we continue to assume that there is something inherent in electronic communication that requires such regulation.

6

WILLIAM E. PORTER

The Media Baronies:
Bigger, Fewer,
More Powerful

Ideas, information, and profit. Hearst and Pulitzer, McCormick and Knight. Newspapers as properties. Print and broadcast communication. Corporate giantism and internal constraint. Pressure groups. Quality and competition. Conglomerates. Consolidation's effect on journalism.

The task of assessing the role of the mass media in American society has been forever plagued by an unresolved confusion between what we know and what we want to believe. Americans have been particularly inclined to force any issue involving money in the mass media into a normative mold before they talk seriously about it, and this has always been true of discussions about *big* money—as represented by big corporations with big profits and big circulations or, in the broadcast spectrum, big audiences.

The epitome of attacks against bigness was written by Morris Ernst and published in 1945, at the end of the second World War. Although most of the book was made up of data on the growth of chains, monopolies, and oligopolies, it was called *The First Freedom*, an indication that the real issue was freedom of expression. Ernst, whose commitment to that cause had been demonstrated in his brilliant defenses in censorship cases including that of Joyce's *Ulysses*, equated the growth of media empires with thought control in fascist societies (World War II was just ending). He adduced as evidence Anaconda's then-monopoly of media in Montana and reported efforts by the Chandler and Newhouse organizations to shape news coverage in their properties with an eye toward protection of the companies' business interests. His basic point was that growth at the cost of diversity was evil, and he found his text in Learned Hand's (1943) famous decision in *Associated Press* v. *The United States*:

[The newspaper] industry serves one of the most vital of all general interests—the dissemination of news from as many different sources and with as many different faces as possible.

That interest is akin to, if indeed it is not the same as, the interest protected by the First Amendment; it presupposes that right conclusions are more likely to be gathered out of a multitude of tongues, than through any kind of authoritative selection. To many this is, and always will be, folly; but we have staked upon it our all.

Bryce Rucker (1968, p. xvi), a professor of journalism at Southern Illinois University, produced a book which followed the outline of Ernst's and carried the same title, along with an introduction by Ernst which sounded the old theme in the familiar rhetoric:

This is the sad story of our cultural trek toward monopoly in the most precious commodity known to man. . . . The most frightening part of Professor Rucker's exploration may well be seen in the simple and dirty fact that the abandonment of the idea of competition of ideas can scarcely be debated in our culture today.

Rucker drew no parallels with fascism, but assumed—even more than Ernst—that evil goes with bigness. Two publications in the late 1970s were somewhat more detached in their attitudes: *The Mass Media: Aspen Institute Guide to Communication Industry Trends*, by Christopher Sterling and Timothy Haight, published in 1978, and *Who Owns the Mass Media?*, edited by Benjamin M. Compaine, in 1979. Both included more extensive data than Ernst and Rucker; they also were set out in language much more pallid than that of the old defender of *Ulysses*.

Yet between the lines of both books the reader could discern a conviction that most of the changes documented in their pages, however symptomatic of health for the media as business enterprises, were danger signs for the society. This endemic concern grows, of course, out of the fact that the mass media deal with information and ideas. Our Puritan inheritance leads many Americans to identify the search for profit as an elemental source of contamination; the more maneuvering and restructuring that goes on in the name of increasing profits, the more suspicious do Americans become.

That may be naive. Since the very beginning of mass communications, ideas, information, and profit have been irremediably mixed. The first books printed in the colonies may have been devoted to piety or pedagogy, but the printers made money out of them. The first newspapers in the colonies were published by printers, more or less as a sideline, and were generally a combination of information and opinion which was designed to sell. Benjamin Franklin may have been one of the great minds of his age, but he also was an extraordinary wheeler-dealer (often to the extent, by modern

standards, of sharp practice) in the business of editing, printing, and circulating publications. Even near sacred texts
from our patriotic inheritance have a strong smell of profit
about them; Tom Paine's *Common Sense*, it has been said,
sold more than a hundred thousand copies, and it is a safe
assumption that some citizens made a neat profit out of
scolding summer soldiers.

THE APPEAL OF NEWSPAPER EMPIRES

It was during the nineteenth century that the first media
barons emerged. These were people who hawked ideology
and a commercially successful product in a single package.
Perhaps the most famous among them was Horace Greeley.
As an ideologue, Greeley was an odd, almost comic, figure; he
was at least briefly attracted to almost every political idea
that floated through his lifetime, and all of them received
some attention in his *Tribune*. Toward the end of the century
William Randolph Hearst and Joseph Pulitzer appeared as
the principal characters in that curious American amalgam
of entrepreneurs who peddled their ideas—or at least their
convictions—at great profit.

The contrasting evaluations of those two large figures in
the years up to our own demonstrate the problems in determining good or bad influences. Pulitzer was the one in the
white hat, our vague tribal memory tells us; Hearst, the one
in black. Yet their business methods were very much alike;
each was, at least in the beginning, not overly concerned
about the role of his circulation battle in bringing about the
war against Spain. Each became, in old age, an irascible
tyrant whose commitments shifted from ideas to idio-
syncracies. Both were deeply committed to reaching a gen-
uinely mass audience; in succeeding, they helped lay the
seedbed for the era of political reform. Their profits ran into
the millions.

In retrospect, that sometimes seems a golden age of American journalism. These were people who worked hard to make a profit, but who would never renounce their right to say what they believed. In great part, that era ended sometime after World War I, although robust exceptions survived. Colonel Robert McCormick of the *Chicago Tribune* could not have been cajoled into saying pleasant—or even neutral— things about the British, nor would Henry Luce allow his magazines to say a favorable word about the Chinese revolution; nor, before his company went public, would John S. Knight countenance the publication of favorable things about the Vietnam war in his newspapers. To reduce the issue to perhaps over-simplified terms, the media barons who were either literally or spiritually of the nineteenth century would *not* do anything for a buck. It is the suspicion that most modern-day empires are concerned with the buck above all else which colors the thinking of current worriers about the state of journalism.

The new style of ownership is not so much a selling out of an honorable tradition as the elevation to positions of authority of money—and people—managers. It is particularly true of companies which have gone public, such as Time-Mirror, Gannett, Knight-Ridder, and the New York Times company. The price of their stock and the size of stockholder dividends have become crucial. But managers, rather than owners concerned with self-expression, also have risen to the control of Hearst and Scripps-Howard. Newhouse, like Lord Thomson, has been interested largely in the business side from the beginning. Most of this country's media are now, like many other businesses, in the hands of marketing specialists and accountants.

Concentration in newspapers has come about not through starting new papers, but through buying established, profitable ones. The single newspaper owned by a single family has all but disappeared. Many have been through three or even four stages which are rather like the ecosystem of the sea:

small fish eaten by bigger fish which are eventually eaten by the biggest (the family-owned paper sold to a small chain, which in turn is sold to a big one). The reasons for this passage are compelling:

1. It begins with the fact that the newspaper industry has been one of the most profitable in this country for several decades, with after-tax profits around 10 percent, well above the average return of business in general and double the median for *Fortune*'s top five hundred. As properties, newspapers are in short supply. The combination of scarcity and high profitability produces phenomena such as Gannett paying $221 per subscriber for a modest daily in western Pennsylvania.

2. Taxes and taxation policies make selling not only desirable, but in many cases imperative. A privately held media property is a taxable asset in the estate when the principals die, and frequently it is necessary to sell the property to pay the taxes. Ernst urged some changes in the way this law is applied to newspapers in his book published more than thirty-five years ago, but today the situation is, if anything, more difficult. Compaine (1979, p. 3) refers to some "speculation" that Dorothy Schiff sold the *New York Post* to Rupert Murdoch because of her family's inheritance tax position.

On the other hand, tax inducements enhance the desirability of selling through two simple principles: the sale price, if received in cash, is taxable only as capital gain, and if payment is in the form of stock shares in the buyer's properties, even that attenuated tax does not have to be paid until the stock is disposed of.

It should be noted that the system sometimes works in such a way that publishers who do not want to sell sometimes find they have been sold. The small, prosperous Booth chain, public owned but family controlled, set out to expand by acquiring the Sunday supplement *Parade* from Whitcom Investment Company, transferring 17 percent of its stock as

the purchase price. Whitcom subsequently put the Booth
shares on the market. They were bought by Newhouse.
When Booth raised cries of alarm, Newhouse management
made soothing noises, saying that they only wanted a small
piece of such a superb little organization. They nevertheless
began the acquisition of more shares, with another substantial block from a charitable foundation with cash-flow problems. Control finally was acquired, despite efforts by Booth
management to get the stockholders to stand fast, by simply
raising the offering price for shares to what many found an
irresistible price. It was the largest cash newspaper deal in
history. Many Booth readers have been protesting ever since
about what's happened to their newspapers.

MEDIA CHANGE
AND THE GOVERNMENT

Acquisitive newspaper chains are not new, of course (the
largest 25 percent of newspaper firms accounted for less of
the total daily circulation in 1978, in fact, than in 1923). The
efficiency, skill, and (to some extent) the objectives of their
managements are, however, new. So is the corporate structure within which most of them function.

The communication empires of the nineteenth and early
twentieth centuries were, in effect, single product—or at
most, two, newspapers and magazines—enterprises; they
were dominated by men interested only in journalism. Newspapers in Europe, expanding at the same time, were frequently adjuncts of huge industrial concerns such as oil and
textile companies, arms and automobile manufacturers; this
is still the dominant structure in Italy and, to a lesser extent,
in France. This seems a dangerous arrangement because
such media, even though they may be relatively free of financial pressure, inevitably serve as mouthpieces for the giants

which rather offhandedly own them. For whatever reason, the great American industries have never sought out communication properties for purchase, although increasing numbers of companies with no interest in media are becoming bedfellows with media companies through conglomeration.

For the most part, however, today's biggest companies based upon the news business have been self-generating; they have begun with newspapers (or, less frequently, with broadcasting stations—Capital Cities Communications is an example) and spread laterally into other news media. Acquisition of broadcast properties has been restricted by outside regulation; Federal Communication Commission (FCC) rules stipulate that a company can own no more than seven television stations (no more than five of these in the VHF band), seven AM and seven FM stations. Further, since the mid-1970s the FCC has forbidden the construction or acquisition of broadcast facilities by any company which owns a newspaper in the same market area, and a court of appeals held in 1977 that existing newspaper/broadcast combinations must be split up.[1]

In contrast to this rigid set of rules, the ownership of newspapers has been lightly regulated, with the antitrust division of the Department of Justice seeking divestiture in cases where a single company has two or more mastheads in the same market area (the Times-Mirror company, owner of the *Los Angeles Times*, for example, was required to dispose of the *San Bernardino Sun* and *Telegram* in 1970; as Compaine points out, the government made clear that geographical proximity was the only standard by approving the sale of the papers to Gannett). Thus there is nothing in broadcasting like the 81 papers owned (as of December 1980) by Gannett, the 36 owned by Knight-Ridder, and the 20 owned by Dow Jones.

An abundance of data and supporting detail about all these changes is available in several places,[2] including the

Sterling, Haight, and Compaine volumes listed earlier. The remainder of this enterprise is for the most part ruminative. Our first concern here is with the news media, and they, along with the other mass media, are increasingly having to cope with a tangle of forces which might be subsumed under the plain word "bigness."

FREEDOM OF EXPRESSION AND CONSTRAINT

We can begin by looking at what might be called the ethical imperatives, beginning with freedom of expression. This is a phrase with rubbery edges, better analyzed by looking at its opposite—constraint. The likelihood of increased visible, official constraint growing with corporate giantism can probably be dismissed. Although corporate publishers and broadcasters have reacted slowly and insufficiently to challenges of freedom of expression, they have eventually moved (in part because they sometimes lose economic advantages when the First Amendment shrinks).

The question of heavy-handed internal constraint seems almost as unlikely; the editor or publisher who wants a distorted news product for political reasons is probably rarer now than before. Support for that judgment is provided in a recent case centering on the Panax Corporation in which editors of the chain's papers were requested to publish two personal attacks on the Carter family originating with the Washington bureau. Two Panax papers did not comply; one editor compressed and rewrote the original story, and the other simply refused to carry it in any form. Both were forced out of their jobs by John McGoff, who controlled the chain. Journalists have been fired for literally hundreds of years in this country because they refused to do what the publisher or editor ordered them to do, but this case provoked a flap which made most of the country's papers and newsmagazines as well as a CBS documentary on the state of the American press. In any event, the heavy hand generally eased its grip as corporations took over from the earlier generation of media barons; such practice leads to inefficiency, difficult labor relations, and even the creation of improbable martyrs. It makes much more sense to pick competent people, as the organization defines competence, and let them apply their own interpretations of management's intentions.

That standard invokes a third kind of constraint, the kind which generally *does* increase as the corporation reaches out to take over more kinds of businesses: the effort to maintain a centrist position in the market to which the maximum number of readers, listeners, and advertisers are attracted, and to gradually push that audience outward, metaphorically speaking, until it includes everyone except the outer fringes which are so small they can be safely neglected. This is what manufacturers of most mass commodities do, and it is sound business. It frequently involves a decline of quality, as in the case of mass-marketed food in this country. It obviously happens to the media product as well. The Swedish government attacked this problem directly in 1963 when it first began providing subsidies for the support of newspaper publishing. The traditional dailies owned by political parties were seeking to build their audiences by soft-pedaling their partisan character; the first subsidies were provided not to the papers themselves, but to the parties. We shall have another look at the quality versus market issue below.

ACCESS TO THE MASS MEDIA

Another ethical imperative to be considered is that of access. What has been, and will be, the effect of giantism and declining media competition upon those societal groups which are not situated on that mass appeal center? The answer varies, depending on the type of outsider. Obviously, the groups which seek access are many. The extent of their success in enlarging access in the future seems to depend largely upon their numbers and the amount of pressure they are able to bring to bear.

This would suggest that groups clustered around ethnic identity will, in fact, do better in the future. These are the people who, in the past, have been invisible, in Ralph Ellison's metaphor—blacks, Hispanics, and now a profusion of groups in such cities as Chicago, New York, and Detroit. In many cases they are substantial populations, and they have been gaining visibility in the media. The first steps generally are the kind bitterly referred to by activists as tokenism— the hiring of minority journalists, for example, in both print and broadcasting (Detroit now has black, Arab, and Hispanic female television journalists, most of whom appear as weekend anchorpersons). But to say that this is only cynical, and that the movement toward broader coverage stops with it, is not accurate. American journalism has been improved by this reaching out, however mixed the motives of marketing and altruism may be. There is evidence in almost every responsible daily newspaper and on television newscasts that coverage of those groups and their neighborhoods has grown steadily.

Sectors of society organized along a different axis probably will find their access diminished rather than improved. In the development of his proposal to support access to the media through the courts, Jerome Barron gave much attention to labor unions, for example, which could not prevail upon newspapers or broadcasters to carry their advertising during strikes. The system of evaluation through which specialized interest groups obtain access to the media is complex. Madalyn Mays O'Hair's attempt to gain broadcast time to reply to church services under the Fairness Doctrine, for example, was dismissed by the FCC apparently without

serious consideration, thus sparing individual stations the
trouble of taking that action. But Mobil Oil Corporation also
has been steadily refused time by broadcasters to reply to
what it considers one-sided treatment of energy issues. The
basic test seems to be what kind of people, with what kind of
clout, will be alienated by lack of access. Those of small numbers and little direct power in the media—a group which in
this context includes oil barons, if one stops to think about it
—will fare no better in the future, and very possibly worse.
Those who inspire significant hostility without substantial
numbers to back them will have increasing difficulty.

That judgment, one must hurry to add, applies to the most
mass-y of the media: commercial television, standard newspapers, consumer magazines. There is every reason to
believe that the developing technology will provide greatly
increased access of all types, and at all levels except that of
wide visibility; obviously, when there are fifty cable channels
available in most homes, space will be available for almost
every group. The print equivalent is the copying shop.
Publication of a handbill, or even an issue of a magazine, is
increasingly cheap and easy. These media help add to the
discourse eddying around the marketplace of ideas, although
they are not what most of those deeply concerned about access are talking about.

CORPORATE JOURNALISM, QUALITY,
AND CONCENTRATION

Ethical imperatives, as they have been called here, are
abstractions for most people most of the time. As corporate
journalism grows bigger, the question of the level of quality is
more real and is regularly faced by even the casual reader or
viewer. What happens to quality when the chain or conglomerate moves in? Definitions of quality vary, but a

baseline can be drawn by paraphrasing the familiar language in the report of the Hutchins commission which, in 1941, charged newspapers with providing a full and fair report of events.

In some mergers and takeovers, fullness obviously has suffered. Two highly acquisitive chains, Newhouse and Thomson, were reported by *Business Week* in 1977 (21 February, p. 59) to be well known in the industry for their inclination to "chop budgets and staff, hold investment to a minimum, and wring the paper dry of profits." This kind of activity is possible only in noncompetitive and already profitable situations, and both these chains seek such properties almost exclusively. The signs of the new regime generally include a smaller news hole, less hard local news and more local features, and frequently a new format which includes larger type and more white space.

When a new corporate owner enters a competitive situation, however, it sometimes must commit itself to improving the product. The most impressive demonstration in recent years has been in Philadelphia, where Knight-Ridder acquired the *Philadelphia Inquirer* and *Daily News* and, just about everybody agrees, improved them greatly. Even the most high-status chains get mixed reviews in terms of quality generally. The pages of such publications as the *Columbia Journalism Review* are filled with anecdotage, pro and con, and the pages of research publications such as *Journalism Quarterly*, with survey studies, more or less balancing one another out. It is clear, however, that most changes imposed from the top are going to be managerial and not philosophical (or overtly political); most chains leave local editors free to make candidate endorsements, for example. Managerial decisions to improve quality tend to be taken when quality is necessary to hold or expand a market.

Competition of itself does not produce virtue; the important factor is what one chooses to be competitive *about*. A great deal of media competition is over trends which have nothing to do with either fullness or fairness. Consider, for example, the spread of the magazine influence in newspapers—the establishment of specialized feature sections, generally on a different subject each day. It is too early to know, except viscerally, whether newspapers promoting this space-selling device are downgrading the traditional marks of quality in a paper, but it seems clear that they are not elevating them.

The worst aspects of competition are demonstrated by television journalism, however. For most of that industry's short life, network news was not a money-making enterprise, and while prime-time entertainment was churning itself into a homogenized product which was to be evaluated in terms of two or three Nielsen points up or down, news departments were free to develop a character of their own, experimenting along the way. They were too poor to do much of it but, as Fred Friendly once said of documentaries, "we had time to be bad."

The possible development of local news into a money-making enterprise, however, brought a great deal more attention from managers and owners, who hired consultants— who, in turn, provided guidance on matters ranging from hairstyles through the need for constant visual excitement to the optimum length and number of stories. Since the tribe of consultants all worked from the same highly limited packet of expertise, local news broadcasts in competitive markets (which is where most television markets are located) have come to resemble each other in most respects, including the perpetual shuffling of on-camera staff in search of just that right touch of personality. In the face of these standards, changes in ownership mean little; everybody is playing the same game.

Big ownership, it should be repeated, can bring improvement. Managements such as Gannett are now moving to provide their papers with services rather resembling the boiler plate of the past. Most Gannett papers are small (average circulation for chain members is 45,000), and it seems probable that many of them will be somewhat better for the help.

Although there are exceptions, one might make a reasonable generalization to the effect that the worst newspapers and news broadcasts are, in terms of overall quality, likely to be improved by chain acquisition; the best are likely to decline, particularly in noncompetitive situations. Great journalism always has been expensive, and there are few ways indeed that the touch of the cost accountant can improve it.

The summary observations set out above seem to indicate that the case against concentration in media, so often set out in tones of alarm, is not particularly damning at first look. There are several varieties of concentration, but by conventional standards none seems presently dangerous. As American business goes, media oligopolies are modest. The most acquisitive chains have concentrated on widely scattered, small but prosperous properties in noncompetitive towns; there have been few cases of independent newspapers driven to the wall by competition. As for broadcasting, federal regulation has kept it, in Compaine's word, "semicompetitive," even though it produces the most striking statistic in the whole field: just three companies (the major networks) collect 50 percent of the total spent for broadcast advertising. That happens despite the FCC's long insistence on localism, and demonstrates the difficulty of trying to legislate virtue. Protected by regulation against any kind of direct pressure from the networks, encouraged by both carrot and stick to go their own way, most station owners still gladly turn the responsibilities for most of their programming over to the assembly lines which manufacture time-killers.

Ben Bagdikian, longtime watchdog of such things as media ownership, has expressed his concern about the multi-industry conglomerates which have a news media component; how well will that component report the other elements of the conglomerate?

There undoubtedly is an impulse to play down the faults of
conglomerate bedfellows, but there also are counterbalancing trends. In the first place, sensitivity to the problem, probably best demonstrated by the furor when International
Telephone and Telegraph proposed acquisition of the American Broadcasting Company in 1965–1967, runs strong;
although twice approved by the FCC, negotiations eventually
ceased. There also is the corporate practice, common
throughout American industry, of the vertical organization
of units essentially in the same field—for example, the independent divisions of automobile manufacturers, or the
spirited competition within the Time, Inc., conglomerate between *Time* and *Life* when those magazines were at their
height. And most newspaper chains, at least, give a good deal
of editorial freedom to each paper.

THE COST OF COMPETITION

To many, the central issue is the decline of competition. Our
traditional attachment to the feeling that this is *per se* a bad
thing is to some extent sentimental. In this country at this
time, when it is possible to receive through a $20 radio not
only scores of AM stations but in many areas as many as 100
FM stations (some of them representing special interests),
when a typical cable setup provides from 30 to 50 channels
—in such a time when psychologists are busily studying
"cognitive overload"—there seems to be little cause for worry about a shrinkage in Learned Hand's multitude of
tongues.

Still, that clutter is not the same thing as competitive
newspapers in the same town. Although small differences in
style are of some importance, the real significance of competition lies in the presentation of an alternative agenda, described long ago as the power of the press to tell people, not

what to think, but what to think *about.* Alternatives in what to think about, set out with the full authority and pervasiveness of major media, on occasion are highly important. Consider the *Washington Post* putting a "second-rate burglary" on the agenda and keeping it there for months while other media largely ignored it, the *Philadelphia Inquirer* making the inequities of that city's justice system a leading civic concern, and literally dozens of similar cases where the pressure of competition added to the thrust for investigative journalism.

And, quite apart from the occasional big story, there is a continuing vigor and zestfulness about most public issues in a city such as Detroit where there are genuine head-to-head competitors. Between the *Detroit News* and the *Free Press* there is a constant crackling interplay which adds vitality to many aspects of the city's life.

But the basis of competition is economic viability, and the cost of running no more than an adequate news operation in the future will inevitably mean more consolidation, more one-newspaper towns, usually after an interval of operation under that strange, sad piece of legislation called the Newspaper Preservation Act. The structure of broadcasting in this country is much better suited to competition, but the industry as a whole decided long ago that the real competition would be in packaging, not in journalism.

The problem is worldwide, and is particularly sharp in Europe, where increasing numbers of countries have—in the name of preserving at least a variety of voices—gone to direct government subsidization. American opinion, both within and outside the news business, is a long way from finding that remedy acceptable. Meanwhile, we must be prepared to see some old and famous papers die, consoling ourselves with the thought that most of them really are not much of a loss. After all, who beyond the immediate family misses the *New York Daily Mirror,* or the *Washington Daily News?*

Competition we miss, and will miss more in the future, but even that is not the largest loss. What we are in the process of losing thus far has been an essential part of the news business in this country—that curious mix of convictions, the desire to tell the world about them, and the desire to make money. It would be unfair to contend that the newer generation of media people are less interested in what they can *do* with a newspaper or radio station and more interested in how much they can *make* with it; that would imply cynicism. It is simply that mass communications is a good business to be in—maybe almost as good as, say, small computers or genetic engineering.

To put it another way, some of us suspect that the emerging news business will become to the body politic what prime-time television already has become to American culture. We are hardly on the precipice, however. Most of us who see journalism students find them still interested in *doing* something; the enrollment pressure indicates that the Woodstein—Lou Grant legacy continues to touch the young. Some occasional systematic investigation—journalism students have been researched even less than journalists—might help us track the change, if it comes. But reporters and working staff are not the first to change. A. J. Leibling once said that he would not believe in journalism schools until they had schools for publishers: publishers are the key.

A year or so ago this writer was at a press meeting at which the young publisher/editor of a small Midwestern daily was to receive a prize, on behalf of his paper, for investigative journalism. His grandfather had started the paper and it had survived the tax collector, at considerable cost. The prize-winning series dug out the details of some complicated municipal cheating in the use of federal money awarded the town; there had been little personal profit in it for individuals, and most of the money had been diverted to the support of good-hearted programs. Some of the town's most prominent citizens were involved, and exposure forced resignations and raised the possibility of indictments. Somebody asked the young publisher if he had not taken painful personal abuse. It was, after all, a small town; everybody knew almost everybody else, and there was the awkwardness of Rotary meetings and church and the country club.

"My family," he replied, "never have had much to do with the people of the town."

He obviously felt no other explanation was needed. His remark could, of course, be interpreted as lacking a sense of responsibility toward others. But it might also be taken as an expression of spirit, of an awesome independence, which has dominated people with a sense of first responsibility to journalism for a long time.

In either case, there are not many like him any more, and there will be fewer in the future.

IV

Analyzing Content

7

EDWARD JAY EPSTEIN

The Selection
of Reality

The news organizations. Targets, coverage, and discretion. News reconstruction. Presentation and bias. Television. Organizational control. The logic of audience maintenance. Assumptions. Adjusting the news.

The daily agenda of reports produced by the media and called "news" is not the inevitable product of chance events; it is the result of decisions made within a news organization. Many of these decisions are made prior to the event itself. For example, deadlines determine in advance the point at which happenings will no longer be considered viable news. The crucial decisions as to definition of news—what will and what will not be covered—are made not by the journalist on the spot but by executives of the news organization. Such decisions include the selection, advancement, and deployment of reporters (and editors), the expenditure of time and resources for news gathering, and the allocation of space for the presentation of the news.

In making such basic decisions, news organizations must consider their own requirements for surviving in a competitive environment. A news organization obviously cannot spend more on news than it earns in revenues for a sustained period of time without going bankrupt. Similarly, a news organization cannot advance the career of journalists who undermine its basic values. Eventually, it may be assumed, the key decision-makers in an organization will identify with the needs of the organization and they will make decisions consistent with its overriding interests. These decisions will in turn shape its product—the news. If these premises are accepted, news must be viewed as the by-product of three factors: events, the journalist's perceptions of them, and the requisites of news organizations.

THE ORGANIZATION CONTROLS THE NEWS

The most predictable part of this equation is the news organization which provides the machinery—including the journalist—for processing reality. News organizations perform in much the same way as does an intelligence service. They collect information concerning a set of targets, analyze the data according to some rules of relevance, and then present it to a particular audience. And, as is the case with intelligence services, news organizations generally operate in an environment of competition that requires secrecy (protection of sources), speed, and precision. Such an admittedly simplified model of the news business provides little room for idiosyncratic or biased reporting.

Consider, for example, the following operation of the Reuters news service. Reporters in twenty key cities around the world are asked each day to call a list of food warehouses and request the temperature at a given hour. This list of warehouse temperatures is then compiled into a table by an editor and made available to a special audience of food shippers who pay for the service; presumably, the service is valuable because it allows them to consign their cargo to the warehouse with the lowest temperature. This news operation is not trivial. Along with similar data compilations on currencies and commodities, it now provides Reuters with more than half its income.

Nor is such "scorekeeping" journalism confined to Reuters. Most afternoon newspapers in the United States depend for their audience maintenance on such computer-delivered scores as the closing prices of stocks on Wall Street, racetrack results (which also determine illegal lottery payoffs in many cities), and weather services. "News," in such cases, is merely reporting the numerical score of some event of interest to a special audience.

In this form of reporting, there is no analysis or journalistic bias. The "targets" are selected by the news organization on the calculus of profitability; the space is allocated to the scores for which audiences will presumably pay the most money—or which will attract the greatest number of readers. Such reporting involves only the decision by the news organization as to the time and place of data collection; it involves no discretion on the part of the journalist.

The news organization may also preselect targets which are necessary to cover to maintain its credibility. The television networks, for example, have a policy of covering presidential announcements and press conferences. If the White House press officer announces there will be a presidential statement, television coverage is automatic. Neither the White House correspondent, the Washington bureau chief, nor the news producer has the discretion to decide *not* to record the president's word. Like warehouse temperature reporting, televising presidential press conferences is merely an exercise in data collection. While different news organizations maintain different policies on such mandatory coverage—and these, of course, change from time to time— a considerable portion of the events covered are preselected by the news organization.

Journalist discretion

To be sure, not all coverage targets are chosen in advance by the news organization. Journalists, and especially the more established journalists in print media, have the discretion to select their own news targets. Even here, however, the organization generally imposes constraints. The journalist may be restricted to a "beat," or to a certain prescribed set of conceptual targets (such as arrests reported at police stations); he may be restricted geographically to targets in a certain bailiwick, or he may be restricted by deadlines to a certain time period. And ultimately, whatever the discretion a journalist may have in assigning himself targets of opportunity, his story must be approved at a higher level before it is printed or broadcast.

The perceptions and biases of journalists assume a far more influential role in the intermediary stage of the news process: the analysis of events. Journalistic analysis involves choosing and ordering the significant aspects of the data collected about an assigned target. Surrounding almost any happening is a confusing, confounding blur of information. The journalist—who seldom, if ever, witnesses the entire event—must reconstruct it from a welter of conflicting assertions, fragments of evidence, and possibly some eyewitness accounts. (The only events that journalists can count on witnessing in their entirety are those staged especially for the media, such as press conferences and interviews.) In sifting through the data surrounding an event, the journalist must have some overall view of reality to help him put together a coherent picture. Some statements might be emphasized and highlighted; others, played down or omitted entirely. Indeed, the journalist often organizes the material to coincide with what he believes is the true meaning of the happening. For instance, television reporters covering a political rally commonly find that from the same audience they can choose a picture either of a participant cheering with enthusiasm or of one yawning with boredom. If they select the former, they provide a visual cue indicating approval; if they select the latter, they signal disapproval.

It is precisely because journalists appear to have this power to reconstruct reality according to their preferences and biases that they have come under increasing attack by politicians and critics. In 1969, it will be recalled, then Vice-President Spiro T. Agnew directed his fury at newsmen's "instant analysis" of presidential statements and suggested that this analysis distorted issues of vital importance to the nation.

Even in analyzing events, however, journalists must conform to the rules and values of the news organization that employs them. They can, of course, assert an idiosyncratic opinion or version of reality in an isolated news report; but if they are to succeed, the analysis they provide must, over the long run, reflect the organization's view of reality. During the Vietnam war in 1965, for example, Morley Safer narrated a dramatic television story that showed U.S. Marines using cigarette lighters to set fire to Vietnamese huts. This report was attacked by the Johnson administration as "unpatriotic" and defended by CBS executives as "the single most famous bit of reporting in South Vietnam." Despite the attention given to this incident, it turned out to be a decided aberration in the reporting of the war in Vietnam. An analysis of network news between 1962 and 1968 revealed few other examples of televised reports depicting the wanton destruction of civilian homes by American soldiers.* During this period American television journalists undoubtedly had countless opportunities to film burning huts and other atrocities; the fact that few such reports other than Safer's were ever broadcast indicates that the values of the news organizations themselves prevailed over the preferences of journalists to depict American soldiers as foes rather than friends of Vietnamese civilians. In this case, television networks had no doubt what the organizational interest was: the Johnson administration, on which television stations depended for license renewals, had declared the Safer report "unpatriotic" (Epstein 1975, p. 213).

News presentation

It is in the final stage of journalism—the presentation of news—that the news organization exerts ultimate control over the product. Before a news story is published or broadcast, it is read—or screened, edited, and okayed—by a responsible executive of the news organization. Until relatively recently, most newspapers had rewrite desks which actually wrote some stories at the central office; reporters telephoned in facts and editors rewrote them into stories. This system permitted centralized control of news writing. As reporters increasingly tended to write their own stories in the field, it became more difficult to enforce the organizational rules. Editors had to gradually inculcate values through conferences, reediting and "spiking" stories that failed to fit the mold. The introduction of word processors and electronic editing of news will again facilitate centralized editing by giving the organization's editors instant access to the reporter's story, previous drafts, and even research.

*The analysis was by Lawrence Litchy of the University of Wisconsin. Quoted in Epstein 1975, p. 214.

On television, the presentation process provides the organization with even tighter control over the news. Most reports are filmed days or hours in advance and sent to an editing room in the central office. Producers thus have the opportunity to review the story, and to instruct the editors and reporters how to construct, "play," and narrate it. And if the editing fails to conform to organizational values, the producer can kill the story with ease. Under these circumstances, there is little opportunity for a report to be aired that contradicts a value of the news organization.

There is a legitimate concern with bias in news reporting. Unfortunately, critical audiences tend to assume that the bias they detect is the personal bias of the reporter whom they see on television or whose by-line is at the top of the article. This reduces the issue to one of personal fairness (or ignorance), and the remedy most often suggested is to replace or educate the newsman. This focus on personal bias tends to distract attention from the far more important issue of organizational bias. Indeed, if the organization is "tilted" in its preferences in one direction, news will tend to be distorted regardless of the fairness—or unfairness—of the individual newsman. Just as a roulette wheel mounted on a tilted table tends to favor some numbers over other numbers no matter how fair the croupier might be, a news organization that is tilted in a certain direction because of the way it is structured will also tend to favor certain types of stories over others. When confronted with such a biased wheel, it would obviously be unprofitable to attempt to explain its outcomes by studying the biases of the croupier. To understand the criteria by which the media decide what is news, it is necessary first to describe the interests and values of the news organizations.

PROCESSING NETWORK NEWS

Television news provides perhaps the clearest case of the
process by which reality is systematically reconstructed by
news organizations. To begin with, network news organizations have, unlike some newspapers and magazines, absolute
control over their product. Av Westin, vice-president of ABC
News, described the process of control candidly in a
memorandum (Epstein 1975, p. 200):

The senior producers decide if the story has been adequately
covered and they also estimate how long the report should run. In
most cases, correspondents deliberately overwrite their scripts giving the producers at home the option of editing it down: selecting
which portions of the interviews are to be used and which are to be
discarded. . . . In some cases, the senior producer "salvages" a report by assigning the correspondent to redo his narration or by
sending a cameraman to refilm a sequence.

Under such a regime, a correspondent has little opportunity
to insert in a news story personal values that run counter to
the network's objectives. Nor does the description in the
Westin memorandum quoted above apply only to ABC. During the year I spent observing NBC's and CBS's news operations, I saw even more rigorous controls maintained on news
stories—including constant review by network executives.

   In controlling the news product, the network organizations
attempt to satisfy certain basic requirements that will allow
them to continue as viable businesses. They must maintain a
national audience for their advertisers, a need which, in
turn, requires that the news programs be accepted by the
affiliated (but independently owned) stations around the
country. They must satisfy the ground rules laid down by the
Federal Communications Commission (FCC), which licenses
and monitors television stations. They also must maintain
credibility as news media. And they must conform to budget-
ary and time restrictions to maintain profitability.

The pressure of time

Out of these basic requisites flow the rules and logic that shape network news. The most obvious constraint is time. The networks allocate only thirty minutes each night for their network news programs. From this time budget, approximately seven minutes must be deducted for commercials and non-news items. This leaves only twenty-three minutes for the presentation of between five to eight filmed news stories and the narration of other news events. Confronted with this reality, the producers of network news programs have no choice but to limit most of the news stories to a duration of two to four minutes. This enforced brevity leaves little room for presenting complex explanations or multifaceted arguments. In practical terms, two to four minutes is not sufficient for providing the historical context or detailed geographic situations of most events. To make news stories understandable to a national audience in this brief slice of time, producers find that they have to be reported almost entirely in the present/future tense. The focus is on what is happening, not why it is happening or what the root causes are. This time requisite ineluctably leads to a picture of society as unstable. If great events happen without cause or historic context, then it appears—at least, to constant viewers of network news—that any institution is capable of foundering, collapsing, or being overthrown without evident cause.

The audience and the advertiser

A second requisite that shapes television news is audience maintenance. It is assumed by network executives that if the stories on a news program are unclear, confusing, or visually uninteresting, a portion of the audience will switch the channel to another network. Such a loss of audience would not only lessen the advertising revenues from the news program, it would—even more important—lessen the revenues from all the network programs that follow, since the news program is regarded as a "lead-in" for the network's evening of entertainment programs. Network executives therefore insist that news stories have both visual interest and visual clarity. In attempting to satisfy this requisite, news producers have come up with a common formula for audience maintenance.

The first assumption made by news executives and producers is that viewers' interest is most likely to be maintained through easily recognizable and palpable images; conversely, it is most likely to be distracted by unfamiliar or confusing images. This has special force in the case of dinnertime news when, according to studies, the audience has fewer years of formal education than the population at large—and when a large proportion of the viewers are children. In practice, therefore, cameramen, correspondents, and editors are instructed to seek and select pictures that have an almost universal meaning. Stories thus tend to fit into a limited repertory of images, which explains why so often shabbily dressed children stand for poverty, why fire—symbolically—stands for destruction, and so forth. Since television is regarded as a medium for the "transmission of experience" rather than for "information," complex issues are represented in terms of human experience; inflation, for example, is pictured as a man unable to afford dinner in a restaurant. The repertory, of course, changes. But at any given time, images—especially emotional ones, which are presumed to have the broadest possible recognition—are used to illustrate news events.

A second assumption in this logic of audience maintenance is that scenes of potential conflict are more interesting to the audience than scenes of placidity. Virtually all executives and producers share this view. Network news thus seeks situations in which there is a high potential for violence but a low potential for audience confusion. News events showing a violent confrontation between two easily recognizable sides in conflict—for example, blacks versus whites, uniformed police versus demonstrators, or military versus civilians— are preferable to those in which the issues are less easily identifiable. Even when the conflict involves confusing elements, however, it usually can be reconstructed in the form of a two-sided conflict. Network news therefore tends to present the news in terms of highly dramatic conflicts between clearly defined sides.

A third, closely related, assumption is that the viewers' span of attention—which is presumed to be limited—is prolonged by action or by subjects in motion, and is sharply reduced by static subjects such as "talking heads." As has been previously discussed, the high value placed on action footage by executives leads to a three-step distillation of news happenings by correspondents, cameramen, and editors, all of whom seek the moment of highest action. Through this process, the action in a news event, which in fact may account for only a fraction of the time, is concentrated and becomes the central feature of the happening. This helps to explain why news on television tends willy-nilly to focus on activity.

A fourth assumption made by news producers is that stories are more likely to hold viewers' attention if they are cast in the form of the fictive story, with a discernible beginning, middle, and end. One NBC vice-president suggested to news producers that all stories should have rising action, a climax, then a falling action, and a seeming resolution. According to analyses done by NBC's audience research experts (see Epstein 1973, p. 263), this form would "lock" the audience into the news story. Since the film is generally reedited by the producers, it is relatively simple to cast most happenings in this fictive form. The net effect, however, is that reality is reconstructed into a series of events that never actually happened in the form in which the audience witnesses them.

Events do not necessarily begin, build, and resolve themselves in terms of the visual data that are available to a television news team. Yet all the behind-the-scenes oscillations, twists, and contingencies of reality are neatly ironed out.

Networks and the local stations

Another basic requisite flows from the demand of affiliated stations that network news be differentiated from their own local news programs. It must appear to be national news. The problem is, of course, that all news is local in the sense that it occurs in some locality. Network producers resolve this tension by combining a series of local reports into a single national story. For example, the opening of a new subway line in Washington, D.C., may be considered a local story; it can be converted, however, into a national story by commissioning and fusing stories about subways in two or three other cities and then subsuming them all under a nationwide theme such as "Can the Cities Survive?" This process of nationalizing the news yields a constant agenda of national crises in place of local happenings.

Finally, governmental regulation of television imposes another basic requisite on producers: they must appear to be fair on controversial issues by presenting opposing views. This requisite is satisfied by soliciting views from spokesmen of two opposing sides in a dispute—and then editing these conflicting views into a "dialogue." To avoid obvious disparities, the producers usually seek the most articulate spokesman for each side. Not only does this treatment tend to reduce complicated issues to a mere debate, point/counterpoint style, but it also gives presumptive legitimacy to both sides.

MEDIA RESTRICTIONS AND REALITY

Organizational requisites cannot by any means explain all the outputs of television news. The personal quirks of producers, editors, and reporters contribute to news programs. There are also indisputable fashions and trends that change the level of consciousness of news reporting. The organizational requisites do explain, however, many of the built-in tilts that influence television news.

Print media have a different set of organizational requisites. Most afternoon newspapers, for example, face the problem of delivery: the news must be reported, written, printed, and delivered to newsstands spread over a metropolitan area before commuters have returned home from their jobs. They also must find news that has occurred after the deadlines of the morning newspapers. This severe restriction on time, coupled with union regulations that restrict periods in which the paper can be printed, have led the afternoon newspapers to focus their coverage on sports, horse racing, and stock markets. Morning newspapers, news magazines, and monthly magazines face different sets of organizational problems.

One question finally must be asked: Given these constraints, do the media present a picture of reality upon which rational men may make decisions? In spending over a year watching the three television networks collect, analyze, and present data in the form of news stories, I concluded that these pictures of reality were systematically distorted by organizational requirements. Dealing with such distortions involves the same problem as dealing with systematic distortions in a map. No map presents a perfect picture of reality. However, if one understands that such areas as Australia and Greenland are reduced in size, it is feasible to use a map to understand the geography of the world. Similarly, news itself requires some adjustments to compensate for systematic distortions.

If news media clearly and honestly stated the constraints and limits under which they operate, the adjustment would be far easier to make. Unfortunately, they tend to hide rather than to explain these constraints. News magazines, for example, print a false publishing date on each issue (usually a week after publication). This deception makes it difficult for the reader to ascertain the point when news had to be cut off because of the deadline. The value of news to the public would be greatly enhanced if news organizations revealed, rather than obscured, the methods by which they select and process reality.

8

WILLIAM A. HENRY III

News as Entertainment: The Search for Dramatic Unity

TV primacy—a headline service. Mentalities on the air and in print. The event. Novelty and the news. The reporter's role. Documentaries. Conveying news, not making it. Failings and values of TV.

The difference between television journalism and print journalism, TV newspeople are fond of saying, is that TV reporters carry a 2,000-pound pencil.

The joke is old. Small, light electronic cameras have made TV news crews far more mobile and have enabled their pro-

ducers to broadcast live from almost anywhere. TV equipment has become far less cumbersome and its arrival far less
conspicuous.

But the joke remains a useful guide to the conflicting feelings of TV journalists toward their craft, which some practice with more arrogance than pride. Among fellow reporters, they tend to be ostentatious and self-important.
They believe their medium has the clout of a ton of pencil
upon audiences and events. At the same time, they are embarrassed at having to impose showmanship not only on
themselves but on everybody with an idea to express. TV
crews lament the logistical awkwardness of what they do—it
can take hours to set up shots lasting mere seconds on air—
and they know their arrival can melodramatize and distort
events. Yet they believe, with the tacit agreement of most of
society and even of most print journalists, that TV crews
may command whatever they wish because TV is the Great
Legitimator. TV confers reality. Nothing happens in
America, practically everyone seems to agree, until it happens on television.

By that definition, the founding and dissolution of businesses do not happen, nor do the forming of unions and the
negotiating of contracts. Bank robberies may happen, stock
frauds generally do not. Protest rallies happen, but the subsequent delivery or denial of social services remains in limbo.
Budget and tax cuts are publicly proposed. Price indices are
announced. Inflation and interest rates are proclaimed.
Those numbers, abstruse and approximate, then become precise graphs telling us life is 8 percent better or 11 percent
worse.

HEADLINE JOURNALISM

Television journalists see life as bursts of distinct, discon-
tinuous events, however much we may live it as a steady

hum. TV is better at telling us "the way it is" than at threading together the several ways things might seem to be, as seen by different cultures or religions or kinds of men. American TV news, like the rest of American journalism, is scrupulously "objective"—which means it does not challenge the prevailing biases of a predominantly white, Judeo-Christian, imperial, internationalist, capitalist society. Executives at ABC sincerely thought they had made a "breakthrough in consciousness," they told me, when they aired a five-minute report on the theme, "What is a mullah?" Watching even the best TV news from the commercial networks, night after night, is more likely to add to a viewer's store of unassimilated facts than to enhance his perception and understanding.

Walter Cronkite, the most respected broadcast reporter of his generation, used to say in nearly every speech and interview that television news was a headline service, utterly inadequate to keep a citizen informed. But he did not express that opinion on the nightly news, where it would have mattered—not even during the most complex periods of Vietnam and Watergate. Cronkite and his colleagues have treated their eminence much as the dog treated the manger: over and over they have absolved themselves of responsibility for directing the public's education, yet have fought for primacy rather than yield that role to any other journalists.

National pageants—conventions, elections, inaugurations, the return of hostages from Iran or of astronauts from the moon—are stage-managed specifically for television. So are major presidential speeches and press conferences, congressional hearings and debates. In a nation without a genuine national newspaper, with no newspaper chain reaching much more than 3 million households and no wire service published unedited, the networks are the chroniclers of record.

Television performs its ceremonial role ably, and perhaps too willingly. During conventions and other ceremonial occasions, one or more dedicated reporters may ensure that the necessary—if controversial—things get said. But the words will be equated with and overwhelmed by their colleagues' gushing enthusiasm and hushed-voice pointless pomp. In short, on the urgent occasions when nearly all Americans (including print journalists) look to television for meaning, they receive instead a dispiriting triviality. The same television executives who can confidently reduce a complex news story to an essential minute and fifteen seconds are unable, or rather, unwilling, to reduce an emotional event to its rational significance. Television's intimacy, they believe, carries with it a compulsion never to offend.

SHAPING THE NEWS FOR
TV AND PRINT

The foregoing pages offer common complaints about television. Many will be alleviated or supplanted by new complaints when all-news cable services expand their reach and networks counter with more and longer news shows. But for the foreseeable future, the people who shape television news will have learned their fundamental methods and values from the people who shape television news now. Just as there is an unmistakable print journalism mentality, a sort of Platonic ideal to which newspaper reporters instinctively aspire perhaps without ever articulating that vision, so there is a broadcast journalist's mentality. It is markedly different. Yet it seems to be as nearly universal within television as the print mentality is among newspapermen. I have never been a television reporter. But I have spent a lot of time with them and their bosses, and feel able to risk a few assertions about what they believe (and about what print journalists do not).

1. An event is always a better story than a trend or an idea, not only because it is easier to report an event in video and sound, but because it is more tangible, more unarguably "news."

A TV reporter can cover an event, can even appear on camera introducing it, without overtly taking a stand. He does not seem to be shaping the news. For a while, a decade ago, Spiro Agnew successfully attacked the networks merely for showing antiwar protest, for acknowledging what he considered to be an unpatriotic reality. The networks gradually regained their nerve as they discovered that the public accepted television's fundamental defense: if it is there on tape or film, it is real, therefore it is news, therefore it merits air time. Local television news subscribes to the same standard, as community groups have happily grasped. Compelling documentation of an injustice is not likely to make a story for the six o'clock news, but a protest rally is. The first kind of story, no matter how valid, requires the station to become a critic of the status quo. That happens only in stories about child abuse, consumer fraud, and a handful of other motherhood-and-apple-pie topics. The protest-rally story, no matter how muzzily documented or clumsily theatrical, permits the station to pose as just the conveyor of news rather than the maker of news.

Newspapers, too, worry about looking like antagonists of the status quo, but that fear does not mute print journalists as much as TV journalists because of the nature of print. Newspapers have much more space available. Their stories are columns of gray type rather than colorful sight and sound. Readers can turn the page, while TV viewers must wait for the end of a controversial story before reaching an innocuous one. And, least obvious but perhaps most important, in print all stories look pretty much alike. Only a shrewd reader will notice whether the reporter initiated the story.

To amplify: Some print stories contain a lot of quotations and attributions; others depend upon a few unnamed sources. Some may be told in inverted-pyramid style; others, in chronological narrative. Some may begin with a time element, an event, that is the main reason the story was put into the paper. Others may use the time element solely as a gimmick, a "peg" on which to hang an overview of static or slowly unfolding events. Only a few stories, as star reporters have sadly learned, contain enough bite or controversy to impel normal readers to notice who signed them. Hardly anyone except veteran targets of the media will notice whether the reporter was following or generating the news.

In television, by contrast, a studio story looks nothing like a report from the field. A reporter on camera by himself, explaining, seems vastly more assertive than another reporter saying much the same thing as he stands in the middle of a crowd. Experts or spokesmen proclaiming their views suggest more balanced treatment by the station than a reporter summing up the same views, although the tape editor may, in fact, have savaged the arguments of one or both sides. Most TV debates, whether chopped into short news clips or allowed to run on for an hour, consist of antagonists talking past one another from different premises, using different facts, appealing to emotion rather than logic. Print reporters, confronted by the same jumble, have no choice by the nature of their medium but to resolve it. Broadcast reporters preserve the appearance of objectivity by letting the chaos be.

All reporters are trained initially to rely on quotations, to get out of the way of the story and attribute every statement. Some print editors, particularly at smaller papers, will not let a reporter say the sun has risen in the east without attributing the statement to someone else. But as print reporters mature, moving up the professional ladder, they learn when to take liberties. Most broadcast reporters don't, or can't. That's why Daniel Schorr, Dan Rather, Mike Wallace, and a handful of other moderately aggressive reporters are spoken of as so many Torquemadas. It's not what they do, it's what their colleagues don't.

2. *A story must be essentially new. It must not repeat its main points no matter how tricky they are to grasp on first hearing. And it must strive to be "definitive"—so that assignment editors, always short of air time, can consider the topics "covered" for weeks or months to come.*

This dictum can be violated for sex, violence, and scandal (for example, the Jean Harris murder trial), and—especially on local television—for running stories of emotional neighborhood conflict (notably integration). The rule is entirely invalid for stories of natural disaster and for those most formular of standbys, sports and weather. Otherwise it applies to nearly every local or national news show. Why? Because it reflects the strongest appeal television makes to us, the appeal that keeps sets tuned in millions of homes for every waking minute: immediate inclusion. If something is going on anywhere in the world, television can make you part of it right away. If you are not watching, you will surely miss (out on) something.

Television's impact on the "real" political world comes less from its scheduled news programs (although their publicizing power is vast) than from its live, on-the-scene coverage of events. Indeed, we remember many of those events as "happening" in front of the cameras more than as being covered. Vietnam, Watergate, the moon landing, the army-McCarthy hearings, the 1968 Chicago police riot, the desperate struggle for and against the nomination of George McGovern—all of these events reinforced our sense of television as a window on reality, not a reportorial tool showing us particular people's perception of events. When we look at everyday nightly news, we bring to it our accumulated sense of television's credibility, its reality. The reporters and editors, in turn, feel a burden to reinforce that reality by emphasizing events, happenings, immediacy.

At its (frequently reached) extreme, the commitment to events drives television to cover what are variously known as staged events, media events, or nonevents. Outside of sports, relatively few of these media events are created by television executives. Most of them are created by subjects (or would-be subjects) of news coverage, at best to convey information, less nobly to attract attention to a cause or personality, at worst to give a politician or other newsmaker the appearance of knowledge and concern.

An example of the first category is the press conference, a device predating television but brought to its peak with the rise of the six o'clock news. An example of the second category is the star-studded opening night on Broadway or the publication party for a book. Recognizable names and faces are lured with friendship, cash, or simply the promise of personal publicity to help promote a venture. A recurring example of the third category is a presidential or senatorial candidate's visit to a nuclear power plant, a factory in a declining industry, or a nursing home. Sometimes the setting is used to propose a legislative remedy, but usually the backdrop is itself sufficient to express the candidate's awareness and to imply his commitment to do an unspecified something.

Occasionally, in the middle of a report about a nonevent, an enterprising reporter will note that it was created especially for the media. But if the station runs the story anyway, the reporter's remarks don't have much impact—indeed, by implication they are contradicted by the news director's judgment.

To some extent, the emphasis on the new and eventful is an attitude inherited from print journalism. Even now, except at a handful of metropolitan newspapers with national pretensions, a front-page news story automatically includes the words "yesterday" or "today" or "tomorrow" somewhere in the lead.

To an even greater extent, the newsy nature of television is dictated by its technology—or rather, by the competitive advantages of its technology. Visual storytelling is best suited to events; in stories of ideas and in chronologies, the pictures become mere illustration—they cannot replace words and carry the story forward on their own. But the visual nature of television has mattered far less to its success than have its speed and its flexibility of transmission and delivery. Newspapers are cumbersome to make and distribute, and each is a discrete event. Broadcast news can be continuous or spontaneous. The competitive advantage of broadcasting dates from radio, which by definition was not visual, but which could bring the news first—as it happened. Newspapers resented the competition, but it ultimately enhanced their prestige; they were forced to become more thorough, more thoughtful, more analytic. Television was at first slower than radio, at least in the accumulation of pictures. Although sound could be carried over the telephone wires in seconds, it took days to fly film in from abroad and hours more to process and edit it. From the beginning, though, television could be quick—immediate—when it was broadcasting live events. The only events that predictably provided enough hours of news to justify installing equipment "on location" were national pageants: inaugurations, conventions, visits of foreign leaders (especially Nikita Khrushchev), and inevitably, the Olympics.

The way television handles events of less than ceremonial weight—in short, terse, compressed, often telegrammatic stories and "minidocumentaries" barely two minutes long—is a product of technology and economics. In the early days, viewers were effectively limited to VHF channels. Thus was the industry effectively limited, because of the pattern of channel allocation, to three viable networks. They, in turn, were limited to twenty-four hours of the day, and in seeking a maximal audience of wage-earner voters they were further limited to the handful of evening hours soon known as "prime time." Some of that time, moreover, was ceded by the networks back to their local affiliate stations. Thus, the amount of time available for news from the networks is now limited to half an hour. That limit is no more absolute than the fifteen-minute limit which preceded it or the old fifteen-minute limit on local news (which expanded to, in some cases, two hours a day). But this limit is rigid enough that the networks have been unable to alter it, despite a clear public appetite and a considerable profit potential (it would cost essentially nothing to produce another half hour of news from the same vast news department, while a half hour of entertainment costs $300,000 or more).

The point at which television news ceases to be a slave of history and science is in allocating the half hour of nightly news among numbers and kinds of stories. All three networks say they prefer to run from fifteen to two dozen items, averaging about a minute each. All three want a sampling of international, Washington, and heartland stories. All three seek "upbeat" as well as gloomy news. All three minimize crime (a staple of local TV news) and emphasize institutional government (apparently out of mingled civic virtue and favor currying among the regulators of broadcasting). All three attribute the basic look of their shows to the preferences of the public.

In truth, the networks have never tried any other basic format, so the public cannot be said to have shown any preference. It seems reasonable to assume from the ratings, though, that a majority of the public would prefer the current smorgasbord, or "headline service," to the approach of ABC's "Nightline" and PBS's "MacNeil/Lehrer Report"—that is, a half hour pursuit of some single topic. What is less clear is that all of the public has the same preference. The networks compete by looking almost identical because it is safer that way. NBC might have more impact, find more satisfaction, and even attract a bigger and more lucrative audience doing some wholly different sort of news show than by doing the least interesting of three headline services. But it would run bigger risks. It would never be able to "prove" that it was better off striking out than aping the others. And its senior executives would be denied their deepest desire—to "scoop" the opposition on the same story, even a set up and ultimately hollow story such as a political convention.

The major variation on the traditional format has been the expansion of the lead story, usually disguised as six or seven related stories, to fill a third to a half of the newscast. All three networks have used that technique more and more to deal both with such major breaking news as the Iran hostage taking and with such complicated continuing stories as an OPEC oil price rise and its political and economic results. The networks know the public wants longer, more thorough, coverage of major stories. Even their ubiquitously cited (but never documented) "research" tells them that. Yet all three are so constrained by the need "to keep the show moving" that they feel they must disguise the extended story as multiple stories, with multiple reporters, told from multiple venues.

All three also require that the lead story be "new," unaided by repetition, and "definitive." A prime example of these criteria at work, with destructive results, is the way CBS News dealt with its two-part Watergate summary in the nightly news shortly before the 1972 election. The story has been told by David Halberstam, Daniel Schorr, and many others in an assortment of books. Most have emphasized the malign influence of the Nixon White House, applying pressure on CBS chairman William Paley or its president Frank Stanton or its news division head Richard Salant. That side of the story is seamy, though hardly unique. Some have also stressed the report's tardiness. It came four months after the break-in, many weeks after the *Washington Post*'s major opening revelations. And CBS did not delay to complete a new investigation—almost all of the story repeated information uncovered by newspapers.

CBS apologists emphasize the legitimizing effect their reports had in making Watergate genuine news. The report reached Middle America directly. At least as important was its indirect effect. Small-town newspaper editors (and some big-city editors) had downplayed or ignored the story for fear of looking partisan or of taking a Washington teapot tempest too seriously. If the story mattered to CBS and to the network's vast viewership in their individual circulation areas, then suddenly it could matter to the newspapers, too.

Both sets of arguments are valid. What matters more in this discussion, though, is what the process of assembling the Watergate story tells us about the thinking and values that go into TV news. Of most direct use is the set of reasons Salant cited to his department for cutting the second report to half its length.

First, he said, the reports were too long for a nightly newscast. That answer reflected both the show-business values of the era and his news judgment (or fear of advocacy). In 1972, certainly, there were fewer stories meriting half or more of an entire newscast than there would be in 1981; the format had not yet been loosened. But there had been some—either overviews, say, about Vietnam, or breaking stories, such as the choice of a new president's cabinet. Salant really was saying CBS should not give Watergate such import.

Second, Salant said, the reports were not new enough. Most of the "revelations" had been aired on CBS before (many in a weekend news broadcast seen by a fraction of the nightly news audience). Others, he said, had been reported in newspapers and had then been adjudged too obscure, too minor, or too ill documented to make the CBS "Evening News." Thus he conquered practically all argument. Journalists, especially TV journalists, passionately want to be up to the moment, to "advance" the story, and to "respect" the audience by providing information only once (even though just a fraction of the audience for any newscast has seen any particular previous newscast).

The process of assembling the evening news is primarily one of excluding, at any number of points from conception to completion, enough stories so that the rest can be crammed into twenty-two minutes. One of the most useful criteria for considering candidates is whether a story is new. If rejected

stories could reappear as candidates every day, or if stories of
great moment could be repeated in trivially altered form, the
process of exclusion would become unmanageably harder.
Suppose, for example, that CBS does six "definitive" nightly
news minutes on the neutron bomb. In the minds of CBS
News, at least, that report ought to free it from having to
look at the neutron bomb again for at least half a year. Never
mind that the neutron bomb may be an issue we all ought to
think about every day. Never mind that the advance of
nuclear technology may bring closer the moment when all
civilized life erupts into holocaust. The arguments do not
change from day to day. It is CBS's job to summarize them
once, not to bullyrag the public into giving the arguments
whatever weight CBS thinks fit.

Salant's third complaint about the Watergate reports was
that they repeated their principal conclusions time and
again, the way a commercial blitz repeats the selling line for
a product. Repetition is taboo because it constitutes advocacy
(in line with Salant's first attack), because it is not fresh and
new (in line with his second attack), and because it slows the
pell-mell pace that the ever-active audience researchers
claim the public demands.

*3. Every story ought to have a dramatic unity, a clear line of
conflict, with definable antagonists (reduced ideally to Homer-
ic epithets) and a tangible prize at stake.*

Television is a medium of drama, whether in thirty-second
commercials or two-hour movies. It is a branch of performed
literature. Like all other performed literature, it is less concerned with the narrative voice or metaphysics than with the
story. It never lets ideas exist in the abstract. Ideas belong to
people who fight for or against them. Ideas belong to groups
whose lives will be enhanced or threatened by them. All of
life is a struggle, and a zero-sum game. Except in scattered
do-gooder stories—mostly about life in small towns or their
microcosm, nuclear families—no one can win without making someone else lose.

Television news stories are told in much the same way, reflecting much the same values. They may look different, but that visual style is often appropriated by advertisers (notably, Mobil) or entertainment producers (as on NBC's "Hill Street Blues") to give a feeling of reality and objectivity. Camera techniques and editing styles aside, news is shaped fundamentally like any other TV drama. News reporters feel compelled to find individual people to symbolize each story. Sometimes they are "spokesmen," sometimes "experts," sometimes random representatives of some beleaguered group. Always they are personally, passionately, involved.

A news story works better if the antagonists are physically different—a man and a woman, a black and a white, a young person and an old one, someone obviously rich and educated and someone else obviously ignorant or poor. These differences may fairly reflect differences between the groups locked in conflict. The differences may be purely incidental but dramaturgically useful in getting the audience to identify with one side or the other. The appearance of a spokesman may even reflect a manipulative choice—by the reporter or the group he is covering—to break down stereotypes and claim a broader than expected base of support for whatever the group advocates.

In any case, the ideal antagonists will shout or sob or shake fists or otherwise convey intense emotion. Television reporters find it easier to persuade the public that a story is important by showing how it disrupts individual lives than by standing back and explaining calmly how it will affect large but unnamed, unseen, groups.

If a television reporter cannot find appropriate people to symbolize a struggle, he may turn to visual symbols, objects in everyday life—a gas pump, a supermarket checkout line—to prompt viewers to project themselves into a story. They join the conflict in their imaginations. The story becomes important because subconsciously they link it to their own daily struggles.

Stories of conflict resolve themselves in a handful of stereotypical ways. One side may be seen to win. That side may be depicted as the good guy, or as the bad guy, or as a combatant no more deserving but luckier than his rival. The conflict may seem insoluble, with the message that ours is a complex and tautly balanced society. The conflict may be settled by the *deus ex machina* intervention of some outside force—the awesome power of nature, the benign or intrusive hand of government, human mortality, politics.

Or the conflict may be resolved by the intervention of the reporter, cast as a Lone Ranger, settling scores in a chaotic, amoral world. That melodrama at its purest is the underlying theme of almost every story on "60 Minutes," a much-praised show which arguably has done more harm than good by pushing reporters to see themselves as avengers and persuading the audience to expect a champion rather than a tutor.

The news reporter (and/or his producer) is always at least an unseen player in the drama of his story. The reporter or producer is, in effect, the writer of the playlet, establishing the shape of the conflict and the narrative voice. The extent to which he also walks onto the stage, making himself an overt performer, is determined largely by the moral lesson he wants the story to tell and the sympathy or antipathy he wants to evoke toward one or another of the antagonists.

He may simply comfort the afflicted. Almost everyone who watches television news has complained about the reporter who thrusts a microphone into the face of a victim of catastrophe and asks, "How do you feel?" But that approach, properly muted, allows the reporter to express the condolences of everyone in the audience. In the process, the reporter endears himself to viewers, seeming sensitive and compassionate.

He may humiliate the wicked, even if he fails dismally in the reporter's basic task of getting answers. By confronting a slumlord or accused embezzler or gang leader who scurries away, the reporter implies he is an agency of justice, a guardian of the public treasury and trust. The person he confronts may have any number of legitimate reasons for not answering a question. His version of events may be too complicated to entrust to a tape editor. He may be a pawn or a victim of circumstance. But in the mind of the viewer, he probably becomes a stand-in for every authority figure who ever embarrassed or frustrated or "ripped off" the viewer and whom the viewer never had the opportunity or the nerve to confront.

Occasionally the reporter may interpose himself as a counselor or conciliator. He will bring the two sides together, in actuality or in appearance, and get them to find crucial points on which they agree. In a subtler way than by catching a criminal or embarrassing a fraud, the reporter/conciliator again casts himself as an agent of moral order. He is the peaceable sheriff rather than the solo gunslinger; like the sheriff, he carries a weapon he hopes not to use—the power of negative publicity. The threat to use it is only implicit, but the subjects in each interview are aware of it and so, probably, is much of the audience.

For many stories, of course, the reporter wants no moral role. A Washington correspondent imperils his job if he appears to take sides in a policy debate. He is unlikely to take on even the role of the chorus in Greek tragedy or the stage manager in "Our Town." He will not comment on events; he may not put them into context. His bias may pervade the process of reporting and editing, but he will not acknowledge his role by performing.

To some extent, the reporter remains a performer, a personality, by the mere fact of his presence and the repetition of his name. The subjects of interviews feel important, and the audience concurs, simply because a familiar face is mingling among unknowns. A series on Japanese productivity becomes important, not because of its content, but because a well-known anchorman or correspondent travels all that way and spends time in all those factories. Occasionally, especially in local news, a story may seem just an excuse for a distinctive personality/reporter to appear on camera. That happens when the reporter or producer fears the story is dull, and covers it only because standard news judgment dictates it ought to be covered. Finding no obvious conflict, having no themes to express, the reporter at most can legitimize the importance of the issue. If he gives himself nothing to play against, he overwhelms the story. All the audience remembers is that they saw him somewhere or other.

Dramatic unity, even in sharply defined stories, is tempered by some journalistic needs—for balance and fairness, for acknowledging key facts even if they do not fit the Procrustean bed of two antagonists' conflict. It is especially difficult to bring many stories to a satisfactory ending. The conflicts may drag on. They may be the kind that can never be resolved. A preponderance of such stories makes a newscast too unsettling. But irresolution, used judiciously, can remind the viewer that the world is an unsettled, suspenseful place, and that the next installment in the serial melodrama of life is available tomorrow night or in film at eleven.

4. The longer a news story, the more it resembles a traditional documentary, the greater the danger inherent in dramatic unity. A long story in print almost always is a chronology, a narrative. A long story in television almost always is not. An hour-long documentary or anything longer must resolve itself into neat, contained packages, allowing viewers to tune in late and commercials to fit naturally. Unless it exposes an undisputed national scandal—in which case it is probably insufficiently new—a documentary must not show the network taking sides.

The obvious exceptions to this rule are the best group of documentaries in recent history, the CBS and PBS adventures of Bill Moyers. He is the quintessential reporter-as-performer. He has cast himself with complete success as thoughtful, compassionate, independent but not iconoclastic. He is an unabashed moralist, asking tough questions of the powerful, shaming the selfish common man. He is not an adventurer among guerrillas like "Gunga Din" Rather, although Moyers mingled with dangerous and occasionally paranoid Cuban exiles to expose the irresponsibility of creating "The CIA's Secret Army." Moyers more often goes down mean streets, as in the decaying South Bronx for "The Fire Next Door." When an old white woman's apartment was burglarized as she stood talking to him, he raced upstairs to comfort her and record the devastation. When a young black woman complained that she could not teach her children standards because they lived among people who threw garbage out the window and let it pile up, he echoed her vacillation between pride in keeping up her apartment and self-pity at its hopeless surroundings.

No other network reporter shapes his documentaries as openly and confidently as Moyers does. None has won such wide respect among opinion leaders, or such trust among ordinary citizens. Perhaps that is because none has tried since Edward R. Murrow. Perhaps the networks have created a self-defeating rule: until a correspondent has such stature, he cannot produce the kinds of documentaries that would give it to him. Moyers first won that stature at PBS. He, in turn, was able to experiment on PBS chiefly because his terms as presidential press secretary and *Newsday* publisher had made him a "bankable star" in movie parlance—a figure who could lend prestige and bring financing to public television.

A few years ago, critics and network executives asserted that the documentary form was dead and would be replaced by "more flexible" magazine shows covering several topics per hour. That argument was both true and false. None of the networks has a regularly scheduled documentary series, and normally none airs more than twenty per year. Most documentaries are bunched in January and the summer, low-viewing periods when the networks have less to lose in terms of ratings. Despite the infrequency of documentaries and the loyalty of their admittedly small audiences, the networks occasionally schedule one documentary opposite another. By contrast, all three have magazine shows, normally in protected, high-viewing spots on the schedule, and all three promote the magazines as the major prime-time outlets for their news divisions.

The Murrow/Moyers style of moralizing documentary is probably dead. Few if any network executives want to appear as assertive on issues as their predecessors occasionally were in "Harvest of Shame" or "Selling of the Pentagon."[1] ABC under Roone Arledge and Pamela Hill has been willing to risk narrative documentaries which take sides and have a point of view. But in those documentaries, the reporter is not a central performer. The camera is. ABC has followed the lives of violent youth or big-city police or open homosexuals by letting them talk. Some scenes allegedly were staged and most were prepared, if not rehearsed, by advance discussion with the subjects about what might be worth recording. All the scenes were edited. Yet the technique allowed the show to appear as unedited reality. Interestingly, almost all the documentaries using this technique were set in big-city streets or abroad (in Ireland, in Palestinian guerrilla camps). Perhaps the sights-and-sounds approach, with no narrator to explain or impose order, recreates the heartland American's feeling of being a stranger in a strange land when venturing out of the United States or into its urban core.

The polar opposite of ABC's style is the two- or three-hour in-studio blockbuster favored by CBS and NBC. At least once a year both networks recently have chosen some omnibus topic—education, energy, medicine, violence—and strung together a series of ill-matched short reports. The producers usually symbolized conflict by showing ordinary people in their homes or offices. The reporters typically were seen only in the studio. They did not attempt to resolve the conflicts, because the underlying message of a blockbuster documentary is always that the United States has long-running problems we ought to worry about.

In 1979-1980 CBS tried a variant of the blockbuster, a series of related documentaries on sex in America: a homosexual documentary, plus "The Trouble with Women," plus an alarmist attack on teenage sex. CBS network president Gene Jankowski conceded to me in an interview that his network—pointedly the most conservative of the three on matters of taste and candor—had appointed itself a guardian of public morals. Although the documentaries were laments, they were not like Murrow's or Moyers's. They did not prod our consciences and did not advocate specific change. They offered no reporter/hero with whom to identify and, except for the homosexual documentary, they took us on no odyssey, no linear drama.

The fundamental fact of the past two decades is the breakdown of common values, of shared presumptions. The networks, which must structure entertainments appealing across gulfs of belief, are as aware of the problem as anyone. They have halfway solved it in the entertainment division. But their inability to carry over the techniques of news drama to documentaries—their inability to make documentaries as narratives—is a direct result of the breakdown of values. Without shared presumptions, there cannot be readily identifiable violations of American values. There cannot be easily definable villains. There cannot be clear-cut heroism. Thus, there cannot be dramatic unity. The reporter-as-performer can be compassionate. He cannot crusade.

5. A local television station should boost its community and succor community institutions. A national network should assert the interests of the nation—normally, as defined by its government—and should love the nation's friends and hate its enemies.

Ultimately all journalism is patriotism. If reporters can be said to share a religion, it is devotion to making democracy work. Some believe they serve that end by building respect for leaders, institutions, social order, and law enforcement. Others believe they advance democracy by challenging those institutions in the "adversary process" or the "marketplace of ideas." A few simply commit themselves to comforting the afflicted and afflicting the comfortable. Whatever the method, the rationale is democracy.[2]

The aggressive, combative approach to democracy is far more common among print reporters than among broadcasters. Newspapers rarely become the official voices of local institutions. They hardly ever turn over their columns to politicians for direct, unedited communication with the public. They hardly ever enter into business partnerships with local athletic teams. And they usually keep some distance between themselves and their advertisers. Moreover, newspapers sell themselves as gadflies or, more piously, as the consciences of their communities.

Television is a surrogate friend to its viewers. Its voice sounds through the home four or five or six hours a day. Its corporate leaders seek affection more than respect. They ally themselves with athletes, politicians, businessmen, charities. Their business, they believe, depends upon being perceived as generally "for" things. Indeed, the bulk of the Channel 4 stations in the United States have used a promotion with the slogan "we're for," linking the station to local landmarks and institutions, to smiling children and sunshine. Other stations lack the easy pun of affirmation, but they strive for the same effect.

A major additional pressure toward upbeat blandness is the Fairness Doctrine of the Federal Communications Commission (FCC). Stations are, in effect, forbidden to crusade the way newspapers do. Broadcasters must give equal treatment to all factions in controversies, except in "bona fide news." Rather than open themselves to claims for time-consuming replies, stations tend to minimize coverage. The Fairness Doctrine mentality pervades television. Most of its executives, producers, and writers are obsessively objective; they think it is an abuse of their power to distinguish between good ideas and bad except when the good ideas are also overwhelmingly popular and the bad ideas comparably unpopular. Not surprisingly, in a business dominated by ratings, the mass will is treated as a moral good. Dissent, however trenchant, is belittled.

BROADCAST AND PRINT CONSTRAINTS

Almost as important as these differences in thinking are the differing requirements between print and broadcast to get the work done. A print reporter's basic need is an understanding of the issue, event, or conflict he will write about. To reach the assigned length with persuasive detail, he needs quotations, statistics, and/or description. He will want to include a few names for attribution, and perhaps in other ways convey to the reader his familiarity with the topic. But if he has trouble fulfilling those requirements in one way, he can usually deal with them in another.

A television reporter will find it far harder, if not impossible, to substitute one kind of film or tape for another. If he cannot reach the central figure in a story, he has fewer ways to distract the audience from that figure's absence. And even if his needs are only routine—getting someone to argue the obvious or quote some undisputed fact—he still must find a person to appear on camera. He cannot rely on library research, as a print reporter can, because he must make the story visual—if only with someone else's talking head to replace his own.

Print reporters, and media-wise politicians and businessmen, often express contempt for television reporters who arrive, ask three or four uninformed questions, record some film or tape, and leave. Those TV reporters are probably on their way to three or four similar assignments. A typical big-city print reporter does no more than one story a day. A TV reporter in the same city will almost always handle several. The TV reporter may want to spend time informing himself before or during an interview, but instead he must move on. If he had the time to linger, there would be no professional reward for his diligence. As a performer, he is not meant to take the place of the expert. He is supposed to stand in for the dull-witted common citizen. Thus, he cannot display new-found erudition. He cannot even act the most subtle, sophisticated portions of his interview, because the viewer supposedly would be left baffled by too much complexity.

Network reporters, especially those on the major Washington beats, are given time to develop a grasp of the political game and its players. They are at least informed, if not always shrewd and analytic. Their problem is getting air time to share that information. They are somewhat more free than local reporters to speak into a microphone—free of spokesmen and experts—and to assert their version of the truth. But that freedom is relative. Their primary job is to find snippets of reality to tell a story, not to tell it themselves.

TV NEWS—NETWORK AND LOCAL

When critics and opinion leaders talk about TV news, they almost always mean the nightly network news. When the public talks about news, it is just as likely to mean local news, for which ratings are generally higher and the total number of hours watched is considerably larger. With rare exceptions (ABC's giving almost the entire show to the capture of the "Son of Sam" killer), network news is sober and responsible. Local news is often a freak show. The most esteemed station in Boston once began its main newscast with five consecutive fire stories. The anchor on another network-affiliated Boston station referred to Teng Hsiao-Ping, twice, as "Mr. Ping." San Francisco's most popular station began one newscast that I saw with a teaser about "what X-rays showed in Adolf Hitler's head." Then it cut to an interview with its own technicians, out on strike. Then it cut to footage of a tornado a thousand miles away that had injured no one but had demolished a root-beer stand. Such trivia are the rule, not the exception. Similarly, the weatherman is a clown almost everywhere, and almost all anchors are hired for "warmth" and ability to make scripted chitchat sound like ad libs.

Why does television veer to such extremes? How can the same stations which demand that network news be good also cheerily let local news be so bad? The answer, as usual, is money. Network news now shows a profit (quickly dissipated on documentaries and late-night specials), but for most of its history it has been a loss leader. Networks regarded news as overhead, as an administrative cost, a sop to Congress, the FCC, and the highbrows. It was just a fee for doing business. Local news, by contrast, came into flower in the last decade chiefly because it turned into a "profit center"—at some stations, news provides 60 percent of the net. For the network, news is a justification for profitable entertainment. At local stations, the network entertainments have become a lure to attract the audiences for profitable news.

Keeping profits high compels the stations to keep the news staff small, and to spend on things that show (anchor desks, fancy electronics) rather than on worthier things that do not (staff and research). News directors use sensational footage, often from far outside the community, because it draws audience and, equally important, because it is cheap or free from the network. Producers feel free to trivialize the show because it does not bear the burden of high-mindedness; the network news meets that obligation. Executives speak of their news performers as "talent," not as journalists. Robert Bennett, whose WCVB in Boston is a four-time winner of the Gabriel award as the best station in the United States, says:

Anchormen are not newsmen. They are not reporters. They are readers. It doesn't matter to the success of the show whether they even understand what they're reading, so long as they sound as if they do. Good reporting is important to a news show, but anchormen have no part in that. And only two or three of the reporters need to be any good. A lot of the stories we treat routinely. Anyone attractive and moderately intelligent can stand there and let the producer or the cameraman get the tape.

THE VALUE OF TELEVISION

In counterpoint to the failings of television news are its unmatched accomplishments. Television, not print, persuaded us of the folly of the war in Vietnam. Despite the dedication of the *Washington Post* and, eventually, other print media, it was television—both on nightly news and in live coverage—that most effectively aroused the public about Watergate and brought Richard Nixon to justice. Television, by playing the Abscam videotapes, enabled the public to push aside congressmen's claims of victimized innocence and see their raw corruption.

The more modest daily achievement of television is so obvious we tend to dismiss it with the words "headline service." Television news enables the whole nation to learn of events within hours, even minutes, to distinguish fact from rumor, to place disasters in context. It is faster and far more nearly universal than newspapers. It links the broad public with events. And despite the claims of "cabal" by Spiro Agnew and others, television news has evolved into entities so big and decentralized that they could not be manipulated into deceit for long, if indeed some executive wanted to do so. If television is neither penetrating nor brave, it is at least generally accurate and customarily fair.

Sometimes television news is a victim of its own credibility. When Ronald Reagan was contemplating asking Gerald Ford to join his ticket, and again when Reagan and press secretary James Brady were shot, the networks reported "facts" that were only rumors, and inaccurate rumors at that. Ranking politicians, with no source of information other than the networks, heard these "facts" on television or heard them from someone else who had heard them on television. Moments later, these politicians recycled the "facts" to the networks as things they had "heard"—from television. Then the networks cited the politicians in proof of their "facts." Thus Gerald Ford was "nominated" and James Brady was "dead" and all America "knew" it.

Most journalists rely on sources to verify a rumor. Most of them figure that if several independent sources confirm it, it must be true. That system breaks down when the sources have already been told, by the reporter's own medium, whatever the reporter seeks to confirm.

That is the heaviest burden on a TV reporter—the persuasive power of his own medium. Television is made by people obsessed with objectivity but biased toward the mainstream. Its stories are largely limited to the new and the obvious. It seeks to fulfill psychic needs of the audience and yields to dramaturgical needs of the reporter. It avoids moral commitment, yet presents itself as an avenging angel. It compromises its detachment with boosterism. It is edited and purposeful. But while print is gray and abstract, TV looks and sounds like spontaneous life.

9

MICHAEL JAY ROBINSON

A Statesman Is a Dead Politician: Candidate Images on Network News

Candidate evaluation on television. The negative bias. Implicit and explicit criticism. Treatment of "the final four." Candidate typecasting. The infidelity theory. The decline of positive feelings.

In Campaign '80 the networks essentially were nonpartisan; they showed flashes of serious attention to issues; they behaved responsibly in most every respect. But when it came to telling us anything at all about the candidates' leadership or personal qualities, the networks did something everybody's mother always counseled against—they said something bad or, more often than not, they said nothing at all.

Having watched more than 600 network news programs in 1980, and having now analyzed in substantial detail 1,500 campaign or campaign-related stories on the CBS "Evening News," I've come away believing that on TV there are no statesmen, only politicians. No matter who the candidate is—despite his party or public philosophy—if he leads the pack or starts to pull away from it, chances are near certain the networks will get tougher with him. And the better he does, the tougher they get. On national TV, losers and challengers may get the benefit of the doubt but winners do not. Videotapes for all three networks indicate that the aggrieved party in Campaign '80 was not the Democrats, was not the Republicans, was not even the National Unity Campaign of John Anderson. As a class, it was front-runners and incumbents who came away with the worst press coverage and the most gripes about the evening news.

EXPLICITNESS ON THE EVENING NEWS

The networks rarely judge candidates directly. When it comes to TV, there is only slightly more explicitness about individual politicians than about sex. To a surprising degree, networks refrain from making explicit evaluations of the candidate's background, credentials, past record, or competence. Among the 788 presidential campaign stories on CBS—stories devoted fully to the campaign—CBS reporters made only six explicit evaluations of candidate competence. Those same reports made only five unambiguous remarks concerning candidate integrity. During all of Campaign '80 on the "Evening News," CBS correspondents drew not one single explicit conclusion concerning the policy positions of a presidential candidate! If reluctance to draw direct conclusions about personal qualities or political philosophy is a test of objectivity—then CBS campaign news was almost purely objective. So, too, both ABC and NBC.

Not surprisingly, the horse race was the one dimension in which the networks did take it upon themselves to make clearly definitive statements about presidential contenders. There were four times as many explicit references to success or failure as there were to all other candidate characteristics combined. CBS—like the national press generally—felt more than free in assessing each candidate's chances of getting elected, felt less than free about evaluating the qualities of "the man," and felt no freedom whatever in judging anybody's political point of view.

But what CBS did say went in favor of the negative. Table 1 presents the complete and explicit "profile" for each of the thirteen candidates who managed at least one story on the "Evening News." The "score" for each candidate is an index—a summary measure—which combines all the explicit references, positive and negative, to the candidate's competence, integrity, consistency, "quality," during the course of the campaign.

Three candidates failed to generate a single complete story. Six of the candidates received not a single explicit comment. Only five candidates received as many as two explicit references concerning their general qualities for leadership.

But for all candidates combined, the aggregate press score is unequivocally negative—minus 18. That number means that having subtracted all the explicitly positive evaluations from the explicitly negative, there was a remainder of eighteen negative references for all of the candidates. (Negative references outnumbered positive references by about three to two.) What is equally apparent in table 1 is that the two front-runners, Carter and Reagan, got the bulk of the evaluation and the lion's share of criticism.

Table 1
Press Evaluation of Candidates,
January to Election Day 1980
(explicit references only) *

Candidate**	Total press scores
Anderson	+ 4
Bush	+ 2
Baker	− 1
Connally	− 1
Reagan	− 5
Carter	−17
Total score	−18

*Qualities evaluated: "competence," "integrity," "consistency," "general quality."

**Candidates not explicitly evaluated: Brown, Clark, Crane, Dole, Ford, Pressler. Candidates not receiving any complete stories: Fernandez, LaRouche, Stassen.

This table does not, however, indicate changes in candidate images over time. Despite the fact that John Anderson and George Bush look "good" here, their press images during the campaign moved toward the negative. In the last three months of the campaign, all the active candidates had, in aggregate, a "bad press" on CBS.

John Anderson, the one man who was able to keep his explicit media image much above the break-even point, got some very hostile press after his newness had worn away. Walter Cronkite stuck Anderson with what may well have been the most negative one-liner of the campaign when Cronkite led a piece in early July proclaiming that "John Anderson was on the campaign trail today—in Jerusalem! —telling the Israelis and, in effect, American Jewish voters a lot of what they wanted to hear."

Cronkite's remark about Anderson ought not to be regarded as typical; Anderson, after all, did better overall than any other candidate in explicit evaluation. And most of the criticism that did appear in the "Evening News" was not quite this direct. But despite the fact that most stories said next to nothing about our potential presidents beyond the issue of winning or losing, what did come across—especially for those at the head of the pack—was an accentuation of the negative. In entertainment television, explicit sexuality is infrequent but sometimes good; explicit campaign coverage, on the other hand, is as conspicuously bad as it is notably rare.

SOFT CORE CRITICISM

Press need not be explicit to be bad press. Implicit—soft core—criticism is as meaningful as the explicit kind. Whether it takes the form of innuendo, unbalanced presentation of sources, or tone, implicit messages do count. And in

Campaign '80 implicit evaluations outnumbered the explicit by a lot.

But despite the fact that there was more of it, implicit evaluation followed the same basic pattern. The bulk of the total evaluations was negative. The index of press on implicit evaluation, not including successfulness of candidate, was −22.

Sometimes the most critical news stories were couched in the passive voice or written with the conclusions unstated. In what may have been the most negative piece of all in Campaign '80, Walter Cronkite and Leslie Stahl together did an analysis of President Carter's performance in office during the first four months of the year—but neither said anything explicit.

In their seven-minute report, neither Stahl nor Cronkite concluded that Carter's campaign behavior had been cynical and manipulative, but no other conclusion could have been drawn.

Cronkite: It's been called the rose-garden campaign—Jimmy Carter's nontravelling bid for reelection. Ostensibly it is dictated by concern about the hostages in Iran. But has it been above the fray of politics? Well, Leslie Stahl reports.

Stahl: The timing of the president's policy decisions and announcements throughout the campaign season has raised a suspicion that a number of them have been made not because of the normal flow of foreign policy or economic events but for practical political considerations.

Stahl then described, with an electronic calendar as visual, how closely Carter's actions as president had corresponded with the dates of the primaries and caucuses. But she never said outright what she meant—that Carter had exploited his incumbency before every major caucus and primary campaign.

In some senses, the rose-garden piece was unusual—unusual in length, unusual in detail, and unusual in investigative scope. But in many respects it was campaign coverage writ large—implicit, indirect, negative toward the incumbent and toward front-runners. Networks generally chose not to draw complete candidate portraits; even the sketches were few and far between. But the sketches they did pen looked more like the cynical caricatures of Daumier than the virginal faces of Renoir.

IMAGES OF ALSO-RANS

Benny Fernandez failed to make the cut—not a single story for Benny on the weekday "Evening News" in 1980. Of course, Benny Fernandez was not legitimate, let alone viable as a Republican candidate for president.

Robert Dole and Phil Crane *were* legitimate and, arguably, even viable. Yet they did not do much better than Benny Fernandez on CBS.

Crane, a formidable member of the Republican delegation in the House, appeared as principal candidate in a total of three stories—stories in which he revised his campaign schedule, failed to qualify for matching funds, withdrew from the race. His total time on CBS in Campaign '80 was 290 seconds—less than five minutes—half of which was given to his swan song retreat.

Robert Dole had been a household word back in 1976, serving as Gerald Ford's ill-conceived choice for vice-presidential running mate. In the late 1970s Dole served admirably—and visibly—in the Congress as ranking minority member on the Senate Finance Committee. But Dole's visibility stopped at the Capitol's edge. He "starred" in only two stories on CBS—stories in which he considered withdrawing and then did drop out of the race. For all his promise, Dole managed 205 seconds of total news time on the "Evening News." His image was, as he proved to be, that of a surprisingly big loser.

Dole and Crane were completely faceless on the news—men without defined politics or image. But there were other also-rans who were "lucky" enough to attract at least one "feature" piece—a full-length campaign story. These second-tier also-rans never seriously challenged for the nomination, but they did elicit something approaching a media "image" in their few moments of news time. The sketches were vague, generally incomplete, and invariably unflattering.

The clearest case is Jerry Brown. Having passed the threshold of newsworthiness, Brown appeared as principal candidate in a not insignificant eight news stories. In almost all of those stories Brown was painted explicitly as a loser or implicitly as a flake—sometimes both. Bernard Goldberg labelled Brown's campaign the year's "political skylab." Roger Mudd presented Robert Dole saying Jerry Brown was a "beep, beep, beep from outer space." Mudd also gave us Reagan saying that Brown was the candidate who plays his records instead of running on them. To Mudd, Brown was "the candidate who rarely tells jokes himself" but is "frequently the butt of them." In his final campaign appearance on CBS, Jerry Brown was portrayed as a possible replacement for Harold Stassen—a boy wonder gone to seed. Even after Brown was long gone from the race, Bruce Morton referred to him as the "only candidate who spent money to appear on television with holes in his head."

John Connally attracted media coverage the same way he attracted voters—fitfully, if at all. Despite his credentials and a telegenic style, Connally was principal candidate in only six stories. His total news time was 490 seconds. Connally was *not* treated as a wheeler-dealer. He appeared as he was—a candidate unable to parlay his wealth and connections into anything approaching success. CBS said little about Connally, the person, but in the words of one South Carolinian quoted on the "Evening News," Connally was nothing more than a "Texas show horse [who'd] been gelded." So much for John Connally.

Baker and Bush are the last of the TV also-rans, and their

cases are different from those of Brown, Connally, etc. Their press images changed during Campaign '80, and changed in a way that is symptomatic of the way in which networks deal with the real potential presidents.

Baker started out as the principal challenger to Reagan. CBS acknowledged Baker's special status by devoting one of its six-minute issue pieces to Baker in the middle of January—*before* it had given any of the other Republican challengers that kind of attention or legitimacy.

The Baker-on-the-issues piece was unique, not just because it lent to Baker the status of major challenger, but also because it provided Baker with a *positive* major piece of press. Cronkite did for Baker what he did for nobody else in the early campaign: he *praised* him. In the introduction to the Baker "issues" report, Cronkite said that Baker "was, perhaps, the only Republican to be helped by Watergate, as his calm, careful reasoning won him overwhelming praise from television viewers." On network news—where bad press is so much the norm—that comment read almost like an endorsement, although obviously it was no such thing.

A few weeks after that encomium, Baker had it all taken away when Betsy Aaron did a seven-minute investigation of the controversy swirling around Baker's most famous TV commercial—an ad in which Baker's media consultants filmed a confrontation between Baker and an Iranian student at the University of Iowa, a filming nobody in the audience knew was taking place. In this extraordinary piece of investigative reporting, Aaron portrayed Baker as wrong in his description of the confrontation, insensitive about his role in the filming, and unethical in his treatment of the Iranian student.

In a sense, Baker's press image never recovered after that investigative report. In February and early March CBS had nothing good to say about Baker, only that he was a candidate "struggling to keep from going out of style." But *after* his loss in Massachusetts—*after* he decided to quit—CBS, like the national press generally, rediscovered Baker. Lem Tucker's piece on Baker's formal withdrawal sounded ever so slightly like a salute to Howard Baker, a man Tucker described as "with no bitterness," and a man to whom Tucker would allow the last word. Although almost all campaign features end with a closer—a sentence or two by the correspondent that explain the candidate's political motive for doing what he did—Tucker gave Baker the chance to offer his misty eyed farewell without a closer and without comment. Baker never looked better. But the Baker case is just the first instance in 1980 in which dead politicians became statesmen at their own media-covered funerals.

Bush's coverage followed a similar path. In his first month, when he was making a reasonably credible challenge for the nomination, Bush's press was relatively good. Later on, after his "dual front-runner" status was established, his press turned sour on CBS, only to become somewhat more respectable again after his nomination's defeat was a certainty. In keeping with the press rule that politicians are statesmen still in the running, Bush's worst press day came on the day of his greatest personal triumph—the day Reagan anointed him as running mate. Resurrected from the status of defeated statesman, Bush was hit twice on that day's edition of the "Evening News"—once by Richard Roth and once by Diane Sawyer. Roth had compiled eight videotapes from the early months of the campaign, tapes showing Bush categorically rejecting the possibility of his becoming Reagan's VP. As Roth rolled the tapes by in rapid sequence, the inevitable conclusion was that Bush was anything but sincere.

The second slap came from Diane Sawyer, who reported that Bush's early statements about Reagan, about ERA, about abortion, were now inoperative. "Nothing like a shot at the White House to clarify perspective," Diane Sawyer began her report. Her conclusion was even tougher: "Ronald Reagan and George Bush have signed their treaty on the issues," she said, and "Bush yielded most of the territory on the theory that it may have been embarrassing today, but if it gets the Republicans to the White House it won't matter." In May the defeated Bush was portrayed as a man at ease with himself—a regular guy. In July he came back on the "Evening News" as a preppy version of Niccolo Machiavelli.

THE PRESS OF THE "FINAL FOUR"

Press coverage given to Anderson, Kennedy, Reagan, and Carter—the campaign's final four—lends considerable credence to the basic premises implied here. The press history for each of the final four, across the months of 1980, indicates that as a candidate's campaign grows more successful, more established, more serious, or even more media-polished, the tougher the press becomes; and that only after he has lost any real hope of winning or has withdrawn from the race can any viable candidate expect to be treated favorably by the news media—and then only if he has passed a fairly high threshold of newsworthiness in the early phases of his campaign.

Anderson

Anderson's case is vintage. No candidate rode the media roller coaster like John Anderson—a man whose image went from nothing, to superb, to miserable, and eventually back to nothing. Figure 1 presents Anderson's personal image score, implicit and explicit on CBS, during the three phases of the campaign—the primary period, the convention period, the general election. In January, Anderson was the principal candidate in only one story. Although that piece was an icebreaker for Anderson, his press did not really begin until February. But by June, Anderson had managed to build for himself the most positive image of any candidate on the "Evening News," his general press index for those six months reaching an impressive +5.

Due to limitations in coding, this index actually understates how favorable Anderson's press was in the early months of the campaign. And because this index does *not* include direct references to Anderson's electoral success, it also underplays the good press he enjoyed early on, when he was doing comparatively well in the liberal state primaries.

Still, compared with the other members of the final four, Anderson could well have been considered the press darling of early Campaign '80. CBS reporters referred to Anderson as "the forthright candidate," "the freshest face," "the candidate standing apart from the crowd"—in the memorable words of correspondent Bob McNamara, "the one many voters see as the most articulate, honest, and best candidate."

During the first three months of the campaign, Anderson's press on CBS fit almost perfectly with Anderson's general campaign strategy. Both stressed the Anderson "difference." To be sure, when Anderson lost his home state primary, CBS fully reported his loss and what it meant to Anderson's slim hope of winning a Republican nomination. And by July it was the same Bob McNamara quoted above reporting again on Anderson—this time calling the Anderson campaign not much more than "an image-building ... tour, designed to show him with famous faces and orchestrated to sell credibility" to doubting voters.

Before his fall from media grace in July, Anderson was the *only* candidate with a decidedly positive personal news image on CBS. That all changed when Anderson became viable— and admittedly, after he started acting the way viable candidates act. Just as Baker was a politician until he was gone, Anderson was a statesman until he arrived.

Figure 1

"Media Images" for Anderson, Reagan, Carter, and Kennedy in the Three Phases of the Campaign
(not including horse-race news)

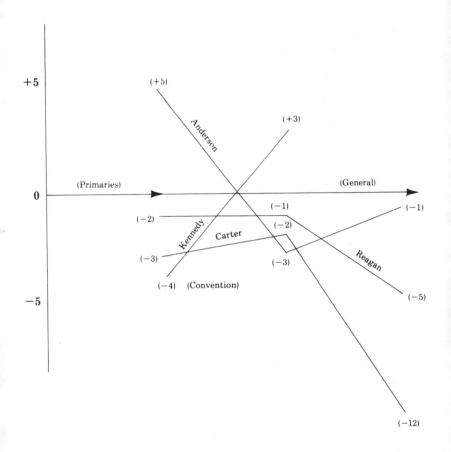

Kennedy

For the most part, Kennedy's coverage parrotted that of George Bush—until Bush was "saved" by Reagan and denuded again by the press. Both Kennedy and Bush had good press while they were developing as front-runners—for Kennedy in the fall of 1979, for Bush in January of 1980. But both candidates lost their glimmer when they *became* front-runners—or near front-runner, in Bush's case. After their falls, Kennedy and Bush went back to basking in the warmth of a sympathetic press.

The now-legendary Roger Mudd interview with Kennedy which took place in November 1979 did not fall within our study, but obviously that episode fits the theory—that the media come down hardest on the guy with the lead. But figure 1 vividly demonstrates for Kennedy's political odyssey what the Mudd interview implies—that he went up and down in image as he went from front-runner to challenger to defeated candidate.

During the primaries—when Kennedy continued to stay alive, if not close to Carter—he did poorly, about as poorly as Carter. By June, however, Kennedy, no longer a potential president, was a courageous champion of his cause; in the words of Jed Duval, Kennedy was a man "in bouncing good spirits," a man finding "devotion in the crowds," a man "not discouraged" and "jaunty as ever."

And, with the coffin nailed shut by 5 June, Kennedy's press score during the convention period rose to a level matched only by that of the early John Anderson when Anderson's campaign was in its salad days. Kennedy's press score jumped from −4 to +3, following his last-gasp effort for nomination.

Reagan

From January through the convention, Ronald Reagan never relinquished his title as Republican front-runner. He paid for it in terms of media image—only Carter got tougher press.

Almost as if CBS were explaining a double standard for front-runners, the very first Reagan story of 1980 was a humorous but biting piece by Bill Plante concerning the headaches front-runners inevitably face. That Plante piece—so clear a statement as to the double standards for front-runners—deserves special attention.

Plante: One of the burdens of being front-runner is that you have to assume that the nomination is yours unless you lose it. So you become rather cautious.

Ronald Reagan is indeed very mindful of the November election. But he does have to get through the primaries.

He was managing with a minimum of exposure until this last week, when he began holding one or more mini—news conferences every day.

That defused the charge that he was hiding, but made more likely the possibility that the candidate would put his foot in his mouth— another problem for a front-runner. . . .

Another problem for the front-runner is that he has to run everywhere, so he is nowhere often enough. . . .

Doing well in Iowa would vindicate Reagan's above-the-battle campaign style. . . . Doing not so well . . . might mean that he would have to jump in and mix it up, just like any other candidate.

What Plante did not say was that front-runners also have to contend with tough pieces like this. Nor did Plante point out that this feature piece was just the opening salvo.

Beyond the "front-runner feature," Bill Plante did two more full-length investigative reports on Reagan during Campaign '80, not including two other long pieces on Reagan's issue positions. Reagan was the only candidate, other than Carter, who elicited two investigative pieces. Howard Baker, in fact, attracted the only other full-length investigative report, the Betsy Aaron piece on Baker's questionable ad.

The second Reagan feature came in early April, following his surprisingly strong showing in the Wisconsin primary. The piece lasted about seven minutes and asserted that Reagan was "wrong" about HEW cost-effectiveness, wrong about federal automobile regulatory policy, wrong about the size of the bureaucracy, wrong about the oil reserves in the United States, and wrong about affirmative action guidelines. Plante ended his fact-filled report by asking, *"Does it really matter?"*—that Reagan refused to "drop the inaccurate facts and figures," that "in instance after instance the campaign failed to go back to the original source" to check out the facts.

Networks do not answer questions like that, and Plante chose not to answer his own rhetorical question. He concluded only that "to some it's a sign that Reagan isn't smart enough for the job he seeks."

Plante also used an indirect conclusion in his third major Reagan report. Coming in early October, this piece portrayed Reagan as a political moving target, one who was "shifting," according to Walter Cronkite's lead-in, "from the right to the center of the political spectrum."

Reeling off an impressive collection of videotape, Plante discussed five major policies on which Reagan had recently reversed field—taxes, labor law, abolishing federal agencies, bailing out Chrysler, and saving New York City. CBS technicians—not Plante—put a white "X" on Reagan's face every time Plante pointed to a change in position. The next night CBS apologized for the Xs—"a very bad graphic," in Cronkite's words. But CBS made no apology for the content of the piece—a very tough piece which proved to be the hardest-nosed feature of the fall campaign. Again Plante chose not to state his conclusion in the active voice, asking only in the last paragraph, "Which is the real Ronald Reagan?" "Does he," asked Plante, "plan to deliver on his conservative promises or is he a closet moderate?"

Overall, figure 1 indicates that Reagan pretty much followed the path of a front-runner challenging the incumbent—starting out with a relatively weak press image and ending up in the general campaign with an even more negative press. But throughout, his press coverage was better than Carter's—something attributable to Reagan's not having been the incumbent and, perhaps as important, also attributable to Reagan's not having been Jimmy Carter.

In one of his convention commentaries on the "Evening News," Bill Moyers actually praised Reagan for his flexibility, his principles (Moyers considered Reagan's decision not to make Ford co-president the constitutionally principled thing to do), his practical conservatism. But that was most of the good news concerning Reagan to appear on CBS in the later phase of Campaign '80—other than coverage of his consistently strong showings in the polls.

Carter

From start to finish, Jimmy Carter got the worst press of all in 1980. His case contradicts three of the old press theories— that networks favor the liberal, that presidents can control their press image, and that more press always helps so long as they spell your name right.

Table 1 indicated that Carter, among all contenders, had the most negative press in aggregate. Figure 1 indicated, with one minor exception, that Carter had the worst press among all candidates in all three periods. Figure 2, which lists total time for all candidates from January to November, implies that people who get the most time pay dearly for it. Jimmy Carter—the man who completely dominated the news hole—was the fall guy in Campaign '80.

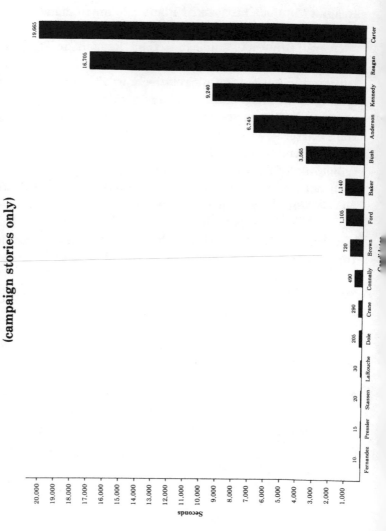

Figure 2
Total News Seconds given to All Candidates Receiving Time
on CBS *Evening News*, 1 January–3 November 1980
(campaign stories only)

Carter, like Reagan, stimulated three extended news features, but all Carter's features, unlike Reagan's, dealt with the same theme: Carter's manipulation of office and administration. Leslie Stahl did all three reports, and each one pointed to the same essential conclusion: that Jimmy Carter had learned to use "the advantages of incumbency with textbook precision."

The first such piece, four minutes in length, came in March, just after Carter's victories in Iowa and New Hampshire. In that piece, Stahl pointed to Carter's political exploitation of network television, his appointment powers, White House news briefings, discretionary grants to cities.

Stahl's second piece came in early April just after the Wisconsin primary, the primary during which Carter had held a 7:00 A.M. news conference in the Oval Office on live television to announce an allegedly imminent breakthrough on hostage negotiations. This second feature examined the questionable use of White House seals and symbols on publications that were arguably campaign literature. "What is involved here," concluded Stahl, "is not necessarily a question of impropriety, but yet another example of how President Carter has learned to use the benefits of incumbency to give his run for election a little boost."

Nine days later Stahl returned to the same topic in what was CBS's *pièce de résistance* concerning Carter's campaign behavior in office. This was the investigative report mentioned above on the rose-garden strategy—the one in which Cronkite and Stahl made it perfectly clear that Carter had made practically all his decisions in 1980 with an eye on the campaign calendar. The piece drew the indirect conclusion that the president had granted exclusive interviews, photo opportunities, public funding, and patronage appointments so that he could do himself the most good in those primary and caucus states where Edward Kennedy posed the greatest challenge.

In at least thirteen separate stories during Campaign '80,

CBS returned to the same basic points—Carter's manipulation of incumbency, or his cynical brand of presidential campaigning. In a medium where direct, pointed criticism is so infrequent—and where follow-up criticism is a real rarity—CBS's continued coverage of Carter's cynical campaign looks especially vivid.

Nor did Carter's bad press stop with his image as cynical politico. After March, Carter got nothing much but bad press in almost every aspect of his office. On the night before Carter would finally finish off Kennedy's challenge for the nomination, Leslie Stahl did an analysis of Carter's keys to victory. One might have expected something approaching praise, given that Carter had vanquished an "unvanquishable" Kennedy. But Stahl read it differently. "President Carter won the nomination by not campaigning, by not debating, by not travelling around the country," she said. And on the convention night in which Carter would accept his nomination, Bill Moyers argued that Carter's career proved that he could do little other than win votes; running, concluded Moyers, is what Carter did best. Overall, given the treatment he received from CBS and from the other two networks—ABC's Sam Donaldson was at least as tough as Leslie Stahl—Carter might well have preferred that all the networks had misspelled his name throughout the year.

TYPECAST CANDIDATES

Most network campaign news is straightforward and descriptive, if not a little dry. For all but the final few candidates, media image never goes beyond that of winner or loser. But over the course of the year Anderson, Reagan, and Carter did come up against news coverage that went beyond description of their day-to-day activities and at least approached typecasting.

Anderson did not elicit nearly as much typecasting as Reagan or Carter. Never a likely winner, Anderson did not merit enough attention to build a fully developed casting mold. But what did come through was John Anderson as a twentieth-century Don Quixote—a man who believed in his own world, not everybody else's. Instead of tilting at windmills, however, Anderson, in the phrasing of Bob McNamara, simply was "going in circles."

In a story about Anderson's address to the National Religious Broadcasters, Bob Faw said that Anderson was acting "in a role he cherishes—Daniel in the lion's den" (the Daniel metaphor because Anderson told those religious broadcasters that the Moral Majority was a political evil, an organization predisposed toward religious intolerance).

Bob Faw said "Daniel" but he implied "Quixote"—given that Anderson could only have assumed that he was hurting himself politically with his remarks but did not care. "Anderson," concluded Faw, "is prepared to endure any political fallout because . . . he strongly believes in what he said and because he's convinced that the country agrees with him."

Rounding out the coverage of Anderson was the press for Pat Lucey—the National Unity Campaign's Sancho Panza. In fact, although Lucey got precious little coverage on the "Evening News," what he did get made him look just right in the role of sidekick to Quixote. Charles Kuralt called Lucey a man with "identity problems," and Bernard Goldberg described him as a candidate who was literally and figuratively out there in the campaign "looking for votes in the dark."

Reagan's typecasting was more direct and detailed. Time and again Reagan was made to look like a Hollywood real-life version of Chauncey Gardner, the unlikely hero of *Being There*—a man who, through his own foolishness and guilelessness, fell into the presidency.

In the early going, CBS treated Reagan's Polish-Italian duck joke as a case study in Reagan's naive trust in—of all people—campaign reporters. Later on, Bill Plante covered in some depth Reagan's silly comments about Mt. St. Helens causing more pollution than cars, trees causing more pollution than industry, air pollution being substantially under control. Plante consistently treated Reagan to some of his most evenhanded and serious press coverage, but Plante and the rest of the network correspondents did, at times, picture Reagan as if he were Chauncey Gardner, if not Peter Sellers in the role. Plante quoted aides as saying they didn't know where Reagan had obtained his questionable statistics on pollution, only that those statistics "must have come from the candidate's own reading"—the clear implication being that Reagan was not much of a reader.

As early as January, Plante had already discussed Reagan's propensity for putting his foot in his mouth. And in April, after Plante had done his extended report on Reagan's tendency to misstate facts or mangle names, Plante again quoted Reagan's staff to support his contention that the candidate never seemed to get the speech or his information straight. "Reagan," aides said, "was hard to program." And how did Plante describe the way in which aides made that assessment? "Ruefully," according to Plante. Rueful indeed—a word that would have fit Chauncey Gardner's closest associates as well as Reagan's.

By now it is not really surprising to find that the networks pictured Anderson as Don Quixote or Reagan as "Chance" Gardner. In fact, most of us—having closely followed the media—accept those images as sound.

But the Carter case is more problematic—not because Carter got the greatest share of typecasting coverage; the incumbent always gets the greatest amount of press and, consequently, the greatest proportion on image news as well. Carter's case is surprising because his 1980 media image contrasted so sharply with his "early" media image—the one given him by the media between 1977 and 1979.

Carter's early media image had been that of a decent man in over his head—unable to be political enough to control professional Washington. But in Campaign '80 Jimmy Carter came out looking very much like the J. R. Ewing candidate. Carter, the man held to be too apolitical for his first years in office, was now consistently portrayed as mean, vindictive, manipulative, and petty.

ABC went hardest on the J. R. theme, especially in the last month of the campaign. On 8 October Barbara Walters led the "World News" in an exclusive interview with Carter, asking the president, in effect, why he was so mean. Although Carter denied it, Walters rejected his disclaimer, noting that he does "strike out so."

Meanwhile, back at CBS, Carter was very much in the J. R. mold. Although Bruce Morton did a balanced and essentially neutral report on the Carter record in office, every piece which looked at Carter as a *candidate* made the Carter White House look suspiciously like South Fork, the Ewing mansion in "Dallas."

Even in the noncampaign stories, the J. R. Ewing image got big play on the "Evening News." In June, Carter went to Europe for the summit meetings and Leslie Stahl, acting as chief White House correspondent, went along to cover the trip. In Europe, as stateside, Stahl characterized Carter as the near ultimate *poseur.*

Stahl: Mr. Carter spent much of the day today moving about Rome being photographed before the city's famous landmarks.

He posed on a balcony of the Coliseum; he posed in an alcove; and he posed again on a ledge outside the Coliseum.

A few months later, Stahl did very much the same story, following Carter's campaign tour to Pennsylvania.

Stahl: What did President Carter do today in Philadelphia? He posed with as many different types of symbols as he could possibly find.

There was a picture at the day-care center—and one during a game of bocci ball with the senior citizens.

Then another with a group of teenagers.

And then he performed the ultimate media event—a walk through the Italian market.

Why a walk in a market becomes an ultimate media event was not especially clear, especially to Carter's advance people who, not surprisingly, really objected to Stahl's report. What is fairly clear is that, despite his early image, after the Wisconsin primary Carter became in all the national media a non-adulterous J. R.—the epitome of the self-serving head of a rich and powerful household.

Carter was also treated as a man unwilling to face up to his manipulative character, his darker side. In one of her heavily researched feature pieces on the cynical Carter campaign, Leslie Stahl, speaking about his use of the advantages of office, noted that "such a practice has been common with incumbents. What is uncommon is Mr. Carter's insistence that he is above politics." What happened to the Sunday-school teacher who didn't know how to be president?

Reality plays a part in media image, of course. Cronkite, Plante, and Stahl, and the network press corps that they lead, did not invent anything. They reported real events and presented important insights. But reality fails to explain why Baker, Kennedy, and Bush were all better men simply by having lost the nomination. Reality does not explain why Anderson was the best candidate—the most articulate candidate—in February and March, yet was none of that in November. And, most important of all, reality does not explain why the media did *not* cover Carter's precision with facts and Reagan's near-constant good humor toward his opponents and the press. It is possible that "mean" Jimmy Carter has the mind of a sage, and dumb Ronnie Reagan has the disposition of a saint. But that horn of the dilemma was conspicuously absent from all the evening news programs. We got to choose between fools and scoundrels. Final choices always seem to look bad on network news—and in the national print media as well.

MICHAEL JA...

Cha...
pres...
medi...
tory in
ing con

My gues...
same way
root for t
is . . . switc...

The reason
want the ga...

do its hardest, most negative pieces about
ter—just after it became clear that
become the nominees.
ter came close
Walter Cronkite's piece on R...
led Bill Plante's piece on R...
Ronald Reagan appears
nomination. Our su...
mitted show him
independent
They app...
detrac...
sho...

184

Peters's *n*   ...rd
for front-run   ...n people who
start moving   . ...ut appealing as the infidelity theory   ...n media—and some of this must be
going on—it makes the media out to be much less serious
than they really are. If they were as impishly unfaithful—as
committed to making it interesting, as Peters believes—they
would not have turned on Anderson as they did in the summer. He was anything but front-runner at that point. But his
midsummer gambol in Europe and his late-summer gambit
with Kennedy in July convinced the press that Anderson had
sullied himself, had denied his own Anderson "difference."

What we have here is a problem with a journalistic norm
or principle—or bias—depending on how one feels about it.
Through this norm, television, much like other media, considers it a mission to get toughest on the most likely winner,
generally the incumbent or the out-party front-runner.

Consequently, CBS was clearly the toughest during the
last two months of the campaign—most eager to find the bad
news about the people most likely to be president. And CBS
followed the same principle in the primaries when it chose to

Reagan and Car-
these two men would

o admitting all this when he
eagan's factual errors this way:

unstoppable right now for the Republican
eys in states where cross-over voting is per-
ttracting significant numbers of Democratic and
oters.

rently like what he's been saying—but some of his
ors claim at least some of what he's been saying is a little
t on accuracy, and we asked Bill Plante to look into that.

As a rule, CBS blasted Reagan when he was doing best, blasted Carter when he was making a comeback. There were no hard, investigative pieces of Carter during the general campaign; only Reagan got that treatment then, implying that CBS realized that it was Reagan's campaign in need of closer scrutiny—because it was Reagan who would win. The CBS Poll, in fact, proved much less accurate than the CBS investigative features in estimating who was really ahead in October.

Anybody inching closer to the presidency faces a great probability of being labeled fool or scoundrel. That is, of course, inherent in the role of the press as watchdog. Watchdogs do not lick the innocent; they bark at everybody, and the closer the suspect, the louder the bark. Asked about the reason front-runners get bad press, Knight-Ridder's Stephen Seplow put it in much those terms: "We don't know how to cover winners very well—we don't do a good job of being gracious. We look hard at a guy when he begins to win."

Acting like journalists, correspondents at CBS feared missing the dark side of any possible president. In the end, Anderson had to be implausible instead of exceptional. Carter had to be mean instead of smart. Reagan had to be dumb instead of nice.

CONCLUSIONS

It seems reasonable to assume that, with media accentuating
the negative year after year, the public will take the hint. It
has. According to the Center for Political Studies at
Michigan, the percentage of positive remarks made by the
public about the final two candidates has declined in every
election since 1952—with just one exception, 1976. In the
1950s two-thirds of the public's comments about candidates
were favorable; in the 1970s the proportion was only half. In
1960, before the era of big media and new journalism, even
Richard Nixon looked great; 71 percent of the public's comments made about him in that campaign were positive!
(Kennedy, by the way, got "only" a 60 percent positive score
in public approval.)

There is no real evidence as yet to indicate that TV is more
hostile than other forms of national press; the hard evidence
indicates otherwise. Richard Hofstetter's work, for example,
shows that in 1972 CBS and the AP wire were practically
identical in their treatment of Richard Nixon and George
McGovern. But we should not lose sight of the fact that since
the age of television—since 1960—there has been a near
linear drop in public affection for the two major party
nominees as expressed in the national surveys.

Television has grown so dramatically in size and scope in
the last twenty years that, even with a message identical to
that of print, the same words have had greater reach. The
overall effect has been even more pronounced because television has come of age in the era of post-Vietnam, post-
Watergate journalism. Correspondents and editors now feel
a greater need to explain policy statements in terms of campaign strategy, and a greater freedom to expose the
blemishes of each prospective incumbent.

None of this should be read as inherently sad, let alone

evil. Obviously, *nobody expects or wants the press to flak for candidates,* or to let the incumbent president garden his roses into reelection. We should not be at all surprised—or displeased—to find the media covering front-runners and incumbents with considerable and growing suspicion. Under the unstated, contemporary rules of the free press, that's the way it is—and, perhaps, should be.

But neither should we be surprised—or much disheartened—when the viewing electorate grows consistently less enthusiastic about the choices, especially final choices, between fools or scoundrels. Given the media messages, that, too, is the way it is. If the press insists that we have to face the reality of our democratic leadership, warts and all, that's understandable. But then we also have to face the reality of our passive democratic electorate in a media system geared to covering the dark side of the major candidates. A critical press and an apathetic public come as by-products of free media, free elections, and a free society.

10

ROBERT L. BARTLEY

The News Business
and Business News

The press and its market. Television and time. Press vulnerability to crisis confusion and the role trap. The profit metaphor. Earnings per share v. return on investment. Accounting concepts. The importance of alternate stereotypes.

Over nearly two decades on the nation's business newspaper no single topic has wasted more of my time than the subject of this essay. In particular, I can barely suppress the memory of endless conferences and conversations with business executives asking, "Can't we educate journalists about business?" The answer is, "No, you can't." I am beginning to wonder, in fact, whether you can even educate business executives about business.

This cynicism arises from my ever-growing conviction that, despite its critics' fears and its own pretensions, the press reflects society far more than it shapes it. You do not get society to understand business by getting the press to understand it; you get the press to understand business by getting society to understand it. The press certainly does have its failings and limitations, but these extend across all of its subject matter. If there is a particular problem about business news, and I think there is, its roots must lie somewhere in the particulars of the subject.

The most important root, I have been increasingly persuaded, lies in business's own self-definition. It lies in the central metaphor around which our thinking about business has been shaped. It lies in misunderstandings—shared by the press, the public, and business alike—about something called "profit."

SOURCES OF PROBLEMS
IN PRESS COVERAGE

This is not written to exonerate the press, which certainly does not cover itself with glory in reporting business. While matters have recently improved with the spread of business sections in major newspapers, the sophistication being nurtured there has not yet spread into the general run of the news, let alone into television. In the general news media, the coverage of business captures less of what is actually going on than the coverage of politics, let alone sports. The point is to understand why this is so, and why it is so difficult to change.

The first instinct of businessmen themselves is to attribute any problem of press coverage to bias on the part of reporters and editors. It is true that through the process of self-selection journalists do, and always will, find their political center of gravity to the left of the general population, just as military officers do, and always will, find theirs to the right. The press is at its worst when it denies this simple fact, but it is far from the most important source of the problems businessmen see. Professional norms of objectivity and fairness and the power of embarrassment, while far from perfect, are far more serviceable than businessmen tend to believe. In any event, far more powerful influences are at work.

These influences are three: the audience, the format, and the news. None of them is going to be much changed by educating or hectoring journalists, as satisfying as such activities otherwise may be.

The audience

To start with the audience: I always instruct my writers that the first duty of a journalist is to get read. Nothing is easier than to stop reading a newspaper; turning off a television set takes a bit more effort, but people will learn that, too. If you do not engage the reader, you are not going to educate him. So you start with what people like to read or watch.

This naturally puts a premium on scandal, personalities, the fall of the mighty, and other perennial themes of drama. As the audience becomes a more popular one, the dose of this sort of entertainment has to go up. Rupert Murdoch, himself an exceedingly serious and sophisticated man, defends the sensationalism of the racy journalistic style displayed in his *New York Post* as educating people who would otherwise read no newspaper (the truth is that many sophisticates read it too). In Australia, Mr. Murdoch publishes a serious newspaper for an up-scale audience, and it is very doubtful that he will take *Post*-style journalism to *The Times* of London. These are aimed at different audiences.

Or, as a businessman might put it, at different markets. Any business executive understands that the demands of the market are the chief forces shaping the product he sells. He understands that he has no power to impose on the market a product it does not want. But many executives seem to think the news business is different, that publishers and editors start with some grand scheme and force it down the throats of their customers. In fact, of course, the demands of the market, the desires of the audience, are the most powerful influences shaping the news.

The format

If the audience shapes the news, so does the format in which it can be presented. *The Medium Is the Message*, Marshall McLuhan proclaimed, as if there were something new under the sun. In fact, the substance of a message has always been shaped by the literary form in which it is encapsulated, and the longer I am in the news business the more impressed I become with the power of this influence.

The standard newspaper format for spot news is called the "inverted pyramid" news story. It starts with a "lead," cramming into the first paragraph the essential facts, the "five Ws"—who, what, where, when, and why. It then proceeds with the next most pressing information, then the next most, and so on, in order that the story will always be intelligible no matter how many of the trailing paragraphs have to be thrown away as it is fitted around the advertisements as the paper is made up.

Sometimes the "five Ws" are supplemented by an "H"—how. The optional character of this ingredient—the odd letter just doesn't fit the format—gives a hint of the implications of the inverted pyramid format for the content of the news. There are some stories that fit awkwardly at best in this literary form—whether a particular political proposal makes any sense, for example, or the impact of the Texas

Railroad Commission on patterns of energy usage. These, of course, are the stories that businessmen and other serious readers would like to see.

The power of a new format is perhaps best illustrated by the history of my own newspaper. As the late Bernard Kilgore laid the foundations that were to take the *Wall Street Journal* from a small financial sheet to America's largest and only national newspaper, he acted on a series of brilliant insights. The most important of these clearly was the identification of an audience—the recognition that the businessman in Portland, Oregon, wants the same news as the businessman in Portland, Maine. But the product was shaped for this audience through the invention of new news formats.

The most notable of these was the *Journal* "leader," the two daily stories in the outside columns of the front page. Typically, these stories start with an anecdote to catch the reader's attention. Then, at least in the classic leader, there appears in the third or fourth paragraph the phrase "up 10 percent from the year before," or "down 15 percent from the year before," or whatever. Instead of a 500-word story on yesterday's event, you have a 1,500-word story on a trend. This focuses the reporters' attentions in entirely different ways and even on entirely different topics. These leader articles, and the training and middle-management demands they produce, are the keystone of the *Journal's* reputation for seriousness and reliability. The impact of Mr. Kilgore's format lives long after him.

The extreme example of the limitations of format is, of course, television. Anyone who undertakes to criticize the network news ought to ponder how *he* would tell a story in 30 seconds, with pictures. As Dr. Johnson remarked about a dog walking on two legs, the wonder is not that it's done badly, but that it's done at all.

Not surprisingly, it is television that has caused business executives the most anxiety. After the experience of trying to

defend themselves in the midst of controversy, they complain bitterly about the severe and often arbitrary editing of
television footage. The usual articulation is that a television
crew will tape a 60-minute interview, then throw away
everything except the 15 seconds when they caught him
picking his nose. The executives' ire is compounded when
they find the networks have a policy of not accepting "controversial" advertising, thus precluding businesses from de-
fending themselves as they sometimes do in print ads.

Many high-profile executives have adopted a policy that,
while they are anxious to defend themselves on TV, they will
accept only those invitations that will be broadcast live, without editing. One concern, Illinois Power Company, simultaneously taped everything shot by a CBS "60 Minutes" crew.
After CBS broadcast a segment quoting critics (the company
said they were fired employees) alleging mismanage-
ment of a nuclear power project, the company produced its
own documentary in refutation. CBS felt forced to broadcast
two corrections of factual errors concerning the company's
rate increase request, and the Illinois Power tape was requested so often that 1,300 copies were distributed within six
months.

These grievances seem to me to have a substantial
justification, but it is instructive to observe that they are by
no means unique to business. Former Secretary of State
Henry Kissinger, for example, had his own shoot-out with
"60 Minutes" after a program built around the accusations of
James Akins, whom Mr. Kissinger had fired as ambassador
to Saudi Arabia. In the waning days of the Carter administration, Robert C. Embry, Jr., assistant secretary of Housing
and Urban Development (HUD), complained about a "60
Minutes" segment on HUD's program of Urban Development
Action Grants (UDAG). The broadcast ridiculed the fact that
the UDAG list of eligible depressed areas included such play-
grounds as Orlando, Orange County, Pasadena, and Santa
Barbara. Mr. Embry complained that the program failed to

note that none of the cities had actually been granted UDAG funds.

When public officials and even liberal bureaucrats come with the same complaint, it is hard to believe that the problem is bias against business. Rather, it is an interaction of audience and format. "60 Minutes" is most often television news at its best; its reporting is typically hard-hitting, accurate, and innovative. Through the dramatic format of exposing scandal, it built itself into television's most popular program. But this creates immense demands of audience or market (keep up the rating) and format (expose scandal). Since it is not easy to find three scandals a week, the pressures create the temptation journalists know as "hyping the story."

It is not impossible, of course, to devise other formats, even for television. The "MacNeil-Lehrer Report" on the Public Broadcasting Service is an obvious example. But to judge by the ratings, most viewers prefer "60 Minutes," and no doubt they are educated in the same way as the readers of Mr. Murdoch's *Post*. In time, though, we will surely see more formats like "MacNeil-Lehrer," simply because of the impending technological revolution. The spread of multichannel cable television will lead to fragmented markets and great program diversity. The next step, presaged by video discs and home recorders, will be even more important. When technology permits audiences that do not have to conform to rigid broadcast schedules, there will be a market for truly serious television programming, and format innovations will follow.

In the print media, the new business sections also represent progress, but the limitations of format will always remain, and they represent an important limitation of journalism. I recall the chief executive officer (CEO) of a large sugar company expressing puzzlement over a reporter who had come to interview him about a sudden run-up in sugar prices. They talked awhile and, despite the pressures on any CEO's time, he wanted to spend all afternoon on it. The reporter had to leave; "I had the time, but she didn't." Of course. She already had "the story"—what would fit in the format she had been allotted. If she learned more, the story would be harder to write.

This limitation and the habits it breeds account for what I personally consider the most telling criticism of the run-of-the-mill journalist—a lack of serious intellectual curiosity. Of course, a reporter who starts to wonder about the story behind the story will seek out new formats—trying to become a columnist, perhaps, or dropping out entirely to write books. If he succeeds, he will leave behind those colleagues comfortable with the strengths and weaknesses of the inverted pyramid style.

The news

With some notion of how severely journalism is constrained by its audience and its formats, finally consider the meaning of "the news." The unordered reality of any given day pours down on the editor or television news director in an unmanageable torrent. He is asked to sort the interesting from the uninteresting, the significant from the insignificant. As Walter Lippmann brilliantly described in his *Public Opinion* decades ago, the editor manages this through "stereotypes." He has in his mind certain metaphors or themes he will use to organize the news, and he imposes these preexisting structures upon reality. This does not mean the press is mendacious. This is the *only* way a day's events can conceivably be sorted out and organized by a night's deadline.

This does mean, though, that once a stereotype is established, it tends to dominate news coverage and may be exceedingly hard to dislodge. An easy example of the process can be found in press coverage of the 1980 presidential campaign. Given Ronald Reagan's age and rather removed leadership style, two or three dubious statements quickly established the stereotype of "gaffes." Everything he said would be scrutinized for evidence of another misstatement. This persisted until his staff shut him off from the press for a week, eroding the theme, and until another stereotype took over.

Given Jimmy Carter's inability to point persuasively to his record as president, his strategic necessity was to run a negative campaign, depicting his opponent as a menace to the republic. Especially given Mr. Carter's well-advertised piety, it was almost inevitable that the next stereotype would be Mr. Carter's "meanness," and his statements soon were subject to the same kind of single-minded scrutiny Mr. Reagan had faced earlier. Neither story was without some substance, but in retrospect both were overdone once the stereotype took hold.

Obviously, the question of where these stereotypes come from is of no small moment in understanding press coverage. A few are, as many businessmen would suggest, drawn from ideology. More important are those drawn from the everyday experience of the reporting press—the frustrations of access to news sources, personal relations with them, the logistics of traveling to the news, writing stories, filing them by deadlines. The press's most persistent complaint about business, for example, is lack of access to corporate chief executives or other spokesmen who have the understanding and authority (or self-confidence) to respond to inquiries competently and candidly. Reporters are less likely to interpret this in terms of the pressures on a CEO's time than in terms of business having something to hide.

Mostly, though, the stereotypes that order news coverage come from the common coin of society. The stereotypes most useful in communicating with readers or viewers are those the readers and viewers already share. These change over time with our national experience, both among the public and in the press. If, in the prosperity of the 1920s, the public is in a mood to hear Coolidge say "the business of America is business," businessmen will be treated one way in the press.

They will be treated quite another way if, in the depression of the 1930s, the public is in a mood to have Roosevelt castigate "the Insulls and the Ishmaels."

None of these major forces shaping the news is easy to change. The audience will evolve only with the slow process of education and generational change. The formats will change with the pressures of the audiences, the ambitions of the publishers, and the ingenuity of the editors. Of the three, the organizing stereotypes are the most pliable. They will change mostly with our national experience, but they might also evolve with greater sophistication of journalists and more careful explanations by businessmen.

THE VULNERABILITY OF THE PRESS

This background provides a vocabulary for discussing the particular problems of business and the news. A handy starting place might be two relatively minor but recurring press/business interactions. One might be called "crisis confusion," and the other might be called "the role trap."

From a public relations point of view, the very worst stereotype that can arise is, "They're lying to us again." Trapped among deadline pressure, the norm of professional objectivity, the need for sharp quotes, and a vulnerable reputation for accuracy, the press is peculiarly sensitive to misinformation. Once it feels it has been misled by a news source, it will scrutinize all further statements for any hint of inaccuracy, denying all benefit of doubt. This habit arises less from ideology or a sense of an adversarial role than from the self-interest and vulnerability of the press.

When some innocent businessman is ambushed by crisis, it is terribly easy for him to fall into this trap. Often he simply will not know, or will sincerely believe something that later proves to be wrong, or will be badly advised by subordinates who themselves are victims of the natural psychological tendency to suppress or minimize bad news. Because of the particular vulnerabilities of the press, it is not likely to interpret any such errors charitably; it is likely to see them as deliberate misinformation and to look for more of the same in any future comments from the same source.

At the same time, of course, the press will interpret failure to comment as an attempt to hide something. Careful statements through public relations departments are little better, since they suggest impenetrability—and anyway are usually attempts to evade the questions reporters recognize as most pressing.

The person to explain a crisis to the press is an honest, patient, sensitive spokesman who has line responsibility for the involved operation and endless time to meet with reporters. It scarcely need be said that such paragons are rare, especially in crisis. But since the biggest business stories are likely to be those of crisis, the lack of such spokesmen taints business news in ways that outlive any particular crisis. This is preeminently a management problem, of course, and ought not to be beyond managerial ingenuity.

Second and similarly, because of its limitations and the pressures under which it labors, the press tends to judge individuals and groups in society by their perceived motives. It seldom has the time to get to the bottom of everything it is told, let alone the expertise to referee disputes among competing experts. By necessity, it has to rely on human instincts, a nose for when it is being told the truth or sold a story.

The credibility of any group is permanently undermined when the press repeatedly hears it talk one way and sees it behave another. And the press is not so foolish as to overlook the incongruity when businessmen mouth slogans about free enterprise and competition, then run to government for protection from every adversity. Watching this, the press will simplemindedly conclude that all the talk about free enterprise is not to be taken seriously, that it is a smokescreen for some ulterior and probably pecuniary motive.

In fact, the matter is more complicated. Businessmen typically do believe, from their own experience, that the system works best when competitors are forced to compete. But when their own business is endangered, they understandably feel that their responsibility is not to the system generally but to the interests of their various constituencies—shareholders, employees, and so on.

As government guarantees for loans to Chrysler Corporation were being considered in late 1980, the American Stock Exchange took a poll of its CEOs, including the question, "The government should give economic assistance to financially troubled corporations if they are among the nation's *major employers* (such as Chrysler)?" Only 21.5 percent of the executives agreed, while 78.5 percent opposed such bailouts. But it is safe to say that if nearly any one of these executives headed Chrysler, he would be lobbying for the same bailout. There are arguments for such policies that deserve a hearing, after all, and from whom will we hear them if not from the chairman of Chrysler?

I remember being visited once by Charles Tillinghast, longtime chief executive of Trans World Airlines (TWA), who was trying to persuade the editorial board of the *Wall Street Journal* that then-troubled TWA ought to have government subsidies to allow it to compete on transatlantic routes with subsidized European carriers. Our forcefully announced position was that if the citizens of Belgium wanted to tax themselves to fly Americans across the Atlantic, the American government should not stop them. But here was Mr. Tillinghast, his personal millions already assured, undertaking this fool's errand. When he crossed his legs, he had a hole in his shoe. I decided then and there not to be personally critical of executives in such a position. Whatever the lack of worth of their arguments, they are driven by duty to make them.

Journalists with less exposure to the problems and foibles of corporate CEOs, though, are not likely to be so understanding. The crisis confusion that besets the big stories, and the role trap that pits the individual interests and responsibilities of businessmen against their larger beliefs, are both perhaps inevitable. But both make a permanent contribution in keeping a certain skeptical edge in press coverage of business.

THE POWER OF THE PROFIT STEREOTYPE

The most powerful stereotype shaping and misshaping business news, though, is far more fundamental. The limitations of the press—the need to find an audience, the constraints of format, the necessity of dealing in stereotypes—apply across the board, not solely to business news. Crisis confusion and the role trap also have their counterparts elsewhere. If there is a particular problem with business news, there must be something wrong particularly with the stereotypes with which the press organizes it, with the metaphors with which society understands it. Where this problem lies does not seem to me a mystery. It lies in certain misunderstandings— shared by the press, the public, and the businessmen themselves—about something we call "profit."

The enormous power of this central stereotype or metaphor has been repeatedly demonstrated. Never more so, I suppose, than in the "oil crisis" that started with the 1973 Middle East war and the Saudi Arabian oil production cutbacks and boycott of shipments to the United States. Oil prices soared, and with them the reported profits of the oil companies. This quickly became "the story"—the gains of the oil companies and not, curiously enough, the big winners, the Saudis. My own hunch is that oil prices did not go up because of the 1973 war, that it is closer to the truth to say there had to be a 1973 war because it was time for oil prices to go up. But the Saudis escaped much of the blame by cloaking their motives as political and racial, which somehow struck a lot of people as more honorable than trying to make a buck.

But the headlines quickly read, "Exxon Profits Surge 170%," "Mobil Net Up 140%," or whatever. Not too surprisingly, the notion quickly spread that the oil companies contrived the crisis to drive up the price. One television station, it was at least rumored, sent a camera crew by helicopter to search for tankers circling off the Eastern seaboard waiting to dock when the price got high enough. Such was the power of the stereotype of profit.

As the oil companies rather vainly tried to explain, much of this initial profit surge was illusory. Much of it was merely "inventory profit," gains that go on the books but must immediately be spent to refill the pipelines with oil at higher prices. The oil companies scarcely tried to explain that, to the extent their real profits did go up, this is how our economic system is supposed to work—when a commodity gets scarce the price rises, the companies producing it make higher profits, the higher profits attract more investment to the field, the investment produces more of the commodity, and the price stabilizes.

Besides, who, after all, benefits from profits? The chairman of an oil company is richly rewarded, but he does not get to put the company's profits in his pocket. Profits are either reinvested in the business or paid out in dividends. In either case, the chief beneficiaries are the shareholders. And who are the shareholders? Some 65 percent of Exxon shares, to take one example, are held by pension funds, insurance companies, mutual funds, and other mechanisms for small savers to pool their resources. Employee pension funds alone own 28 percent of Exxon. Profits are used principally to prepare for and support retirement. Yet the notion persists that if they get too high someone is getting away with something.

This drama is repeated in ways large and small throughout the culture. In the wake of the Three Mile Island nuclear power accident, Jane Fonda's "The China Syndrome" depicted utility employees suppressing warnings of danger in order to increase profits. This image of a profiteering electric utility is ludicrous. A utility has its consumer prices regulated by rates of return, so that if it has a big profit it gets lower rate increases. Conversely, though, its rate base reflects its capital costs, which move inversely with shareholder returns. So if the shareholders' dividend is cut, the ratepayers ultimately have to pay more for electricity. The confusion is not merely a matter of movie scripts. In the real world, the Nuclear Regulatory Commission punishes utilities for accidents by fining them, as if this could have some meaning in a regulated industry that depends on continuous access to the capital markets.

In short, the profit stereotype teaches the press, the regulators, and the public to envision businessmen as motivated solely by greed. Fair enough, of course, to some extent. But the stereotype is so powerful that the actions of businessmen are examined far more closely for evidence of overreaching for pecuniary gain than, say, the actions of a politician are examined for evidence of overreaching for power. And far more than the actions of a Ralph Nader are examined for overreaching for publicity and personal glory. Miss Fonda makes more money than your typical businessman, yet scarcely anyone notices that her political posturings are good for her box office. In her case, other stereotypes apply.

What, then, is the source of the stereotype under which businessmen labor? As with all stereotypes, there is, of course, a substantial vein of truth. Market economies are indeed based on the principle of harnessing the acquisitive instinct, while nonmarket economies profess to harness altruistic motives. Yet given the historical irony that market economies provide room for higher motives while nonmarket economies rest on fear, this in itself cannot account for the pervasiveness of the profit-seeking stereotype. No, the stereotype draws its extraordinary power from generations of bragging by businessmen.

"XYZ Corporation Profits Up 140%" is the headline, after all, that the XYZ Corporations of the world dream about four times every year as they release their quarterly earnings reports. As with so much in life, your troubles start when you get what you want. Businessmen complain that the public opinion polls show that the public has a grossly exaggerated notion of profit margins, and yet when they report their financial results, businessmen like to exaggerate their profit margins.

The inflation that started in 1965, in particular, served to exaggerate profits in a number of ways. First, of course, profits are stated in nominal dollars, so that inflation makes them seem to grow even if their real value is stagnant. Beyond that, inflation creates phantom profits—income that shows up on the books but must be immediately spent merely to keep the business where it is.

The simplest type of phantom profit is "inventory profit." If a corporation spends $1 on horsehide and tallow to make a widget and sells the widget for $2, it can claim a profit of $1. But if, because of inflation, it then has to spend $2 for the same amount of horsehide and tallow to make its next widget, it clearly is in a losing game.

Even more important, the same thing happens with the widget-bending machines. When a business buys new plant and equipment, it charges these expenses as depreciation— that is, rather than subtracting the whole cost from gross income in calculating profit for the year in which a plant is built, these deductions are spread over a number of years presumed to approximate the plant's lifetime. Thus, when the plant wears out, the business should have been able to hold enough money in reserve to buy a new one. But depreciation is based on "historical cost" (the cost of the plant in the year it was built) rather than on "replacement cost" (the cost of the same plant in the year the deductions are taken). The result over time is to make profits look much larger than they really are.

One would think that businessmen would rush to explain their dire predicament. In inflation-adjusted terms, many leading companies have recently met their dividend payments only by dipping into capital or by gradually liquidating the shareholders' property. Yet year after year the typical company, far from complaining, bragged of "record" earnings—records established not by the skill of managers but by the vagaries of inflation. It was not until October of 1979, with Statement 33 of the Financial Accounting Standards Board, that businesses were led kicking and screaming to the modest step of publishing supplementary inflation-adjusted results.

Worse, many businessmen are so intent on reporting high "profits" they are willing to sacrifice real—as opposed to reported—money to do so. Accountants give businesses the choice of valuing inventories on two different bases—FIFO (first in, first out) or LIFO (last in, first out). Without delving into accounting technicalities, in times of inflation FIFO will show higher reported profits, but these lead to higher tax liabilities. Under LIFO the company reports lower profits, but pays less tax and has more money left to put to work for shareholders. Yet late in the 1970s a survey by the American Institute of Certified Public Accountants showed only 10 of 600 major companies had switched entirely to LIFO, while 268 remained entirely on FIFO.

The usual justification for this behavior is that reporting higher earnings will boost a corporation's share price and improve its borrowing power. This is almost surely not the case. It is most difficult to conceive that the stock market would value a company more if it gave a larger portion of its cash flow to the government. As early as 1974, in fact, a study by Shyam Sunder at the University of Chicago showed that companies switching from FIFO to LIFO, with lower reported earnings but higher actual cash flow, outperformed the market averages. More broadly, the best academic work on the stock market has produced the "efficient markets" hypothesis—that share values quickly and accurately incorporate all available information on a company. Because the shares are so intensely studied and so widely traded, vagaries of human judgment wash out and the facts prevail, leaving little room for cosmetics.

(Consistent with efficient markets, the Sunder study showed that the share-price gains from switching to LIFO came before the effective date of the change; by then everyone knew of the impending development and it had been "discounted" into the share price. The same effect has been documented with stock splits.)

In their internal management, modern businesses make little use of "profit" in the sense of "earnings per share." They are interested in ROI—return on investment. Rates of return are also the relevant measure for the macroeconomic function usually assigned to "profit"—maximizing economic growth by attracting investment into the high potential areas. Many businessmen recognize the contradiction, of course, but it seldom stops them from bragging about record earnings if the occasion presents itself.

One of my favorite CEOs jokes about renaming his bottom line; instead of calling it "profit" he would call it "savings." While this is precisely the way the item is treated in the National Income and Product Accounts, for my friend it remains a joke. His accountants and the Securities and Exchange Commission would not hear of it. Similarly, the chief executive of a major oil company once complained to me that his company always reported its rate of return as well as its earnings per share, and asked why our news accounts always emphasized the latter and often omitted the former. A good question, I thought, and when I inquired I found the reason is that no two oil companies calculate rates of return the same way. Earnings per share, by contrast, is the product of an accounting system designed (though not always successfully) to state results on a consistent basis from company to company and industry to industry.

As the reader may by now be starting to suspect, what we commonly call "profit" reflects economic reality perhaps even less than it reflects accounting fiction. The fundamental problem is that accounting practices were first developed for the great joint trading companies that were the ancestors of the modern corporation. Investors bought shares in financing a ship, and when it returned the cargo was sold and the profits divided in proportion to the investment—an eminently logical measure for such an enterprise was "earnings per share." It still is, in one circumstance, for the modern corporation—in liquidation.

For an ongoing enterprise, though, the principle has been adapted into a curious beast. An ongoing enterprise must constantly replace its ships, and this leads to a charge called "depreciation," which is excluded from profit though it leaves the company with actual cash to invest. Inventory profits are included, though they vanish when the inventory is replenished. Interest on debt is deducted as an expense, but dividends on stock come out of profit. I suggested to my friend that when he called "profit" "savings," he should call "dividends" "interest on equity."

The de facto decision on what is included as "profit" is made by the tax collector when he decides what is and what is not a deductible business expense. Peter Drucker instructs us that earnings are what is left after the charges the tax collector has allowed you to deduct. "Profit" is that portion of a corporation's cash flow the government has decided to tax.

This confusion, while monumental, probably does little direct material harm. We have developed a whole industry, called securities analysis, for the purpose of translating accountants' reports into something economically meaningful. Efficient markets are a testimony to this profession's success.

Nor is it likely to be feasible to dream up entirely new accounting concepts that would more nearly reflect economic reality. The Financial Accounting Standards Board (FASB) has, in fact, sponsored a project on Financial Accounting Concepts, already a huge undertaking without the enormous changes suggested by the above analysis. To the credit of the FASB, its conceptual project's reports are notable for their modesty and sense of limitation, in decided contrast to the hoopla with which earnings per share figures are often treated.

It is probably illusory to expect accountants to come up with any single figure to sum up the performance of so complicated a social organism as the modern corporation. If we need such a number, we should look to share prices in efficient markets. The movements of an individual company's stock would have to be set against broader market movements reflecting general influences such as the business cycle and government policy.

Yet as a central organizing metaphor for thinking about business—as the most powerful stereotype organizing business news—profit in the sense of earnings per share is mischievous. You think about business one way, write about business one way, if you envision profit as someone's direct gain. You think in an entirely different way, write in an entirely different way, if you think of profit as one species of cost in an ongoing enterprise.

THE VALUE OF ALTERNATE STEREOTYPES

All economies, whether or not they recognize anything called businessmen, have to deal with fundamental problems of savings, investment, growth, and returns. Monies must be saved now to finance investments, and the investments must generate the returns to repay savers, with a bonus for deferring consumption. Around these necessities all economies are organized.

In Sweden in the 1960s, the government started a pension system by taxing workers and investing the proceeds in the bond markets. These forced savings were made available for investment, first in bonds but later also in equities. In effect, the savers would indirectly own the companies, and this would finance their retirement. This was called socialism.

In the United States in the same years, pension funds and other institutional investors were buying up American industry. In the end, the savers would indirectly own the companies, and this would finance their retirement. This was called capitalism.

In market economies, the key decision of which investments will produce the greatest return is left to decentralized capital markets. While they are so subtle and complex that they elude the understanding of any one man—indeed, precisely because they are so subtle and complex—they are able to direct investment far more efficiently than the best central planner. Decentralized price signals from the consumer level up have the same sort of power. This has allowed such economies to dramatically outperform their competitors. And historically it is only in such economies that personal freedom and political democracy flourish.

The concepts of profit as saving, of efficient markets as decision-makers, of the necessity of returns to finance personal retirements, these are the raw materials for an alternate set of stereotypes for organizing thought and writing about the role of business in society. They are the metaphors in which I think about business, and in my experience they are valuable in "finding news" other stereotypes miss. That is to say, they have a real market value. If they became the prevailing stereotypes, businessmen would be happy—except, perhaps, when they are attacked for backing wage/price controls, wanting import protection, or seeking federal bailouts.

A more sophisticated metaphor for understanding business will not be easy to propagate. In any event, it will remain hard to encapsulate in a 30-second television report. But this kind of metaphor surely will never be established without a lot of help from business itself. When businessmen tell the public and government that profits are low, then tell investors that profits are high, they forfeit the right to complain that no one understands them. Least of all should they expect to see the matter set straight by a *deus ex machina* called the press. The press has too many limitations, and the confusion runs too deep. The press can, of course, do better. It will gradually do better with new business sections, different electronic audiences, a general growth in education and sophistication, a different national mood. If businessmen want to speed this process, the first step is to recognize that what is needed is a greater sophistication throughout society about those questions of economic organization that are encapsulated in the concept of profit—and that if businessmen want to get this clear in journalists' minds, they have to start by getting it clear in their own.

V

Issues

11

JOHN L. HULTENG

Holding the Media Accountable

Dangers in media power. Print and broadcast independence. Libel law and the right to privacy. Monitoring by commission, council, and the reader. Competition as a balance. Consolidation or diversity? Codes, the ombudsman, media policy. Journalist motivation.

Ever since the dissemination of news began to significantly influence the way human society functioned, efforts have been made to hold the press accountable for its performance—efforts initially exerted chiefly by such agencies of authority as the crown and the church. These agencies correctly perceived that the unregulated circulation of news and ideas would jeopardize their sources of power, so they instituted means of control through monopolization, licensing, or intimidation.

The gradual spread of libertarian concepts over the centuries undermined the rationale for such controls, and in lands where these concepts were honored, government restrictions on the press were greatly weakened or effectively abandoned. They survive intact, of course, in totalitarian societies of various ideological hues.

In this country the independence of the press has been constitutionally affirmed and many times reaffirmed; open expression of ideas and the unfettered circulation of information are understood to be essential catalysts of representative democracy. When a branch of government does reach out to limit press freedom, as the executive in various ways attempted to do during the Nixon years, it is rebuffed.

But if the issue of press accountability to government has been largely resolved in the United States, questions remain about the responsibility of the news media to other elements in society—in particular, to the various publics that these media are intended to serve.

UNSUPERVISED POWER

These questions arise from a recognition that a press guaranteed against government interference—and also effectively shielded from most other forms of external supervision—represents a massive power center. Such power, if wielded irresponsibly, is capable of inflicting damage on individuals, on institutions, and on society in general. That damage may be only an annoyance in some instances; it may be mortal in others.

The harm can be done in many ways and in varied circumstances. It can happen when an erroneous report is amplified disastrously by the great media megaphones. It can happen when an individual's privacy is invaded in order to hype a story or a photograph. It can happen when the news is systematically shaped so as to distort the public's perception of reality.[1] Even dedicated libertarians acknowledge that some means should exist, some effort should be made, to minimize the damage caused by the willful or careless misuse of media power.

(Benjamin Franklin observed that "abuses of the freedom of speech ought to be repressed, but to whom do we dare commit the power to do it?" That was, and still is, the pivotal question. We certainly do not dare commit such power to an agency of government, since in that way lies the destruction of liberty.)

To be sure, we have accepted a degree of government intervention in many other areas to assure standards of quality and responsible performance: pure food and drug laws, trade regulations, utility rate making, and collective bargaining among them. But government has no significant stake in the grading of meat or pills or in the ground rules for strikes and lockouts. It has an enormous stake in the definition of news and the policing of media performance, as the ominous object lessons of authoritarian states repeatedly remind us.

HOW ABOUT BROADCASTING?

On the surface, the special case of radio and television broadcasting seems to suggest that government supervision of media performance does not necessarily lead to totalitarian excess. Radio and TV are news media as well as entertainment and advertising channels, and an agency of government—the Federal Communications Commission (FCC)—does indeed exercise an overview role. Despite that, the journalistic independence of these media does not appear to be threatened. While the expression of editorial opinion may be less robust than in the print media because of the implications of the Equal Time and Fairness doctrines,[2] news broadcasts certainly are not censored by government and the Dan Rathers and Roger Mudds are in no way intimidated. That seems to suggest that government supervision and media freedom are not necessarily incompatible.

The argument does not really hold. The broadcast media — insofar as news is concerned—are *not* effectively under government control. As they have grown in economic strength and audience allegiance, they have successfully worked toward achievement of nearly as much journalistic independence as that enjoyed by the print media. FCC licensing requirements (which apply only to stations, not to networks) have not been manipulated in recent years to limit the freedom of broadcasters to report the news. Had there existed genuine government control of broadcast news, consider how eagerly it would have been applied to prevent TV from bringing the Vietnam war into America's living rooms or to suppress coverage of the Watergate exposures.

Still, even the limited government leverage on the broadcast media that persists is unwholesome and is a condition that should be corrected. So long as *any* arrangement is in place that might give an arm of government the potential for control of the news media, the freedom of the press—and our political liberties as well—are at unacceptable risk.

THE ALTERNATIVES

Yet if not to government, where else can we turn for some guarantee of responsible media performance? How effective are alternative approaches to ensuring that the consumers of news media products will get unadulterated goods? Is it possible to safeguard the rights of individuals against media abuse without sacrificing the independence of the press?

Various attempts have been made, not based on government oversight or control, to establish media accountability. Some have depended on external apparatus; others have been generated from within the press itself.

The longest-standing outside approach is the remedy of civil law. In all of the fifty states there are libel laws (there is no federal statute), and in most of those jurisdictions the right of privacy also is recognized, either in common law or in specific statute.

The reasoning underlying libel law begins with the assumption that if an individual's good name and reputation are damaged by material published or broadcast, that individual should have some recourse in the courts. The concept of a right of privacy, less well established, holds that all of us deserve to be shielded from unwarranted intrusion on our personal lives, whether by the press or any other agency.

Libel laws provide a means whereby someone who has been held up to "public hatred, contempt or ridicule" may sue the offending publisher or broadcaster for financial damages. If the case is won, the injured party presumably is made whole, partly by the damage award and partly by the public vindication the trial and verdict represent.

Thus simply described, the libel laws would seem to provide significant leverage to hold the news media accountable. But the reality is more complex and less reassuring from the standpoint of the public.

Those handy loopholes

Numerous defenses are afforded publishers and broadcasters under the law; if successfully mounted, these defenses can frustrate a high percentage of libel actions that are brought. A series of Supreme Court decisions beginning in 1964, for example, made it exceedingly difficult for public officials—or persons who had for some reason become widely recognized as public figures—to recover any damages at all under the libel laws unless they could prove gross carelessness or malice on the part of the newspaper, magazine, or broadcast outlet that had disseminated the damaging news or picture. That proof is very hard to come by.

Some more recent decisions of the Supreme Court have moved the pendulum back somewhat in favor of plaintiffs, but the various defenses against libel actions still constitute wide and accessible loopholes for the news media and make the law an uncertain protection for individuals who consider themselves wronged by those media.

The common law protection against invasion of privacy (only a few states have enacted privacy statutes) is equally porous. Someone seeking redress for a publication that violated privacy (for example, by publishing a gruesome accident photo showing a mangled body, or a feature profile that revealed embarrassing details of an individual's personal life) might well be frustrated if the defendant publication could demonstrate that the picture or story in question was newsworthy and of general public interest.

Still, despite the loopholes, the libel and privacy laws do represent a means of punishing the grossest forms of media injury to individuals. Perhaps more important, the fact that such recourses exist constitutes a restraining influence on those elements of the press that might otherwise wield their power irresponsibly. And so far as the loophole defenses are concerned, it should in fairness be acknowledged that the court decisions defining these defenses were taken in an effort to make sure that the libel laws would not be exploited to intimidate and muzzle the press in its role as a watchdog of the public interest.

In sum, at least a modest degree of accountability is achieved by the libel and privacy concepts as interpreted by the courts, without invading media freedom in the process.[3]

APPOINT A COMMITTEE

Another approach involving an agency outside the press is of more recent origin than the libel and privacy laws. It is based on the notion that a commission or council of disinterested but informed citizens could function as an ongoing monitor of press performance, identifying unethical behavior, coming to the rescue of individuals injured by the media, and uplifting standards generally. Since such an agency would not be governmental, the specter of First Amendment infringement would not be invoked. The commission members would represent the public, not the media, and thus would be uninhibited in the role of critic and arbiter.

When the idea was advanced in 1947 by the Hutchins Commission on Freedom of the Press, it did not exactly take off like a rocket—not even like a World War I biplane. Most of the nation's editors were either skeptical or flatly negative, sensing a regulatory foot in the door.

During the next couple of decades, however, some newspapers experimented gingerly. Local press councils were set up, typically with foundation financing, in Oregon, California, Illinois, and Washington. Statewide councils were established in Hawaii and Minnesota, and a National News Council—also launched under foundation auspices—came on the scene in the 1970s.

Preaching to the converted

All of the experimental monitoring efforts have been of some value. At the local level, the councils contributed briefly (most were short lived) to the education of community members and in some instances made the editors more sensitive to reader concerns and grievances. But, as might have been predicted, those newspapers that cooperated in the local

trials were, for the most part, run by already law-abiding
journalistic citizens doing a commendable job for their communities. Those who most needed the monitoring and sen-
sitizing—the news twisters, the media monopolists, and the
cash-register journalism crowd—never let the council concept get a toehold on their turf.

On the national level, the council mechanism has had the
opportunity to deal with complaints involving any journal or
broadcast outlet anywhere in the country, responsible or irresponsible, cooperative or defiant. It has taken up a wide
range of cases, sometimes finding for the media and sometimes for a complainant who has charged media abuse. Some
sample cases:

—Was an NBC News report on Exxon activities in Florida
unfair? Decision: it was.

—Did the *Louisville Courier-Journal* misrepresent the fees
charged by a Louisville doctor in a survey story of medical
charges in the area? Decision: it did not.

—Was a Gannett News Service story about the Paulines, a
religious order, inaccurate? Decision: it was not.

The council has addressed only a relatively small number
of cases and has been cautious in its judgments, although it
has grown in confidence as it gained experience. But its impact has been limited, as with all of the commission experiments at whatever level. None of the councils has had any
enforcement power. A defendant journal or editor could be
given a critical tongue-lashing, but that was about the end of
it. Whether the aggrieved readers would even know of the
negative verdict was pretty much up to the newspaper involved, which could acknowledge or ignore the council's finding as it pleased. Some media, notably CBS News, have been
conscientious about reporting council decisions unfavorable
to them; others have been less forthcoming.

Council cases are reported in such professional journals as
Editor and Publisher and *Columbia Journalism Review* (the

latter quotes the full text of decisions and dissents) but are rarely mentioned in the general news flow where the public might find out about them. In short, the press councils have had no real bite; energetic gumming is about as much punishment as they can hand out.

Despite this, the council approach deserves to be sustained and expanded. Moral suasion and peer pressure may have little short-run effect, but they can build cumulatively, particularly among journalists, who are oddly thin-skinned about their own professional standing, however cynical and calloused they may be about the news events and the news figures they cover. Perhaps the most fruitful area of expansion of the press council idea would be at the state level, where jurisdiction would not be limited to a single community but where the council still would be close enough to the scene to be able to accommodate most grievances filed. Foundations could find few more significant ways in which to channel their largesse, not only for start-up and maintenance costs, but also for the dissemination of council findings to the general public — by paid ads if necessary.

CRITICS AND CRITIQUES

Another approach to media accountability has been undertaken through the years by a changing cast of press critics ranging from the muckraker Upton Sinclair (*The Brass Check*) through the late A. J. Liebling with his *New Yorker* commentaries and on to present-day counterparts such as Ben Bagdikian and Edwin Diamond. The individual critics' books, articles, TV commentaries, and magazine columns have been biting and well targeted, but their relatively small and select audiences have not often included those who most needed the scolding.

The opinion journals *(National Review,* the *New Republic,* and others at various points on the ideological spectrum)* and general circulation periodicals such as *Time* and *Newsweek* occasionally pass judgment on media performance. So do numerous agencies representing causes and constituencies, ranging from the American Civil Liberties Union to Accuracy in Media.

A more systematic critical oversight has been provided by specialized media reviews, the longest-surviving and most widely read of which is *Columbia Journalism Review,* published by Columbia University. Neither the individual critics nor the reviews have wielded more effective leverage than have the press councils. But again, the sting of knowing criticism, particularly from the Columbia journal, cannot be dismissed as ineffectual; it represents a spur to more ethical media performance, even though few media consumers may be aware of its existence. This is another avenue along which foundation investment would richly benefit the public interest.

THE PEOPLE SPEAK

Some publishers and owners contend that media accountability to the public already is achieved—and on a daily basis—by means of the newspapers' letters-to-the-editor columns and their occasional and irregular counterparts on the broadcast media. Through such feedback, they argue, errors can be corrected, arguments rebutted, and omissions filled in, all without recourse to cumbersome press councils or obnoxious government intervention.

Although there is some substance to the argument, it is considerably overstated. There is, for one thing, the question of access. On very small newspapers, the flow of letters is light enough so that a fairly high proportion of those received can be accommodated in the paper's columns — provided the editor wants to assign them space. But on metropolitan dailies and national news magazines, only a tiny fraction of the total of letters received ever get into print, as few as 1 or 2 percent in some cases. That considerably waters down the accountability contention.

Even those letters that are printed may not come very close to achieving their objectives. The readers' comments are typically set out in abbreviated, edited form; the size of type used for letter sections is usually a modest 8 point. But the paper's commentaries over in the editorial column are set in more imposing 10- or 12-point type, given top billing under provocative headlines and placed cheek-by-jowl with the editorial cartoon, the best-noticed item in the paper. The letters are signed by Mary or John Citizen, 245 Rye Lane, while the paper speaks with a corporate voice behind which can be sensed the vast power of a major media institution. It is hardly an equal contest.

PUT IT IN THE CONSTITUTION?

One attempt has been made to improve the odds for the reader, but it has thus far made little headway — for a couple of good reasons. Jerome Barron, a law professor, has proposed that anyone who wants to respond to a press attack on an individual or a cause should be guaranteed access to newspaper letter columns as a constitutional right.[4]

If there were such a guarantee, however, who or what would enforce it? The only effective agency would be the courts, and that would install an arm of government as a kind of supereditor, deciding what should go into the paper and at what length it should be printed. This would be clearly violative of the First Amendment. In fact, the Supreme Court specifically rejected the principal of guaranteed access when a case involving a state law to this effect came before it (*Miami Herald* v. *Tornillo*, 1974).

Even if the constitutional problem could somehow be bypassed, the Barron concept has another strike against it. If newspapers were required to print reader comments, their columns would likely be choked with such copy to the point that news would have to be severely curtailed. And as a practical matter, the glut of feedback would be self-defeating; how many readers would take the trouble to plow through page after page of nothing but letters to the editor?

So as matters stand—and as they are likely to remain— letters from readers and equivalent rejoinders from broadcast listeners and viewers can be looked upon as a useful if limited safety valve. But they cannot be represented as a practical means of insuring media accountability.

A BUILT-IN GYROSCOPE

The early architects of the free press concept believed that accountability would be effectively achieved by the factor of competition and that no form of external supervision or monitoring would be needed.

John Milton, Thomas Jefferson, and John Stuart Mill all subscribed to the notion that if the dissemination of news and opinion were truly unfettered, truth would emerge victorious over falsehood in the open marketplace of ideas— provided, of course, that all members of the community had access to that marketplace. Competition would function as a gyroscopic force, compelling the media toward a responsible heading, and the public would be able to identify the reliable information being circulated and to reject the false or misleading.

The theory was appealing, but the reality has been somewhat of a disappointment.

From the beginning, the marketplace of ideas has been considerably less accessible than the theorists wanted it to be. The mechanical facilities—whether the hand-operated presses of colonial days or the offset monsters of today—have always been limited and costly in terms of their times. Typically, relatively few persons have controlled the media facilities, and they have been the ones who have enjoyed freedom of the press in a practical sense.

As the trend to consolidation of the ownership of the news media has accelerated in recent years, the significance of competition as a check-and-balance force has declined. In only 3 or 4 percent of cities where daily newspapers are published does any head-to-head competition between separately owned publications survive. In the other 96 or 97 percent of the cities there is only one newspaper, or two papers published by a single owner. More and more newspapers have been swallowed up by chains and groups controlled by corporate owners or conglomerates. The independent daily is an endangered species.

In the broadcast field similar consolidation is evident, with only three major national networks and widespread group ownership of individual stations. It is true, however, that more direct competition continues among radio and television stations at the local level than exists in the print medium. In a major market city with only a single-owner morning/evening newspaper combination, there may be three TV stations battling among themselves for viewers and perhaps as many as twenty radio stations trying to stay alive in their specialized field. And in a cross-media sense, significant competitive forces are still at work, achieving some of the balancing effect envisioned by the theorists.

Although there may be only one daily in a community, its readers also have access to regional newspapers, national news magazines, and local radio or television broadcasts. Distortions or misrepresentations in the hometown daily may be corrected or offset by different versions disseminated by these other media, pretty much as Milton, Jefferson, and Mill had hoped would happen. The corrective balancing brought about by such cross-media competition is admittedly uneven and erratic, but it is certainly better than we could expect from a complete media monopoly—single ownership of all of the news and information channels.

Something resembling that unhappy possibility may even now be slouching toward Bethlehem. Experimenters are working on the hardware for an electronic newspaper which would be brought into the home by cable rather than by paper carriers on bicycles and would be displayed on the TV screen rather than on pages of newsprint. Presumably the same system could be made to work for magazines, advertising shoppers, and perhaps even for books. Then the way would be open for the consolidation of all media under one vast information network—and that single network might well turn out to be under government regulation.

This grim prospect may be years off, if it materializes at all, but we ought to be thinking about its implications now while we still have a chance to anticipate them. We should be preserving and nourishing such diversity as still exists in news media ownership. And we should be keeping a close eye on the backstage maneuvering for control of the cable medium, since it would likely be the nucleus of any all-embracing information monopoly.

But let us turn from unsettling visions of the future and back to the quest for accountability in the news media as they are today. With the various external influences itemized and evaluated, we can consider what forces are at work internally to encourage responsible and ethical performance by the press.

GRAND PROMISES

Longest evident among these forces have been the codes of ethics formulated by individual editors or by professional journalistic associations.

Such avowals of faith and promises of right conduct showed up early as newspaper masthead credos. Later they were institutionalized in more elaborate and detailed statements of principles adopted by organizations of journalists. Invariably they read well, asserting that truth will be venerated, that service to the public will be a paramount consideration, and that journalists as a class should be as far above suspicion as Caesar's wife.

Among the earliest of these behavioral guides was the Canons of Ethics of the American Society of Newspaper Editors (ASNE), subscribed to by that group shortly after its founding in the 1920s. A half-century later the ASNE updated the canons as a "Statement of Principles." By then numerous other trade and professional associations in both the print and broadcast fields had developed similarly high-sounding codes.

But all of them suffered from a critical anatomical defect: they had no teeth.

No provision was made for enforcement of the lofty principles set out in the various organizational codes. As a practical matter, what enforcement machinery *could* there be? Journalists cannot be disbarred, like errant lawyers, or deprived of their licenses to practice, like incompetent physicians. The First Amendment rules out admission or licensing requirements for those who seek to exercise freedom of expression through the press.

Theoretically, professional associations could administer at least a wrist slap to backsliding members by expelling them from the organizational ranks. But this has almost never happened, even when flagrant transgressions of the codes were involved. Association memberships have been unable to bring themselves to blackball one of their fellows, perhaps concerned that such an action would constitute a compromise of journalistic independence.

So the utility of the codes as guarantors of media accountability would seem to be limited. Their principal influence has been as guidelines to right conduct for those conscientious journalists who were looking for such guidance; it is doubtful that they have had much impact on the black sheep and the exploiters.

THE READERS' CHAMPION

Another attempt to develop an internal quality control for press performance was based on the Scandinavian institution of the ombudsman.

In the European version, the ombudsman is a kind of people's champion, empowered to hear citizens' complaints about government infringement on their rights and to take corrective action where necessary. As the concept has been adapted to American journalism, the ombudsman not only receives and responds to readers' grievances, but he also functions as a monitor of the publication's overall performance. Through staff memos or in published columns on the paper's editorial page, the ombudsman points out professional lapses and suggests remedies.

It is not an enviable assignment. An ombudsman who is doing the job properly is certain to alienate colleagues and ruffle management's fur; journalists are experts at handing out criticism but are not very graceful about taking it in their turn.

In order to function at all, the ombudsman must be a seasoned professional whose credentials are acknowledged and respected. And the office must be insulated and independent. The in-house critic has to be perceived not as just another cranky editor but as a detached, authoritative observer and arbiter whose tenure is not at the whim of the staff *or* the publisher.

For obvious reasons, it is not easy to find the right person to fill the ombudsman's shoes; it is equally difficult to set up the necessary working conditions. So it is not surprising that there have been very few ombudsman offices established on American newspaper staffs. One survey in the late 1970s found fewer than two dozen on the approximately 1,750 dailies in the country.

The *Washington Post* was among the earliest to try the ombudsman approach. The first three persons appointed to the job, all of them drawn from other departments on the paper's staff, had brief and not entirely successful tenures. Then an outsider was brought in, an experienced metropolitan newsman but not one who had worked at the *Post*, and he was able to achieve the necessary detachment.

When the ombudsman concept works it works very well indeed. Readers become aware that they have a friend at court to help when a name is misspelled or a news situation is distorted, and this improves the publication's credibility with those it serves. Staff members are kept on their toes, since they know that a lapse will bring a public chiding before their peers. It is a promising approach to the achievement of press accountability, and it deserves a wider trial than it has thus far had. This is a third point at which the efforts and resources of private foundations could be soundly invested. Media consumers could help, too, by making it clear to managers and owners that they need and want an ombudsman to represent their interests.

Publishers and editors who have been unwilling or unable to install an ombudsman on the premises have taken other, less dramatic steps toward improvement of the relationship between the news media and their publics. On some papers, for example, the editorial page fixtures now include an editor's column addressed to reader concerns. Backstage journalistic operations are described and explained; apologies are offered for slipups in coverage; questions are answered. Such columns are, of course, not adequate substitutes for an ombudsman office. They are basically public relations exercises. But they can result in some useful consciousness raising among both readers and staff members.

OOPS, SORRY!

Heightened media sensitivity to the rights and needs of the public has been evident in a gradual but steady improvement in the error-correction policy of newspapers. News is gathered and disseminated at high speed and in an atmosphere of deadlines and tensions. Mistakes are inevitable. Some are the result of carelessness or malice, but most are attributable to craft conditions. However they happen, they cause anguish and embarrassment to those who have been misrepresented in the news. Anyone so wronged is entitled to have the damage mended as fully as possible by a correction of the original error.

It once was standard operating procedure for newspapers to print corrections of error only grudgingly, if at all, and to place the correction notices in odd corners where few would notice them. A misstatement published on page 2 under a large headline might be corrected a few days later in small type and on page 59, next to the classified ads. This disreputable practice still survives on some papers.

But it is now increasingly the case that corrections are acknowledged regularly in a special section set aside near the front of the paper and displayed under a standing head so that they will be readily recognized. Although corrections never can catch up completely with the original error, the standing head approach is far more responsible than the old policy—or lack of policy.

Some well-heeled complainants, dissatisfied with the standard error-correction procedures, have sometimes resorted to taking out ads in the paper to set the record straight. But that is an expensive option available to very few. One corporation produced a full-dress documentary film and showed it around the country in an effort to rebut a story aired on a network television program.

HELP FROM WITHIN

There is, finally, one other internal force working to improve the performance of the news media and to make them more accountable to the public welfare. It is generated by the motivations of the men and women who write newspaper copy and headlines, produce the news broadcasts, and edit the news magazines.

It is not a force that can be isolated or quantified. But it is real and meaningful.

Individuals are drawn to journalism as a career by a variety of motives. Some see it only as an adequately satisfying, nonmenial job. Others look on it as a path to power and fame as television anchors or syndicated pundits. Many are fascinated by the sense of immersion in the flow of events, by being on the inside, by knowing more than most others about what is happening. And a great many more—perhaps the majority—are attracted by the opportunity to perform a significant public service, by the chance to provide the people with a window on the world.

There obviously is no way to prove statistically that more journalists are motivated by the public service ideal than by a lust for power or money. There certainly have been periods in journalistic history when this did not appear to be the case. But my experience through a lifetime of involvement with the news media as a practitioner or a close observer has satisfied me that in journalism today the idealists are indeed more numerous than the exploiters and self-servers.

Those journalists who recognize that the jobs have a public service dimension are likely to behave responsibly and ethically in their own niches, and that of itself is all to the good. Whether they also exert a larger influence depends, of course, on how much leverage they happen to have.

An Otis Chandler, inheriting power on a vastly profitable but stodgy and undistinguished paper, had plenty of leverage and he used it constructively. Attracting able people and giving them both professional freedom and financial support, he built the *Los Angeles Times* into one of the nation's most respected and significant journals. Similarly leveraged and well-intentioned owners such as Barry Bingham of the *Louisville Courier-Journal* and Katharine Graham of the *Washington Post* helped to give scores of others the opportunity to create fine and responsible journalism.

Most men and women who work in the news business do not have the advantages of ownership to reinforce their contributions. Yet the best among them are very much a part of the internal quality-control apparatus.

What they do, day by day, may not be particularly apparent from outside, or perhaps even much noticed within the organization. The reporter who makes several extra calls to be sure that she has gotten the story balanced and fair to both sides, the picture editor who turns down a dramatic news shot because it trades on a moment of personal tragedy, the editorial writer who struggles again and again for the right phrase that will make a complexity meaningful to the reader—that sort of constant nudging and reaching in the direction of quality and responsibility makes for better journalism.

Occasionally the nudging generates enough friction to catch the public's attention, at least momentarily. A group of reporters on the *Cleveland Plain-Dealer,* disturbed because they believed that their editors were dragging their heels on a proposed series of articles exposing the political machinations of a local utility, staged an informational picket and a by-line strike and finally got the series into the paper.

David and Cathy Mitchell, youthful proprietors of the tiny weekly *Point Reyes Light* in California, felt that the major news media were failing to give adequate coverage to the activities of the litigious and violence-prone cult, Synanon, which had its headquarters in the *Light*'s circulation area. So they took on the story themselves, and their exposures of the cult's abuses of individual rights earned them the Pulitzer Prize for public service.

The editors of two newspapers belonging to the Panax chain in the Midwest rebelled at the efforts of the chain's owner to inject opinion into the news columns and refused to print the offending articles. They lost their jobs as a result, but attracted so much national attention that the chain owner was put on the defensive and obliged to modify his tactics.

Most of the time, however, the push toward responsible and ethical journalism is exerted within the precincts of the news organization, without much fanfare. And it is exerted not because some outside monitor is pointing a finger or because a threat lurks in the background, but because the journalists involved are acting on conscience and conviction, responding to the public service ethic.

I do not mean to overdo this theme. Certainly there are plenty of money-hungry publishers and venal chain owners, plenty of shoddy newspapers and rip-and-read news programs, and plenty of journeymen in the ranks who are self-serving or indifferent. Their destructive influence can easily be documented.

But there are also the Chandlers, the Grahams, the Mitchells, and the unnoticed thousands of others, motivated by a belief in the public service function of the news media.

Their influence represents a persistent and ponderable force for responsible, ethical journalism. Without that force, our newspapers and broadcast news programs would be far, far worse than they are.

If press performance is to be further improved and the media made more accountable, these objectives will not be achieved at a stroke by legislative fiat or executive order. They will be attained incrementally, through the encouragement—by the foundations and the public—of such promising ventures as the press councils, the analytical reviews, and the in-house ombudsmen. And improvement will also depend—perhaps most of all—on the survival of the public service ethic among the men and women who choose to make their careers in journalism.

12

GEORGE COMSTOCK

Social and
Cultural Impact
of Mass Media

**Attracting an audience. Properties and functions of
the mass media. Media interaction. Television and entertainment. International use of television. Transforming media content: audience reaction. Distinctive
aspects of mass communication. Children and
television.**

Machiavelli's admonition, "When you strike at a prince,
strike to kill," is appropriate in exploring the social and
cultural impact of the mass media. Boldness at least has the
merit of willfully embracing the consequences. Let us then
entertain seven propositions, arguably supported by history
and empirical investigation.

I. The mass media are not mere technologies for disseminating information. They are a distinctive social innovation.

A contemporary American might assume that the mass media merely do what was always done, only more efficiently. But this is not so. Mass communications did not exist when Gutenberg published his 42-line bible in 1456, drawing on the development of movable type in China and cast-metal type in Korea during the preceding five hundred years. The birth of mass communications is more accurately traced to the appearance of the first newspapers in the seventeenth century than to Gutenberg's innovation.

The distinction is between technology and the social innovation to which technology may sometimes lead. Today's mass media are remote in scope and character from anything that existed when the initial technology was developed. The distinction, in essence, is the calculated creation of messages and symbols for transmission to the largest possible audience.

The innovation does not reside in the message, although parallels can be drawn between the content of contemporary mass media and certain ancient texts. Nor does it reside in the fact of one or a few communicating to many. It resides in three places: (a) in the calculated attempt to devise something to which a large number of people will wish to attend; (b) in the criterion of as large an audience as possible, given the nature of the message and the specific means of dissemination; (c) in the stepwise regularity by which, as the media have evolved, their audiences have grown larger.

It is through this last prism that the role of television in the evolution of the media can best be explained. First, television has increased the amount of time people spend each day on the mass media. This simple fact is documented in a study of life in the mid-1960s in twelve countries by three sociologists—Philip Converse, John Robinson, and Alexander Szalai (Robinson et al. 1972, pp. 113–44). They compared the ways in which thousands of people in eastern and western Europe and northern and southern America spent each day. When they compared those who owned television sets with those who did not, they found that television had increased attention to the mass media by an average of an hour a day per person. Second, hours of television use per day in the average household have increased steadily since the 1950s. They pointed out that television combines ready access with audiovisual stimuli, thus overcoming barriers that restrict the reach of other media. Newspapers, magazines, and books require literacy and normally must be paid for at the time of use; movies require the act of entering a theater; television has to be paid for only once, and is always available in the home.

As they evolved, the media assembled increasingly large audiences, and television is a good example of the mass media's tendency to maximize their audiences. Television has achieved its success in two ways. First, it has won increasing popular acceptance as an appropriate way to spend time. Second, the television industry has applied two other innovations—random sampling and computer analysis—to produce an accurate record of what people in fact watch, thereby permitting it to discard what they do not watch in acceptable numbers.

II. The distinctive properties of the mass media are unevenly distributed. Each medium therefore functions differentially in society.

Sociologists posit as the distinctive properties of the mass media the largeness, heterogeneity, and anonymity of the audience, the rapidity of transmission, the transitory nature of the experience, the public availability of the message, and the fact that the communicator is an organization, not an individual. Among the functions mass media serve, they argue, are the surveillance of the environment, or newsgathering; interpretation and prescription, or analysis and editorializing; transmission of culture; enforcement of norms; and diversion and entertainment. These characteristics apply broadly to all media, but a clear division of labor has emerged.

Television worldwide has become largely an entertainment medium with scant pretense to art. In the United States and elsewhere, newspapers are used for information by the better-educated and higher socioeconomic groups. Since its introduction in the 1950s, however, television has risen in public esteem as a news source. Survey evidence shows that the public names television as the source of most of its news, the most rapid disseminator of news, the most fair and unbiased of sources, the most comprehensive in coverage, and the more credible when two media disagree on a report. Newspapers, magazines, and radio all rank lower, although they once either rivaled or exceeded television. Mental set and actual behavior, however, are two different things. When people are queried—not simply about "news" but about different kinds of news—it turns out that, for regional and local news, newspapers equal or exceed television as the principal source. Furthermore, far more people actually see a daily newspaper within any two-week period than watch a national network evening news program. This is as true today as it was a decade ago.

Voting studies have found that the reading of newspapers—but not the viewing of television news—is generally related to knowledge about candidates and issues, the accurate recall of specific stories, and the rational use of information to reach a voting decision. But viewers do appear to learn from brief, paid-for, political spots on television. Lucas and Adams (1978, pp. 120–31) found that in a close election, such as the 1976 Carter-Ford contest, viewing the evening news regularly apparently gave undecided and wavering viewers the confidence to reach a decision.

When people are questioned closely about the news media, the one dimension on which television remains dominant — regardless of the kind of news at issue — is its credibility. This, and the sense it can convey of a candidate as a living being instead of just a name, enable television to give voters confidence. Newspapers, on the other hand, apparently figure more prominently than television news in defining which issues are important. But even they take second place when personal experience intervenes, as when a gasoline shortage moves energy and the Middle East to center stage. Television, in contrast, is unrivaled in its ability to draw and hold the attention of the public on a single event. These events often come to be perceived as inseparable from their television coverage — space shots, assassinations, state funerals, coronations, the Super Bowl, and presidential debates are examples. Part of television's ability to focus public attention lies in its capacity to entertain in almost any context. The public's faith in television as an information source thus does not diminish its entertainment value.

About three-fourths of the time that people spend with the mass media is devoted to television. Much attention is focused by the other media on television as an institution. Consequently, the social role of mass entertainment has been enlarged, a fact nowhere more apparent than in the way that entertainment values set the framework within which news and public affairs broadcasts must be designed as well as provide the organizational milieu within which such broadcasting must occur, and this entertainment is of a special order — *mass* entertainment, objectionable to few, acceptable to all. According to sociologist Paul Hirsch, television is "the K-Mart" of culture.

*III. Differentiation among the mass media is neither
static nor additive: they change each other.*

A new medium does not simply add to the existing media network. A new medium can succeed only by diminishing the
existing media—by withdrawing revenues from advertising,
admissions, or sales, and by consuming time once spent on
them. During the fight for survival, the older media evolve.

Again, television is a prominent example. It has
transformed the other media. Radio listening has declined,
and radio has changed from a three-network medium offering entertainment and news, on a schedule much like that of
network television today, to a largely local medium primarily—although not exclusively—devoted to music. Before
television, the radio audience was national and heterogeneous; today, each station reaches a fairly homogeneous segment of the public attracted by its particular format, so that
across stations there is a diversity unknown in television.

Movie attendance has declined. By 1970 the annual figure
for the United States was about 19 million, compared to 41
million a decade earlier and 82 million in the mid-1940s.
Movies have lost their status as family entertainment and, in
order to compete with television, moviemakers have turned
increasingly to material unacceptable on the home screen;
sexual explicitness and violence have become more prominent. Television, in turn, has become a major outlet for
movies, so that a variety of forces has been shifting television
toward more liberal standards—competition from the
movies, the standards set by them, and the lucrativeness of
presenting films at the frontiers of taste.

Some of the great national magazines—*Saturday Evening
Post, Life, Look*—have reemerged since their demise after
the arrival of television, but with comparatively puny circulations. It is clear that people spend less time reading
them, making advertisers skeptical of their effectiveness
relative to television. Specialized magazines—such as *Ski-*

ing, Gourmet, Playboy, Road and Track, New York—that appeal to an interest or a locale, have largely supplanted them.

Television also affected other print media. As humor- and thrill-seeking youngsters turned from comic books to television, sales fell from 600 million in 1950 to half that in 1970. Libraries found less demand for fiction, while the demand for nonfiction, which television was ill-suited to deliver in much quantity or detail, remained about the same. Television delivered fantasy to many people in a way they found more convenient, economical, or entrancing. It is not surprising that in the three decades since the appearance of television the proportion of book titles devoted to fiction, poetry, and drama has declined while that devoted to nonfiction has increased.

Predictions that television would quickly destroy book publishing because people would no longer read have proved false. Nevertheless, the shift toward nonfiction is not the only way in which book publishing has been affected by television. As early as 1959, when Alexander King's *Mine Enemy Grows Older* became a best-seller through the author's guest appearances on the Jack Paar show, it became apparent that television was a superb vehicle for promoting books. It is a case of mutual exploitation among talk show, author, and publisher. The equation, however, includes a mass audience nonliterary in taste, so that what can effectively be promoted to best-seller status by television is largely circumscribed by boundaries of factuality, self-cultivation, titillation, and accessible prose—the how-to book, promising mastery in sex, mind, soul, and finance; the how-it-was book, usually in entertainment; and the how-it-*really*-was and is in finance, art, politics, the cosmetic business, television, and other pinnacles of glamour and notoriety.

Accompanying the rise of television as a means of book promotion has been the increasing dominance in book distribution of chain stores. Like television itself, their outlets, often in suburban shopping centers, reach a public that is not particularly literary—a public, in fact, that would not enter a bookstore were it not brought to them and made to look like a supermarket. Television has made mass promotion possible; the chains have made mass sales easy; and together, the two have increased the popularity of the "big" seller.

The film industry has more recently joined this partnership, promoting movies through commercials and books related to movies through authors' talk-show appearances and commercials. A key date is 1976: the concept and script for *The Omen* had just been sold to Hollywood by the author, David Seltzer. He obtained the right to base a novel on the script, which was published as an original mass-market paperback at the same time the movie was released. The movie drew attention to the book; the paperback displays in bookstores, newsstands, and supermarkets promoted the movie; television, variously, was used to promote both. The movie did very well, and the book sold 3.5 million copies.

There are two broad lessons here. One is that—in the television age—the other media have emulated television. The other is that television's tendency to make entertainment more prominent in our society is not limited to the time people devote to television viewing.

Some newspapers at first refused to print television schedules for fear of aiding a competitor, but they soon found that people wanted to read about television as well as watch it. *TV Guide*, for example, has become the magazine with the largest circulation in the United States at more than 18 million copies a week. Television has played a continuous role in reshaping U.S. newspapers, but in ways not readily observable from gross circulation figures. For the first two decades of television's existence as a household medium, per capita daily newspaper circulation kept pace with population growth. The decline in the number of big-city dailies seemed to have more to do with the post—World War II shift to the suburbs where distribution was more expensive and difficult, and where people often preferred the local daily—with its community coverage and advertising—to the metropolitan newspaper. Yet television certainly increased the vulnerability of big-city afternoon dailies by providing more recent national news and by reducing the amount of evening time people were willing to spend with a newspaper. It is quite possible that, in the absence of television, rising education levels since World War II would have resulted in an increase in per capita daily newspaper circulation. In any case, three decades after the appearance of television it is clear that daily newspaper circulation—and, more significantly, the amount of attention people give to the various parts of a newspaper—have fallen because of television.

IV. Despite the enormous social, cultural, and political differences that are observable from society to society, the mass media evolve everywhere in a strikingly similar way.

The twelve-nation study found considerable variation in access to television sets (see Robinson 1972, pp. 410–31; Robinson and Converse 1972, pp. 197–212). In Yugoslavia, for example, only 35 percent of all households owned one. When the examination was confined to set owners, however, the international differences in time spent viewing were almost eliminated. Despite the differences in programming and hours of broadcasting in the twelve countries, television took up about the same amount of time each day among those who had access to it. In addition, the division of social functions among the media is much the same everywhere: television, for example, universally emphasizes entertainment.

This tendency of the media everywhere to move in the same direction is attributable to the similarity of the circumstances they confront and to their own functional imperatives. Newspapers, books, and magazines cannot escape the fact that literacy is required for access, and television everywhere seeks a large audience because—not so burdened—it has high operating costs that must either be covered or justified. Television tends to emphasize entertainment whether it is a private or a public enterprise and whether it is financed by advertising revenue, viewers' contributions, government subsidies, or some combination of these. Entertainment becomes a priority because it is the best way to attract a large audience. With private enterprise, it is a matter of maximizing profits; a public enterprise must justify its expenditures to the controlling authorities. The demographic pattern of television viewing in the Soviet Union thus resembles that of the United States—those of lower income and education, women, and children are higher-than-average viewers—because programming strikes a similar social chord by using such familiar devices as game shows to attract audiences.

The hegemony of the media is also exemplified by the steady increase in average daily hours of television viewing that has occurred almost everywhere. Israel is a good example of a medium dictating its terms. Katz and Gurevitch (1976), two sociologists, traced the history of television and public reaction there. They found that the proportion of people who expected television to have some cultural value was greater when television was first introduced than after a few years of broadcasting, but that television had become acceptable on religious holidays from which it had originally been barred. And there are countries where the inverse relationship between education and average daily viewing that has always held for the United States did not hold at first; but as the content of the medium shifted toward satisfying a broader audience, much the same pattern appeared.

V. The mass media are not vessels impassively conveying content. They frame, transform, and invent what they purport to convey.

Two sociologists—Kurt Lang and Gladys Lang (1953)—by comparing the observations of those on the scene with what appeared on the television screen, long ago convincingly documented that news coverage may give an impression of an event far different from what actually occurred. The occasion was the public welcome given General Douglas MacArthur when he visited Chicago after his dismissal by President Truman as commander of American forces in the Korean war. Television gave the impression of seething masses, exuberance, and a tumultuous welcome, with the general at the center; those on the scene experienced curious, uneven, and somewhat indifferent crowds that occasionally had a glimpse of MacArthur. The explanation, of course, is that television covered the event in accord with its expectations and with its vested interest in conveying something exciting.

More recently, a Berkeley media scholar, Todd Gitlin (1980), has focused on the "frame" employed by the media to introduce a story—that is, the context and implied rationale for coverage—to analyze coverage of the "New Left" during the 1960s and early 1970s. He concluded that these "frames" emphasized dangerous extremism, immature adventuresomeness, and counterbalancing pro-war protesters. The result was to give the reader or viewer the impression of drama and a balance of public expression that was not there. At the same time, the exposure motivated the movement to act so as to seek additional coverage, while the media's continuing emphasis on opposition to the Vietnam war and draft resistance portrayed the New Left as outraged over specific issues readily resolvable by the establishment, rather than as opposed to the basic tenets of the society on a broad front as it saw itself doing. By choosing one from a variety of possible ways of covering the New Left, the media defined for the movement options of how to reach a broader public.

Entertainment, similarly, is constantly reinvented to fit the needs of a medium. Television, by and large, requires comedy and drama accessible and acceptable to the many. Magazine, book, and newspaper publishers have the option of cultivating a narrower audience. The same genre, or even the same story by a particular author, will change in order to fit the needs of different media. This is what film critics perceived when they wrote that *Kramer vs. Kramer* had the structure of television drama; like television, it emphasized a few characters, delimited scenes, and close interpersonal exchanges.

These transformations are involved in a medium's implicit message. The notion that media transform "content" would be inconceivable were it not possible to think of content as distinct from its vehicle. But it is also sensible to think of media as having a second message in the way that they convey content and the responses evoked among their audiences. As Marshall McLuhan argued, print implies a certain linear orderliness and the necessity of some effort to discover the reward of its message, while television and film serve up the message with little cognitive effort. Although television and film are more effective instructional vehicles than the other media in producing immediate gains in knowledge, those gains—as the recent research of Gavriel Salomon (1979), an Israeli psychologist, has shown—may occur at the expense of reasoning skills that would otherwise develop as a consequence of the mental exercise imposed by the absence of cinematic qualities.

VI. Television represents the distinctive characteristics of mass communication at a higher order than

previously known. It has consequently increased the
social and cultural impact of the mass media.

Television has brought about a sizable advance in the
penetration of society by the mass media. The anonymity
and bureaucratic organization that categorize the communicator, the rapidity, transientness, and public nature of
the communication, the size and heterogeneity of the audience—all these are more extreme in the case of television.
Compare a newspaper or magazine with the television network that separates its executive and financial headquarters
in New York from the studios in Los Angeles where much of
the "product" is turned out, and contrast the filmic sweep of
television news with the medium of record that is the goal of
the *New York Times.* Television is to date the ultimate mass
medium, as is apparent when it assembles an audience of 100
million for the Super Bowl. Television in the United States
pursues with vigor the largest possible audience, a ubiquitous
tendency restrained in the other mass media by the profitability or recognized merit of serving a select audience. By
adroit emphasis on entertainment, television has achieved a
dramatic increase in the degree of attention given to all the
mass media. The quantitative shifts upward on almost every
dimension by which a mass medium might be assessed constitute together a qualitative change in the position of the
media in society. They are now more central to the thought,
leisure, and reflection of the public. The publications *People*
and *Us*, talk shows put to print and inescapable in their
strategic positioning at the supermarket, make the point.
And in the course of this change, the balance between information and entertainment in the mass media has tipped
away from information.

VII. Whenever information is a factor in social activity, there is a potential role for the mass media. The degree to which a medium assumes such a role depends on its particular characteristics, as shown by research in the role of television in socialization.

Television has markedly heightened the place of stories and entertainment in the lives of the young, and has transferred authority over such experiences from the home, the community, the church, and the school to distant and diverse influences—corporate interests, government regulation, and a comparatively few persons employed for the most part in Los Angeles and New York. Television has moved the media from the background to the forefront of children's lives.

Social and behavioral scientists have compiled an extensive empirical record of children's relationships with television, but there is one point on which there is no clear answer. That is whether television is essentially threatening to children's welfare.

The initial impact of the new medium in the United States and England was documented by Schramm (1961) and by Himmelweit (1958) with their coauthors, who interviewed thousands of children and their parents and teachers. The amount of time that the average child spent viewing television each day was not a matter of minutes but hours. It was far less, however, than it is today, when the average recorded by the A. C. Nielsen Company for the typical winter week is thirty-one hours for children aged two to eleven and twenty-four hours for teenagers aged twelve to seventeen. Schramm and Himmelweit found that the averages for brighter children were below those for less-intelligent children—a difference that is no longer so clear, now that television is more and more accepted by parents and children alike. They were also greater for children of lower socioeconomic status, a distinction that remains today because the children of more-affluent, better-educated parents have more options and more sophisticated parental encouragement to make use of those options. Children gained in knowledge, but these gains were largely limited to knowledge about the stars and the programming of television. A minor gain in vocabulary attributable to viewing vanished as children advanced in school—although it has become clear that children do learn from television news about public events that might otherwise have escaped their notice.

When television first arrived, there was little empirical support for the speculation that viewing might be a cause of poorer reading and lower intellectual achievement, although—from the first—higher viewing, poorer reading, and lower achievement went together. Perhaps it was simply that less-able children watched more television. With television firmly and universally accepted and with more time spent viewing each day, it appears likely that television *does* interfere with such attainments—simply by taking up time that might otherwise be spent in intellectual exercise.

Then, as today, the amount of time spent viewing television typically increased through the elementary school years and declined somewhat as children entered high school. This illustrates a lesson about television that applies to adults as well: viewing is to a large extent a residual activity, falling when one is taken away from the proximity of a television set and rising when one is not. High school, in American life, means greater personal freedom, increased social activity, and fewer hours in the home.

Schramm and Himmelweit also found that, while children were not usually frightened by routinized violence such as that portrayed in the westerns which were popular at the time, they were often frightened by violence that was not stereotypic, that employed implements found in their own homes, and that was directed at another child, a parent, or a pet.

Two issues, however, did not at first receive much attention—the effects of television advertising, and the possible contribution of television violence to aggressive and anti-social behavior. The first was placed on the public agenda by Action for Children's Television and other advocacy groups in the early 1970s. The second emerged as empirical evidence began to accumulate in the mid-1960s.

The average child sees about 20,000 television commercials a year, the equivalent of three hours a week of continuous viewing. Only about 10 percent of these are aimed primarily at children. Three issues have become prominent: (a) whether the advertising of foods high in sugar content encourages harmful dietary practices, (b) whether the fact that younger children do not understand the self-interested intent of advertising implies deception, (c) whether an excessive burden is placed on parents when advertising encourages a child to want some product which a parent might prefer not to purchase.

There is hardly any doubt that children learn brand names and ask their parents for advertised products, and that some conflict may occur when a parent does not accede to such a request. Experiments have demonstrated repeatedly that the viewing of a commercial for a product that a child might want increases its value for him. And when Rossiter and Robertson (1974), two professors of marketing, examined the toy preferences of several hundred first-, second-, third-, and fifth-grade boys between November and late December — when toy manufacturers advertise heavily — they found that by Christmas, preferences had shifted toward advertised items.

Some have argued that the high frequency of commercials for over-the-counter remedies encourages the young to turn to illegal drugs and to overconsume those that are legal. Milavsky, a sociologist employed by NBC, examined exposure to commercials and drug use among several hundred young people (Milavsky et al. 1975, pp. 457–81). He found use of over-the-counter products slightly associated with greater exposure to drug commercials, but there was no association between exposure to drug commercials and illegal drug use. The data thus do not support the first charge, but they are ambiguous in regard to the second.

The interaction of federal regulation, citizen advocacy, and defensive self-regulation has now changed the advertising that accompanies children's programming. Vitamin advertising has been banned, pitches by hosts have been prohibited, neutral "bumpers" have been inserted before and after commercials to make them more readily identifiable as distinct from the program itself, and the minutes per hour devoted to advertising have been reduced. It has been proposed that advertising be banned entirely by federal regulation when there is some stipulated proportion of children under the age of eight in the audience, and that advertising of heavily sugared foods be banned by a similar yardstick applied to children under twelve. Such action is unlikely in the foreseeable future, but the effects and propriety of directing advertising at children are certain to remain controversial.

The empirical record on the possible contribution of television violence to aggressive and antisocial behavior began in 1963 with the publication in a highly respected scientific journal of two experiments, one by Bandura and his colleagues (1963), the other by Berkowitz and Rawlings (1963). In the first, nursery-school children imitated violent behavior they had seen in real life, in a videotape of the real-life violence, and in a videotape in which the violence was performed by a "Cat Lady" resembling a character that might appear in children's entertainment. The fact that the level of violent imitation was lower after viewing the "Cat Lady" sequence than after the real-life violence suggests that fantasy-like entertainment may be less likely to influence behavior than a real-life experience or a videotape of apparently "real" events. But the fact that the "Cat Lady" sequence was followed by some degree of imitation supported the view that violent fantasy might encourage children to behave violently. In the second study, the hostility that college-age subjects displayed toward another person who previously had mildly provoked them was increased by exposure to a film episode of a violent, retributive prize fight in which the retribution was perceived as justified. In this case, the subjects did not imitate what they had seen; instead, they apparently applied the message that retribution is acceptable behavior. The film lowered their inhibitions against such behavior.

Several dozen similar experiments since then have confirmed these findings. Repeatedly, exposure to violent television episodes has been followed by increased aggressive or antisocial behavior on the part of young viewers. Why, then, does the controversy continue?

The explanation lies in part in the central place that violence has had in fiction—oral tale-telling, folk drama, fairy tales, the stage, novels, radio, and film. For centuries it has been an element acknowledged as not inconsistent with the highest artistic intention. It ensures excitement, suspense, conflict, and resolution, and it is particularly useful for television because physical conflict between persons poses no problems for visual storytelling. It has also, of course, proved effective in attracting large audiences to television, and it is an essential part of the formula that permits the continuing concoction of action-and-adventure drama to fill the ceaseless weekly schedules of new programming each fall and winter. Thus, a conceivably misplaced aesthetic and the vested interests of those who purvey television entertainment have combined to create opposition to the notion that violence in television entertainment might be harmful.

Legitimate questions have also been raised about the application of experimental findings to everyday life. The experiments take place in an artificial setting in which behavior may not be truly representative; the brief exposure differs from the endless unreeling of television in the home; the measurement of effects immediately after viewing precludes the possibility of intervening experience; and there is no possibility, if aggressive or antisocial behavior is displayed, of retaliation by the victim or of punishment by authority. It is because of these objections that the Surgeon General's Scientific Advisory Committee on Television and Social Behavior based the conclusion of its 1972 report, *Television and Growing Up: The Impact of Televised Violence*, on the "*convergence*" of findings from the laboratory-type experiments and from surveys of everyday behavior.

The experiments, by demonstrating the certainty of causal influence within the experimental setting, demonstrated the very real possibility of it elsewhere. The surveys added the important ingredient of information from everyday life. By documenting that young people high in the viewing of violence were also somewhat higher in the aggressive behavior observed by classmates, and by giving no reason — after careful analysis — to believe that this positive association was fully explicable without attributing some influence to television, the surveys confirmed the possibility of generalizing from the experimental findings.

From these experiments, it is clear that television violence achieves whatever influence it has on aggressive and antisocial behavior by giving examples, by suggesting such behavior that is socially approved, efficacious, or rewarding, and by presenting victims who resemble people in the viewer's environment who might become targets and perpetrators with whom the viewer might identify. There is likely to be little or no influence when violence is portrayed as unrewarded, punished, socially disapproved, abhorrent, set in an irrelevant context, or beyond emulation. Many of the conventions of popular drama, however, provide little protection against some harmful influence — much of the violence is for a good cause and performed by admired heroes; physical hurt, repugnant injury, and grief are minimal; and punishment following a series of successes is easy to ignore.

In sum, the evidence is unambiguous that under some circumstances television and film violence can increase the aggressive and antisocial behavior of viewers. Young people are more likely than adults to be affected; the possibility that they might observe something novel is greater, and they are more likely to risk experimenting with something novel to test the public reaction. What is not clear is how frequently such influence occurs, how pervasive it is, and how often it results in behavior which goes beyond mere unpleasantness, bad behavior, verbal conflict, and minor transgressions of the law into the territory of brutal crime. For these reasons, research on television and controversy over the medium are certain to continue. Certainly a new and ambiguous note in the rearing of children to become good citizens has been registered by television news, which adds to the consensual symbols emphasized by the schools (the presidency, the Constitution) dissensual messages (riots, protests, disgraced public officials) that children previously avoided.

Film may match or exceed television audiovisually, but not in ubiquity and ease of access. Radio may match it in ubiquity, but not in ability to simulate direct experience. Newspapers, books, and magazines are handicapped by their cost —and by the requirements of literacy, intellectual ability, and concentrated attention—from reaching as deeply or widely into the process of growing up.

Television, however, does not escape the rule that mass media have the greatest likelihood of impact when they have a monopoly on information. For example, a study of several thousand northeastern elementary and high school students during the Vietnam war found that they got far more information from television news than from parents or teachers, but that in attitudes toward the war, their opinions conformed far more to those of their parents than to the opinions of television newscasters, who were often perceived to be partisan. Similarly, when, in an experiment, the violence in a television portrayal is criticized, the level of aggressiveness displayed by those who see it is reduced. And in examining children's beliefs about various occupations, television has proved most influential when children have had no direct contact with the occupations portrayed. The social contract which exists between audiences and the mass media imposes limits on both. The mass media invariably construct a message that serves their needs in reaching a sizable audience, but the impact of the message depends on the extent to which other voices and contrary forces are operating. The capability of parents, teachers, and other authority figures to intervene in the communication between television and the child is thus a specific illustration of a general principle.

SUMMARY

These seven propositions draw together a myriad of historical periods and specific events. They serve as landmarks for the observer of the media. Nothing, in fact, changes when we think of the media as distinctive social innovations, as functioning differentially, as dynamically changing each other, as indifferent to social and cultural variation, as transforming and inventing what they convey, as enhanced in their influence by the advent of television, and as having become factors in socialization because of the unusual characteristics of television. What *is* changed is our ability to understand what has happened since 1456.

VI

Conclusion

13

ELIE ABEL

The Last Word

Media anxiety in 1981. News—printed or broadcast— and public confidence. Peer groups, ombudsmen, and news councils. Newspaper groups (chains). Economics and cable/satellite TV. Visual stereotypes and clichés. Regulation and funding. Reform.

The spring of 1981, as I write, is a time of anxiety in the media. Reporters, editors, and their electronic counterparts known as producers, are deeply troubled. The "Jimmy's World" episode at the *Washington Post*, involving the belated exposure of a fictionalized account of drug addiction among children and the return of a Pulitzer Prize, has given rise to a climate of doubt and self-questioning in the trade. The editor of the *New York Daily News*, concerned for the credibility of his newspaper, recalls a young columnist from Northern Ireland, confronts him with the accusation of faking a dispatch, and the columnist resigns. Newspapers across the land rewrite their ethical guidelines to make them tougher. Difficult questions are raised: Is it fair to blame reporters alone for false—or at least misleading—accounts in the media? Have editors become too trusting? What, and whom, can the reader believe? Are we sliding back into a period when fact and fiction are woven together into seamless narratives designed to amuse or shock, rather than inform, the public?

Consider this example, the work of a New York columnist named Jimmy Breslin:

I kept listening to the car radio tell about the malfunction in a nuclear plant near Harrisburg, Pa., yesterday. There was a broken valve somewhere in the nuclear reactor, and this caused, the power company man announced, "a puff of radioactivity" to be released into the atmosphere. I loved that. "A puff." That's what they hit the east ward of Nagasaki with. "A puff." "Step on it, Dennis," I yelled. "It could be the end of Pennsylvania."

So Dennis the driver took a chance and started to gun the car toward the holocaust. My heart jumped when I heard the lieutenant governor of Pennsylvania say over the radio, "The incident is minor. There is and was no danger to public health and safety."

"That means there must be thousands dead," I yelled. "Hit it, Dennis."[1]

MEDIA ACCOUNTABILITY

Breslin more recently has delivered himself of the opinion that it is a graver sin to write a boring story than one that has been "piped."[2] His blithe attitude, a throwback to the age of Hearst and Pulitzer as they fought for street sales at the turn of the century, is not widely shared among Breslin's contemporaries. When a Hearst reporter invented a little girl who ostensibly was handed an all-day sucker by a warm-hearted bandit in the act of robbing a candy store of $40, there was no moral outcry. "Find the girl," was the immediate response of competing editors to their reporters at police headquarters. The men of the press, who knew a piped story when they saw one, quickly found another little girl, presented her with a lollipop, and photographed her skipping rope in front of the candy store. It was the era of wonderful nonsense when newspapermen did not take themselves, or their readers, too seriously.

Newspapers today strive for respectability. They have understood that they cannot compete with television as media of popular entertainment. The more earnest approach of the 1980s is exemplified by Benjamin Bradlee, executive editor of the *Washington Post* (quoted in the *Washington Journalism Review*, April 1981, p. 21):

We made our peace with television 20 years ago. We have to work on the assumption that we probably don't bring readers their first knowledge of an item in the news. But we do provide the first in-depth report, giving relevancy and impact to the story.

Ironically, it was Bradlee's newspaper that gave us "Jimmy's World," an embarrassment to the industry and a cataclysm for his own staff. The loss of credibility that followed the *Post*'s apology to its readers is likely to be brief, in spite of the hand-wringing in newsrooms across the country. The apology itself, and the immensely detailed inquest published a few days later, humbled a proud institution.

But a brief show of contrition by the paper that brought us Watergate ought not to end the matter. There is more at stake here than burning ambition on the part of a gifted but unscrupulous young reporter and her too-complaisant editors. The trouble has to be traced back, I suppose, to the first editor who failed to spike a story based in large part upon the testimony of an unidentified source. The plague of Washington sources who demand and get anonymity in exchange for information did not begin with Watergate. It was a game played in the first instance by government officials, Democrats and Republicans, high and low, long before Vietnam. The Vietnam crisis increased the dependence of many Washington reporters upon secret briefing and interviews. With the best of intentions, they passed along the lies and half-truths disseminated in this undercover fashion. Feeling badly used in the aftermath, much of the Washington press developed an obsession with official dishonesty. Exposure became a sacred mission and, of course, the counterinformation had to be put in the mouth of a countersource. Sandy Close (1981), executive editor of Pacific News Service, diagnoses the problem this way:

Ironically, journalism suffers less from arrogance than from an enormous inferiority complex which locks it into a dependency on the very sources that, at other times, it seeks to expose. Thus the reporter depends on the source for describing and confirming the reality he seeks to report; the editor depends on the reporter for discovering the source; the reporter depends on the editor for making the assignment leading to the source; and the editor depends on the good faith of both the reporter and the source. What results is a network of dependent relationships that reinforces the passivity of everyone involved.

Newspapermen are notoriously thin-skinned creatures. If they have been humbled, their confidence shaken, by the fraudulent case of Jimmy, the eight-year-old junkie, they have a great deal to be humble about. The *Post*'s confession came late in the day. It does, however, suggest a grudging recognition that newspapers may, after all, be accountable to their readers if not—in the American scheme of things—to governmental authority.

PROPOSED REMEDIES IN
THE NEWS BUSINESS

The notion of media accountability too long delayed has given rise over the years (as John Hulteng points out) to a variety of proposed remedies: peer-group criticism through such journals as the *Columbia Journalism Review*, newspaper ombudsmen, and news councils. Their advent, beginning in the 1960s, brought a dyspeptic—sometimes downright hostile—reaction from many editors and publishers. The National News Council, in particular, was 'reated with double disdain.[3] Some said the council had no enforcement powers—no "teeth"—which was true, save the power of exposing malpractice where it was found to exist; even that power remains somewhat theoretical, others argued, so long as the majority of American newspapers refuse to publish the council's findings, also true. These attitudes seem to me broadly representative of what Irving Kristol has called an "underdeveloped" profession. Both evade the issue of accountability.

I believe that our newspapers can only increase respect for their product by reconsidering their stubborn refusal in many cases to acknowledge the possibility of human error and to cooperate with such bodies as the council in assuring the public that its complaints will be thoroughly investigated. The silence treatment is hard to reconcile with the industry's periodic genuflections toward "the people's right to know."

Higher ethical standards are not, of course, a matter to be legislated in the American system. Editors and publishers have the crucial responsibility of demonstrating to their staffs that they are aware the news business is not a business like any other. Every great newspaper has, I believe, a distinct character. It dare not ignore the bottom line, yet there are times when it must be prepared to rise above the bottom-line mentality. It lives by a system of values that the staff understands and respects. Such a system cannot be based on blind trust. Editors have a right—and a need—to take a decently skeptical attitude toward unverified and unverifiable sources. Reporters may grouse when questioned, but the greater risk (as the *Washington Post* discovered) is to gamble with the credibility of the institution. And reporters, in turn, need to know that editors are not exempted from the code of conduct they impose upon lesser mortals.

George Comstock reminded us in his chapter that, in survey after survey, the Roper Organization has found that the public trusts television news more than it does newspapers, magazines, or radio. The sample questioned credits TV as its main news source. It also rates TV as the most fair and unbiased of media and, incredibly, as the most comprehensive. That finding may tell us more about the audience than it does about television news. It tends to contradict other findings that, at least during election periods, newspaper readers tend to be better informed than TV viewers about candidates and issues and to use that information rationally in deciding how to vote. Opinion surveys frequently raise more questions than they answer definitively, but they appear to point in the direction of Disraeli's two nations, non-readers and readers divided along class lines.

ECONOMIC PRESSURES ON PRINT AND ON THE AIR

Newspapers in America are not (as James Rosse has observed) big business by the standards of the Fortune 500 list. But the newspaper groups—they prefer not to be called chains in this modern era—grow steadily larger. The independent family-owned newspaper, whose passing has been deplored for decades past by reformers if not by economists, is most of the way to oblivion. In the San Francisco Bay Area, for example, only the *San Francisco Chronicle* remains family owned. The afternoon *Examiner* is part of the Hearst empire. The *Oakland Tribune*, which belonged to the Knowland family, is part of the Gannett group. The *San Jose Mercury* is owned by Knight-Ridder. The *Redwood City Tribune* and the *Palo Alto Times* were bought by the Chicago Tribune Company and merged into a single regional paper called the *Peninsula Times Tribune*. Benjamin M. Compaine (1979, pp. 33–34) attributes the increasing concentration of newspaper ownership across the country to several factors, among them weak management, family squabbles, and the effects of our tax laws.

Of these factors, only the tax laws are within the reach of national policy. William E. Porter, in chapter 6, suggests that for many owners, selling to a chain or group has become not only desirable but imperative. There is the inheritance tax problem, compounded by the fact that the value of the estate tends to be determined less by the newspaper's earning record than by the price a chain is willing to pay. Not all newspaper families are so well endowed with cash or marketable securities as to pay the estate tax without strapping themselves. So they sell, for the most part to the highest bidder. The proceeds of a cash sale qualify for treatment as capital gains. If, on the other hand, an exchange of stock has taken place, no tax has to be paid until the seller decides to sell the purchasing firm's stock. Representative Morris Udall, the Arizona Democrat, has been sufficiently alarmed by the trend to hold hearings and call for legislative remedies, but Congress has failed to act. For all the lamentation on the subject of media concentration and the passing of the independent newspaper, there is a real question whether newspaper owners, or any other category of citizen, should receive special treatment under the tax laws.

Television has its own catalogue of problems, few of them financial so far as the national networks and their VHF affiliates are concerned. The doctrine of localism enforced by the Federal Communications Commission (FCC), which goes back to the early days of radio, has given us more stations in out-of-the-way places than some markets will support and less local programming than the commissioners had hoped to see. Rosse has explained the economic reasons why the typical station operates more like a relay for network programs than as a distinctive local voice. Until the recent advent of satellite-linked cable systems, our three commercial networks had every reason for gratitude to the FCC. The long-term effect of the localism policy had been to entrench their profitable position; few markets have more than three channels.

The advent of cheap satellite communications, together with the cable explosion, has darkened the long-term outlook. As they look ahead nervously, the networks have reason to fear an erosion of their audience base and their revenues. Estimates vary, but few TV executives question recent forecasts of an increasingly fragmented national audience as cable and other new technologies take hold. There are published estimates that by 1990 network television will have lost no less than 10 percent and as much as 50 percent of its aggregate audience, a severe jolt for an industry that has known more ups than downs over the past quarter century. Apart from the competition of cable, there is the distinct possibility of local over-the-air stations creating their own ad hoc networks through the cheap and universal linkages offered by the satellite to share the cost of acquiring programs. The technology exists. It is used every day, in fact, by the Public Broadcasting Service to distribute its programs without depending on microwave relays or land lines.

TECHNIQUES IN NEWS
AND PUBLIC AFFAIRS

The news and public affairs output of the networks, which is examined critically by William Henry III and Edward Jay Epstein, is more likely to survive the threatened shakeout than other features of the program line-up. Entertainment, for the most part, is bought from production companies in Hollywood. The network news programs and documentaries are in-house products fashioned by staff technicians, reporters, and producers. Twenty-five years ago, when NBC put the "Huntley-Brinkley Report" on the air for the first time, it was regarded as a loss leader, a way of building prestige and earning merit with the FCC. Newspaper critics liked the program; some station owners were reluctant to carry it, lest they suffer a loss of revenue. In Boston, a major market, NBC was reduced to negotiating an arrangement with the ABC affiliate to carry "Huntley-Brinkley" when its own affiliate station refused. The program ran fifteen minutes, commercials included. Its rapid success, reinforced by what then seemed a novel approach to covering national conventions and election nights, thrust NBC into the leadership in news. A dogma was born: that the network with the best news ratings would sooner or later establish its primacy in the three-network race. NBC showed the way, to be supplanted by CBS (after Walter Cronkite became the anchor). ABC, after many years in third place, started moving up in the 1970s when it greatly increased the network's commitment to news.

As TV news came of age, the innovations of the 1960s ripened into traditions in the 1970s and, in the 1980s, are fast becoming tired stereotypes. Consider, for example, the balcony of sorts that overhangs the flag-draped lobby at the diplomatic entrance to the State Department in Washington.

Watchers of the evening news know it well. When Marvin Kalb was the diplomatic correspondent of CBS News he used to deliver many of his reports from that balcony, with the array of flags at his back. That unvarying camera shot established the authenticity of the locale. Kalb still uses the balcony from time to time now that he has shifted to NBC.

His CBS successor, Robert Pierpoint, wanting to put his own stamp on the job, reads his pieces to camera from the State Department briefing room. A few feet to his right and behind him is the familiar podium bearing the Great Seal of the United States in replica, the podium from which a succession of secretaries of state have spoken to the media and, through them, to the people. Other times, other clichés.

TV makes much of these "establishing shots." The White House lawn is reserved for each network's White House correspondent. Less-favored reporters use the same backdrop from time to time, but they have to stand in Lafayette Park, on the far side of Pennsylvania Avenue, while the camera provides a misty over-the-shoulder shot of the executive mansion in the middle distance. Reporters assigned to the halls of Congress have their own setting, with the wedding-cake bulk of the Capitol behind them. When rising gasoline prices are in the news, the reporter's piece has to be taped in a busy filling station; wheat sales to the Soviet Union are reported from a field of ripening grain in Kansas or the Dakotas. Should the story of the day have to do with inflation, then the correspondent will tell it, somewhat awkwardly, as he pushes a shopping cart filled with groceries toward the checkout counter. Choose your own network, the setting will be the same. It is a form of validation, designed to lend a certain weight, a sense of place, to a report that is so compressed, so stripped of nuance and perspective, that few newspapers would find it adequate for publication. Time is the enemy here. How much information or insight can the most gifted reporter cram into a piece about rising food prices in seventy-five seconds while standing in front of a pile of grapefruit in a Maryland supermarket?

The pieces I have been describing are what used to be called "talking heads." There is no action unfolding as the correspondent talks his piece. These are stories that must be told in words, and the iron rule of network television is that pure talk—unless it is the anchorman talking—must be strictly rationed. The same piece could be done from the studio at considerably less cost, as it used to be ten or fifteen years ago when the first generation of TV directors and producers was in charge. The new breed, far more skilled in the manipulation of images and symbols, has taken the curse off the talking head by inventing its own clichés.

The new 24-hour news and information service offered by Ted Turner's Atlanta-based Cable News Network is one alternative. Its prime-time newscast, called "Prime 120," runs two hours instead of the networks' uniform half hour. That frees it from the tyranny of the clock. When one of the networks recently allotted five minutes to the budget debate in Congress, "Prime 120" gave the story ten minutes. Anchormen or women have not been abolished, but they rotate through the day in various combinations on the Cable News Network, contradicting (in the words of one critic) "all that is sacred to TV news." Another alternative, favored by many who get their news from the papers, is the "MacNeil-Lehrer Report" on PBS. It devotes a half hour to a single topic, which can be explored in some depth by a knowledgeable panel divided between Washington and New York.

REGULATION AND FUNDING

Although television remains a regulated industry, the FCC does not attempt to regulate questions of format and content. New approaches to presenting the news on television call for experimentation, an expensive business for the commercial networks with their large overheads. They are likely to go on resisting any but cosmetic changes until the day their audiences start declining sharply. The Cable News Network, on the other hand, can better afford to develop new methods of presentation. It has less to lose and much to gain from testing fresh approaches to storytelling on TV.

PBS, on the other hand, because it has come to depend increasingly upon federal money, faces an uncertain future. The Reagan administration proposes to reduce congressional appropriations for public broadcasting from $162 million for 1981 to $100 million by 1985. Local news programs, several funded at the outset by the Ford Foundation, have shriveled and died in San Francisco, Dallas, New York, Boston, Chicago, and Pittsburgh.

The scheduled cuts in government funding have generated a certain amount of debate about whether and how the public system can long survive. When the system was young and self-consciously educational in tone, the notion of an excise tax on new TV sets was rejected after study by a presidential commission. License fees on TV and radio receivers, of the sort used in Britain and West Germany to support public broadcasting, seemed inappropriate when the bulk of the national audience clearly preferred network programs, in spite of the commercial interruptions. A more recent idea—attributed to Henry Geller, a Washington lawyer and former government official—is a "spectrum use tax" to be levied on commercial broadcasters. It is based on the theory that the broadcast spectrum belongs to the public and those who use it should pay for the privilege. Geller concedes that the commercial networks would fight such a levy, but he is prepared to offer them a powerful inducement: an end of federal regulation. Nothing would be lost, he argues, because present-day regulations are "a charade." The FCC does not regulate program content, in any event. It requires stations to schedule public affairs programs but does not balk at the common practice of putting them on Sunday mornings, when the audience is small. "So why not just let them do what they do anyway, in return for a spectrum fee of one or two percent of gross revenues?" Geller asks.

It is a bold proposal, one that might have seemed a good bargain to commercial broadcasters a few years back. But that outlook changed with the all-but-total deregulation of radio within the past year—a move that dates back to the Carter administration—and with the promise (as broadcasters see it) that the Reagan administration will favor doing as much for television before 1985.

THE MATTER OF REFORM

Since the not-too-distant prospect is for a media industry wholly or substantially free of federal regulation, it follows that whatever reforms we may see adopted will be voluntary measures enforced by market pressures, peer-group criticism, citizen action, and, one hopes, the occasional prick of conscience. There is early evidence that Evangelical Christian groups will be among the first to put pressure on the networks by mobilizing consumer power against corporations that sponsor programs the so-called "Moral Majority" finds offensive. It is a tactic used in the recent past by parents' groups objecting to violence in children's programming.

As for the print media, the recent shocks we have discussed could have a wholesome effect. Editors will, I suspect, tighten their newsroom procedures, demand more careful verification of verifiable facts, and be far less inclined to publish information they cannot vouch for from anonymous sources, in or out of Washington. Joseph Kraft (1981), in an article drawn from the Jefferson Lectures he delivered at the University of California, Berkeley, in 1979, went a step farther:

It is no longer good enough to say that we mirror the world, or merely report things as they are. If things go wrong, we bear some blame. And it seems to me vital that we admit—to ourselves at least, and in public as much as possible—when we do go wrong. And I don't mean just misspelling the name of the Vice-Premier of China. I mean seeing that at times, anyway, we went overboard on the Great Society, and on civil rights, and the Imperial Presidency. I mean that some of the consequences of our noblest efforts have turned sour.

That kind of responsibility, it seems to me, is required, because it is only by admitting our larger mistakes that we can deserve public support.

It is, I suspect, a sentiment shared by many journalists who, like Kraft himself, plead guilty to the indictment.

NOTES

1. Elie Abel: "The First Word"

1. The *American Heritage Dictionary of the English Language* put the medium/media question to its Usage Panel, as in: "*Television is* an *unpredictable media.*" The panel members were emphatically negative. Ninety percent found the use of "media" as a singular noun unacceptable in writing; 88 percent found it equally unacceptable in speech.

2. The Los Angeles market is served by two metropolitan newspapers of general circulation. It has fourteen television stations and thirty-two radio stations. The same pattern obtains in other large cities such as New York, Chicago, Philadelphia, Detroit, and Washington.

3. James N. Rosse: "Mass Media: The Economic Setting"

1. I am indebted to several generations of graduate students at Stanford who have helped me study mass media industries. The list is too long to be replicated here and to name some would devalue the contributions of those not named. However, I am deeply indebted to Ray Olszewski for assistance in the preparation of this chapter.

2. In phonograph and video recording processes, the master tape contains the public good which is then embodied in a private good as discs or tapes for marketing and distribution. Movies are also a public good; the mode of transmission—movie theaters—is what one might call a "congested public good." Consequently, the content of movies can be thought of as a pure public good, but the means of transmission is a public good sufficiently congested to be, essentially, a private good.

3. In monopolistic competition, each producer sells products that are distinguishable, in the minds of the consumers, from those of other producers. Hence, in contrast to the case of perfect competition, at least some discretion in pricing is possible. In contrast to the case of pure monopoly, that discretion is limited by the existence and possible entry of close substitute products. We return to these matters below.

4. First developed by Chamberlin nearly fifty years ago, the theory of monopolistic competition has been updated by Spence, Dixit and Stiglitz, and others. It seems to have been first applied systematically to a media industry by Reddaway. Spence and Owen have developed an insightful normative application to television programming. See Chamberlin 1960; Spence 1976; Dixit and Stiglitz 1977; Reddaway 1963; Spence and Owen 1977. A useful introduction to the quite technical modern literature is Lence 1978.

5. A recent paper by Rosse and Panzar (1977) shows that this presumption is valid for daily newspaper firms in spite of the fact that almost no American newspapers face direct, local, newspaper competition.

6. These and subsequent figures concerning advertising shares are based on the McCann-Ericksen time series on U.S. advertising expenditure.

7. A cynic might note that this also seems like a policy to put licenses in as many congressional districts as possible. One might also note that bringing licenses as close to the grass roots as possible in the rural areas means that considerable distance gets opened up between license holders and the man in the street.

4. Benno C. Schmidt, Jr.: "The First Amendment and the Press"

1. I am grateful to the Markle Foundation for continuing support of my research and writing on problems of the First Amendment and the press. I want to express my appreciation also to my colleague, Louis Henkin, who organized a conference on French and American conceptions of human rights in Paris in December 1979 at which some of the ideas in this chapter were presented.

2. The law of the First Amendment concerning injunctions barring publication of defense secrets remains in a state of confusion. The government recently persuaded a federal trial court to enjoin the *Progressive* magazine from publishing an article on how to make a hydrogen bomb, but before appeals could run their course, the government dismissed the case because other publications had revealed the same information. Had the case not aborted, and had the magazine been unable to prove that the information it sought to reveal was already public, the Supreme Court might well have sustained an injunction on the theory that the publication could have caused grave and irreparable harm.

6. William E. Porter: "The Media Baronies: Bigger, Fewer, More Powerful"

1. There has been no widespread rush to conform to this ruling, which has yet to be confirmed by a higher court. Thus far, the response has been limited to barter arrangements such as that through which the *Washington Post* and the *Detroit News* traded television stations in 1977; the *Post* paid additional compensation of $3 million because the Detroit market area is larger.

2. For a good brief account, see Bishop 1972, pp. 14–16.

8. William A. Henry III: "News as Entertainment: The Search for Dramatic Unity"

1. When CBS was that assertive in George Criles's and Grace Diekhaus's diatribe about homosexual political influence in San Francisco, the network was denounced by critics and formally censured by the National News Council.

2. And whatever the normal detachment, in times of crisis reporters spontaneously become nationalists. In the early days of the Iran hostage trouble, print—and especially broadcast—reporters, including the networks, readied us for war.

11. John L. Hulteng: "Holding the Media Accountable"

1. For citation and discussion of specific news media lapses, see Hulteng 1976 and idem 1979.

2. The Equal Time Doctrine stems from Section 315 of the Communications Act, the basic federal law dealing with broadcasting. It provides that if a broadcasting station allows one legally qualified candidate for public office to make use of its facilities, it must make available an equal opportunity to all other legally qualified candidates for the same office.

The Fairness Doctrine is a ruling issued by the FCC rather than a part of the basic statute. It provides that broadcasters must devote a "reasonable" amount of air time to public affairs programming and that such programming must be fair in the sense that opportunity for the presentation of contrasting views of public issues must be provided. The Fairness Doctrine does not speak of equal segments of air time; it tries to make sure that all sides of a controversial issue will be reasonably aired. The doctrine contains much flexible language that is subject to FCC interpretation.

3. For a detailed examination of libel law and the right to privacy, see Pember 1977.

4. For an explanation of his proposal and its implications, see Barron 1973.

13. Elie Abel: "The Last Word"

1. Cited by Public's Right to Information Task Force 1979, p. 305.

2. The term "piped," no longer in common use, refers to the not uncommon practice among New York City newspapermen some sixty years ago of passing off fiction as fact. The prevalence of opium dens in the vicinity of police headquarters explains its derivation.

3. The author feels bound to disclose his own membership in the National News Council, a wholly unofficial, voluntary organization which should not be held responsible for his private opinions.

REFERENCES

Bandura, Albert. 1973. *Aggression: A Social Learning Analysis.* Englewood Cliffs, NJ: Prentice-Hall, Inc.

———, Ross, Dorothea, and Ross, Sheila A. 1963. "Imitation of Film-Mediated Aggressive Models." *Journal of Abnormal and Social Psychology* 66.

Barron, Jerome A. 1973. *Freedom of the Press for Whom? The Rise of Access to the Mass Media.* Bloomington, IN: University of Indiana Press.

Berkowitz, Leonard, and Rawlings, Edna. 1963. "Effects of Film Violence on Inhibitions against Subsequent Aggression." *Journal of Abnormal and Social Psychology* 66.

Bishop, Robert L. 1972. "The Rush to Chain Ownership." *Columbia Journalism Review* (November/December).

Business Week. 1977. "The Big Money Hunt for Independent Newspapers" (21 February).

Chamberlin, E. H. 1960. *The Theory of Monopolistic Competition.* Boston, MA: Harvard Press.

Close, Sandy. 1981. "News 'Sources'—The Crutch That Cripples." *Los Angeles Times* (26 April).

Commission on Freedom of the Press. 1947. *A Free and Responsible Press.* Chicago, IL: University of Chicago Press.

Compaine, Benjamin M., ed. 1979. *Who Owns the Media? Concentration of Ownership in the Mass Communications Industry.* White Plains, NY: Harmony Books.

Dixit, A. K., and Stiglitz, J. E. 1977. "Monopolistic Competition and Optimal Product Diversity." *American Economic Review* (June).

Epstein, Edward Jay. 1975. *Between Fact and Fiction.* New York: Vintage Press.

———. 1973. *News from Nowhere.* New York: Random House.

Gitlin, Todd. 1980. *The Whole World Is Watching: Mass Media in the Making and Unmaking of the New Left.* Berkeley, CA: University of California Press.

Hand, Learned. 1943. *Associated Press* v. *United States.* 52 F. Supp. 362, 372 (D.C.N.Y., 1943).

Himmelweit, Hilde T., Oppenheim, A. N., and Vince, Pamela. 1958. *Television and the Child.* London: Oxford University Press.

Hulteng, John L. 1976. *The Messenger's Motives: Ethical Problems of the News Media.* New York: Prentice-Hall, Inc.

———. 1979. *The News Media: What Makes Them Tick?* New York: Prentice-Hall, Inc.

Katz, Elihu, and Gurevitch, Michael. 1976. *The Secularization of Leisure.* Cambridge, MA: Harvard University Press.

Kraft, Joseph. 1981. "The Imperial Media." *Commentary* (May).

Lang, Kurt, and Lang, Gladys E. 1953. "The Unique Perspective of Television and Its Effects: A Pilot Study." *American Sociological Review* 18.

Lence, R. 1978. "Theories of Television Program Selection: A Discussion of the Spence-Owen Model." Studies in Industry Economics Discussion Paper, Department of Economics, Stanford University.

Lucas, William A., and Adams, William C. 1978. "Talking, TV, and Voter Indecision." *Journal of Communication* 28.

McLuhan, Marshall. 1964. *Understanding Media: The Extensions of Man.* New York: McGraw-Hill.

Milavsky, J. Ronald, Pekowsky, Berton, and Stipp, Horst. 1975. "TV Drug Advertising and Propriety and Illicit Drug Use among Teenage Boys." *Public Opinion Quarterly* 39.

Pember, Don R. 1977. *Mass Media Law.* Dubuque, IA: William C. Brown Company.

Public's Right to Information Task Force. 1979. *Report to the President's Commission on the Accident at Three Mile Island.* Washington, DC: Government Printing Office.

Reddaway, W. B. 1963. "The Economics of Newspapers." *Economic Journal* (June).

Robinson, John P. 1972. "Television's Impact on Everyday Life: Some Cross-National Evidence." In *Television and Social Behavior,* ed. E. A. Rubinstein, G. A. Comstock, and J. P. Murray. Vol. 4: *Television in Day-to-Day Life: Patterns of Use.* Washington, DC: Government Printing Office.

———, and Converse, Philip E. 1972. "The Impact of Television on Mass Media Usage: A Cross-National Comparison." In *The Use of Time: Daily Activities of Urban and Suburban Populations in Twelve Countries,* ed. Alexander Szalai. The Hague: Mouton.

———, Converse, Philip E., and Szalai, Alexander. 1972. "Everyday Life in Twelve Countries." In *The Use of Time: Daily Activities of Urban and Suburban Populations in Twelve Countries,* ed. Alexander Szalai. The Hague: Mouton.

Roper Organization. 1979. *Public Perception of Television and Other Mass Media: A Twenty-Year Review, 1959–1978.* New York: Television Information Office.

Rosse, James N., and Panzar, J. C. 1977. "An Empirical Test for Monopoly Rents." Studies in Industry Economics Discussion Paper, Department of Economics, Stanford University.

Rossiter, John R., and Robertson, Thomas S. 1974. "Children's TV Commercials: Testing the Defenses." *Journal of Communication* 24.

Rubinstein, E. A., Comstock, G. A., and Murray, J. P., eds. 1972. *Television and Social Behavior.* Vol. 4: *Television in Day-to-Day Life: Patterns of Use.* Washington, DC: Government Printing Office.

Rucker, Bryce W. 1968. *The First Freedom.* Carbondale, IL: Southern Illinois University Press.

Salomon, Gavriel. 1979. *Interaction of Media, Cognition, and Learning.* San Francisco, CA: Jossey-Bass.

Schramm, Wilbur, Lyle, Jack, and Parker, Edwin B. 1961. *Television in the Lives of Our Children.* Stanford, CA: Stanford University Press.

Smith, Anthony. 1980a. *Goodbye, Gutenberg: The Newspaper Revolution of the 1980s.* New York: Oxford University Press.

———. 1980b. *Newspapers and Democracy.* Cambridge, MA: MIT Press.

Spence, A. M. 1976. "Product Selection, Fixed Costs, and Monopolistic Competition." *Review of Economic Studies* (June).

———, and Owen, B. M. 1977. "Television Programming, Monopolistic Competition, and Welfare." *Quarterly Journal of Economics* (February).

Surgeon General's Scientific Advisory Committee on Television and Social Behavior. 1972. *Television and Growing Up: The Impact of Televised Violence.* Report to the Surgeon General, U.S. Public Health Service. Washington, DC: Government Printing Office.

Szalai, Alexander, ed. 1972. *The Use of Time: Daily Activities of Urban and Suburban Populations in Twelve Countries.* The Hague: Mouton.

ABOUT THE AUTHORS

ELIE ABEL came to Stanford University in 1979 as Harry and Norman Chandler Professor of Communication after nine years at Columbia University, where he was Godfrey Lowell Cabot Professor and Dean of the Graduate School of Journalism. Formerly with the *New York Times* as national and foreign correspondent and head of its Balkan and South Asian bureaux, in 1961 he joined NBC News as State Department correspondent, London bureau chief, and diplomatic correspondent. He is the author of three books—*The Missile Crisis* (1966, reprinted in nine languages), *Roots of Involvement: The U.S. in Asia* (1971), written in collaboration with Marvin Kalb, and *Special Envoy to Churchill and Stalin* (1975), written with W. Averell Harriman. Abel has received two awards from the Overseas Press Club, a Peabody Award, and he shared the 1957 Pulitzer Prize for coverage of Eastern Europe. He served as the U.S. member of UNESCO's MacBride commission which recently concluded a two-year study of international communication problems, and in 1980 he attended the 21st UNESCO General Conference at Belgrade, Yugoslavia, as a member of the U.S. delegation.

ROBERT L. BARTLEY, editor of the *Wall Street Journal*, took responsibility for that paper's editorial page in 1972, and in 1980 won the Pulitzer Prize for editorial writing—the *Journal*'s eighth Pulitzer. He has personally written a large number of the editorials while working on staff development and on the creation of new editorial page features—including the "Board of Contributors," the Monday letter page, and the Friday section on leisure and the arts. He received the 1977 Citation for Excellence from the Overseas Press Club for dispatches filed from China and Tibet after the death of Mao Tse Tung and, in 1979, the Gerald Loeb Award for editorials on international monetary problems. His memberships include the American Society of Newspaper Editors, the Council on Foreign Relations, and the American Political Science Association.

GEORGE COMSTOCK is S. I. Newhouse Professor in Public Communications at Syracuse University. He was senior social psychologist at The Rand Corporation where he compiled the three-volume *Television and Human Behavior* series and was senior author of the book of that title published in 1978, and he has continued his studies on the subject with *Television in America* (1978). As science advisor and senior research coordinator to the Surgeon General's advisory committee on television and social behavior, Dr. Comstock was senior editor of the five-volume series, *Television and Social Behavior* (1972); the committee's report is entitled *Television and Growing Up: The Impact of Televised Violence.* He has written numerous studies and journal articles on the impact of television, serves on the NBC social science advisory panel, and is a member of the National Council for Children and Television and of the editorial boards of *Public Opinion Quarterly,* the *Journal of Communication,* and the new *Journal of Applied Communication Research.*

EDWARD JAY EPSTEIN is a free-lance author and head of E. J. E. Publications, Ltd., in New York. A former Regent's Professor of Government at UCLA, he has also taught political science at Harvard and the Massachusetts Institute of Technology. His books include *News from Nowhere, Between Fact and Fiction, The Warren Commission and the Establishment of Truth,* and *Cartel.* His articles have been published in *The New Yorker,* the *New York Times Magazine,* and *Commentary.*

WILLIAM A. HENRY III is an associate editor at *Time* magazine and holds the 1980 Pulitzer Prize in criticism for his work as television critic of the *Boston Globe.* He has written about television for *Horizon,* the *New Republic, Panorama, Sportscape,* and other magazines, and he contributed a chapter on the media and the elderly to *Small Voices, Great Trumpets: The Media and Minorities* (1980). Former critic at large for the *New York Daily News* and contributor to a number of major magazines, he won several major journalism prizes as a political and investigative reporter when he was with the *Boston Globe.*

JOHN L. HULTENG, Professor of Communication at Stanford University, is former Dean of the University of Oregon School of Journalism. He is an editorial writer, foreign correspondent, and columnist, was assistant director of the East-West Communication Institute in Honolulu in 1975, and holds a lifetime honorary membership in the Oregon Newspaper Publishers Association. He has written numerous journal articles, and his books include *The Fourth Estate* (with R. P. Nelson, 1971), *The Opinion Function* (1973), *The Messenger's Motives* (1976), and *The News Media* (1979).

THEODORE PETERSON, Professor of Journalism at the University of Illinois, was Dean of the College of Communications there for more than twenty years. He received the Sigma Delta Chi Award for research in journalism in his book *Magazines in the Twentieth Century*, and is coauthor with F. S. Siebert and Wilbur Schramm of *Four Theories of the Press*, winner of the Kappa Tau Alpha Award for distinguished research on journalism. He has coauthored and contributed to several other books and has written for many periodicals, including the *Columbia Journalism Review*, the *Saturday Review*, and the *Journal of Communication*.

ITHIEL de SOLA POOL is Arthur and Ruth Sloan Professor of Political Science and Director, Research Program on Communications Policy, at the Massachusetts Institute of Technology. In 1976 he was visiting professor in communications at Keio University, Tokyo, and the following year was a Fellow at Churchill College, University of Cambridge. At Hoover Institution, Stanford University, he held the position of associate director of the RADIR Project. His memberships include the American Political Science Association, the Council on Foreign Relations, the American Association for Public Opinion Research, and the American Sociological Association, and he is trustee for the International Institute of Communications and the Graphic Arts Research Association. His book, *American Business and Public Policy*, won the Woodrow Wilson Award as the best political science book of 1963.

WILLIAM E. PORTER, is Professor and Chairman of the Department of Journalism at the University of Michigan, and visiting professor of Communication at Stanford University. His work as a writer of fiction led to faculty appointments at the State University of Iowa and New York University, and he spent a year as a Fullbright lecturer in publicity and journalism at the Univeristy of Rome. He was national president of the Association for Education in Journalism, and has authored numerous scholarly articles and the book *Assault on the Media: The Nixon Years* (1976).

MICHAEL JAY ROBINSON is Research Professor at George Washington University, where he is Director of the Media Analysis Project. His dissertation, *Public Affairs Television and the Growth of Political Malaise*, received the American Political Science Association Award for 1973. His articles and commentaries on television, the media, Congress, and the presidency have appeared in the *Wall Street Journal*, the *Washington Post*, and other newspapers, and his academic research is published in the *American Political Science Review*, *Political Science Quarterly*, *Public Interest*, and *Public Opinion*.

JAMES N. ROSSE is Professor of Economics and Associate Dean of Humanities and Sciences, Stanford University. He spent several years in the newspaper business before training as an economist, and is consultant to government organizations and to private clients in such fields as communication regulation and antitrust matters. He has written a number of articles for the *American Economic Review* and *Econometrica*, and is the author or coauthor of discussion papers and monographs published in the Stanford series entitled Studies in Industry Economics (SIE). He is also author of "The Sustainability of National Monopoly," in *Pricing in Regulated Industries: Theory and Application II*, edited by J. T. Wenders (1979), and "The Decline of Direct Newspaper Competition," *Journal of Communication* (1980).

BENNO C. SCHMIDT, JR., Professor of Law at Columbia University, specializes in constitutional law, the regulation of mass communications, and the history of the U.S. Supreme Court. A former clerk for Chief Justice Earl Warren and a special assistant in the Office of Legal Counsel of the Justice Department, he is the author of *Freedom of the Press v. Public Acess* (1976), and at present is writing a volume of the Holmes Devise *History of the Supreme Court of the United States*.

INDEX

PUBLICATIONS LIST*

THE INSTITUTE FOR CONTEMPORARY STUDIES

260 California Street, San Francisco, California 94111

Catalog available upon request

BUREAUCRATS AND BRAINPOWER: GOVERNMENT
REGULATION OF UNIVERSITIES
> $6.95. 170 pages. Publication date: June 1979
> ISBN 0—917616—35—9
> Library of Congress No. 79—51328

Contributors: Nathan Glazer, Robert S. Hatfield, Richard W. Lyman, Paul
> Seabury, Robert L. Sproull, Miro M. Todorovich, Caspar W.
> Weinberger

THE CALIFORNIA COASTAL PLAN: A CRITIQUE
> $5.95. 199 pages. Publication date: March 1976
> ISBN 0—917616—04—9
> Library of Congress No. 76—7715

Contributors: Eugene Bardach, Daniel K. Benjamin, Thomas E.
> Borcherding, Ross D. Eckert, H. Edward Frech III, M. Bruce Johnson,
> Ronald N. Lafferty, Walter J. Mead, Daniel Orr, Donald M. Pach,
> Michael R. Peevey

THE CRISIS IN SOCIAL SECURITY: PROBLEMS AND PROSPECTS
> $6.95. 220 pages. Publication date: April 1977; 2d ed. rev., 1978, 1979
> ISBN 0—917616—16—2/1977; 0—917616—25—1/1978
> Library of Congress No. 77—72542

Contributors: Michael J. Boskin, George F. Break, Rita Ricardo Campbell,
> Edward Cowan, Martin S. Feldstein, Milton Friedman, Douglas R.
> Munro, Donald O. Parsons, Carl V. Patton, Joseph A. Pechman,
> Sherwin Rosen, W. Kip Viscusi, Richard J. Zeckhauser

*Prices subject to change.

292

THE ECONOMY IN THE 1980s: A PROGRAM FOR GROWTH AND STABILITY

$7.95, (paper). 462 pages. Publication date: June 1980
ISBN 0–917616–39–1
Library of Congress No. 80–80647
$17.95 (cloth). 462 pages. Publication date: August 1980.
ISBN 0–87855–399–1. Available through Transaction Books,
Rutgers–The State University, New Brunswick, NJ 08903
Contributors: Michael J. Boskin, George F. Break, John T. Cuddington,
Patricia Drury, Alain Enthoven, Laurence J. Kotlikoff, Ronald I.
McKinnon, John H. Pencavel, Henry S. Rowen, John L. Scadding,
John B. Shoven, James L. Sweeney, David J. Teece

EMERGING COALITIONS IN AMERICAN POLITICS

$6.95. 524 pages. Publication date: June 1978
ISBN 0–917616–22–7
Library of Congress No. 78–53414
Contributors: Jack Bass, David S. Broder, Jerome M. Clubb, Edward H.
Crane III, Walter De Vries, Andrew M. Greeley, S. I. Hayakawa, Tom
Hayden, Milton Himmelfarb, Richard Jensen, Paul Kleppner,
Everett Carll Ladd, Jr., Seymour Martin Lipset, Robert A. Nisbet,
Michael Novak, Gary R. Orren, Nelson W. Polsby, Joseph L. Rauh,
Jr., Stanley Rothman, William A. Rusher, William Schneider, Jesse
M. Unruh, Ben J. Wattenberg

THE FAIRMONT PAPERS: BLACK ALTERNATIVES CONFERENCE, SAN FRANCISCO, DECEMBER 1980

$5.95. 174 pages. Publication date: March 1981
ISBN 0–917616–42–1
Library of Congress No. 81–80735
Contributors: Bernard E. Anderson, Thomas L. Berkley, Michael J. Boskin,
Randolph W. Bromery, Tony Brown, Milton Friedman, Wendell
Wilkie Gunn, Charles V. Hamilton, Robert B. Hawkins, Jr., Maria
Lucia Johnson, Martin L. Kilson, James Lorenz, Henry Lucas, Jr.,
Edwin Meese III, Clarence M. Pendleton, Jr., Dan J. Smith, Thomas
Sowell, Chuck Stone, Percy E. Sutton, Clarence Thomas, Gloria E. A.
Toote, Walter E. Williams, Oscar Wright

FEDERAL TAX REFORM: MYTHS AND REALITIES

$5.95. 270 pages. Publication date: September 1978
ISBN 0–917616–32–4
Library of Congress No. 78–61661
Contributors: Robert J. Barro, Michael J. Boskin, George F. Break, Jerry R.
Green, Laurence J. Kotlikoff, Mordecai Kurz, Peter Mieszkowski,
John B. Shoven, Paul J. Taubman, John Whalley

GOVERNMENT CREDIT ALLOCATION: WHERE DO WE GO
FROM HERE?
$4.95. 208 pages. Publication date: November 1975
ISBN 0−917616−02−2
Library of Congress No. 75−32951
Contributors: George J. Benston, Karl Brunner, Dwight M. Jaffe, Omotunde
E. G. Johnson, Edward J. Kane, Thomas Mayer, Allan H. Meltzer

NATIONAL SECURITY IN THE 1980s: FROM
WEAKNESS TO STRENGTH
$8.95 (paper). 524 pages. Publication date: May 1980
ISBN 0−917616−38−3
Library of Congress No. 80−80648
$19.95 (cloth). 524 pages. Publication date: August 1980
ISBN 0−87855−412−2. Available through Transaction Books,
Rutgers−The State University, New Brunswick, NJ 08903
Contributors: Kenneth L. Adelman, Richard R. Burt, Miles M. Costick,
Robert F. Ellsworth, Fred Charles Iklé, Geoffrey T. H. Kemp, Edward
N. Luttwak, Charles Burton Marshall, Paul H. Nitze, Sam Nunn,
Henry S. Rowen, Leonard Sullivan, Jr., W. Scott Thompson, William
R. Van Cleave, Francis J. West, Jr., Albert Wohlstetter, Elmo R.
Zumwalt, Jr.

NEW DIRECTIONS IN PUBLIC HEALTH CARE: A PRESCRIPTION
FOR THE 1980s
$6.95 (paper). 290 pages. Publication date: May 1976;
3d ed. rev., 1980
ISBN 0−917616−37−5
Library of Congress No. 79−92868
$16.95 (cloth). 290 pages. Publication date: April 1980
ISBN 0−87855−394−0. Available through Transaction Books,
Rutgers−The State University, New Brunswick, NJ 08903
Contributors: Alain Enthoven, W. Philip Gramm, Leon R. Kass, Keith B.
Leffler, Cotton M. Lindsay, Jack A. Meyer, Charles E. Phelps,
Thomas C. Schelling, Harry Schwartz, Arthur Seldon, David A.
Stockman, Lewis Thomas

OPTIONS FOR U.S. ENERGY POLICY
$6.95. 317 pages. Publication date: September 1977
ISBN 0−917616−20−0
Library of Congress No. 77−89094
Contributors: Albert Carnesale, Stanley M. Greenfield, Fred S. Hoffman,
Edward J. Mitchell, William R. Moffat, Richard Nehring, Robert S.
Pindyck, Norman C. Rasmussen, David J. Rose, Henry S. Rowen,
James L. Sweeney, Arthur W. Wright

PARENTS, TEACHERS, AND CHILDREN: PROSPECTS FOR CHOICE
IN AMERICAN EDUCATION
>$5.95. 336 pages. Publication date: June 1977
>ISBN 0−917616−18−9
>Library of Congress No. 77−79164

Contributors: James S. Coleman, John E. Coons, William H. Cornog, Denis
>P. Doyle, E. Babette Edwards, Nathan Glazer, Andrew M. Greeley,
>R. Kent Greenawalt, Marvin Lazerson, William C. McCready,
>Michael Novak, John P. O'Dwyer, Robert Singleton, Thomas Sowell,
>Stephen D. Sugarman, Richard E. Wagner

POLITICS AND THE OVAL OFFICE: TOWARDS
PRESIDENTIAL GOVERNANCE
>$7.95 (paper). 332 pages. Publication date: February 1981
>ISBN 0−917616−40−5
>Library of Congress No. 80−69617
>$18.95 (cloth). 300 pages. Publication date: April 1981
>ISBN 0−87855−428−9. Available through Transaction Books,
>Rutgers−The State University, New Brunswick, NJ 08903

Contributors: Richard K. Betts, Jack Citrin, Eric L. Davis, Robert M.
>Entman, Robert E. Hall, Hugh Heclo, Everett Carll Ladd, Jr., Arnold
>J. Meltsner, Charles Peters, Robert S. Pindyck, Francis E. Rourke,
>Martin M. Shapiro, Peter L. Szanton

THE POLITICS OF PLANNING: A REVIEW AND CRITIQUE OF
CENTRALIZED ECONOMIC PLANNING
>$5.95. 367 pages. Publication date: March 1976
>ISBN 0−917616−05−7
>Library of Congress No. 76−7714

Contributors: B. Bruce-Briggs, James Buchanan, A. Lawrence Chickering,
>Ralph Harris, Robert B. Hawkins, Jr., George W. Hilton, Richard
>Mancke, Richard Muth, Vincent Ostrom, Svetozar Pejovich, Myron
>Sharpe, John Sheahan, Herbert Stein, Gordon Tullock, Ernest van
>den Haag, Paul H. Weaver, Murray L. Weidenbaum, Hans
>Willgerodt, Peter P. Witonski

PUBLIC EMPLOYEE UNIONS: A STUDY OF THE CRISIS IN
PUBLIC SECTOR LABOR RELATIONS
>$6.95. 251 pages. Publication date: June 1976; 2d ed. rev., 1977
>ISBN 0−91716−24−3
>Library of Congress No. 76−18409

Contributors: A. Lawrence Chickering, Jack D. Douglas, Raymond D.
>Horton, Theodore W. Kheel, David Lewin, Seymour Martin Lipset,
>Harvey C. Mansfield, Jr., George Meany, Robert A. Nisbet, Daniel
>Orr, A. H. Raskin, Wes Uhlman, Harry H. Wellington, Charles B.
>Wheeler, Jr., Ralph K. Winter, Jr., Jerry Wurf

REGULATING BUSINESS: THE SEARCH FOR AN OPTIMUM
$6.95. 261 pages. Publication date: April 1978
ISBN 0—917616—27—8
Library of Congress No. 78—50678
Contributors: Chris Argyris, A. Lawrence Chickering, Penny Hollander
Feldman, Richard H. Holton, Donald P. Jacobs, Alfred E. Kahn, Paul
W. MacAvoy, Almarin Phillips, V. Kerry Smith, Paul H. Weaver,
Richard J. Zeckhauser

TARIFFS, QUOTAS, AND TRADE: THE POLITICS
OF PROTECTIONISM
$7.95. 330 pages. Publication date: February 1979
ISBN 0—917616—34—0
Library of Congress No. 78—66267
Contributors: Walter Adams, Ryan C. Amacher, Sven W. Arndt, Malcolm D.
Bale, John T. Cuddington, Alan V. Deardorff, Joel B. Dirlam, Roger
D. Hansen, H. Robert Heller, D. Gale Johnson, Robert O. Keohane,
Michael W. Keran, Rachel McCulloch, Ronald I. McKinnon, Gordon
W. Smith, Robert M. Stern, Richard James Sweeney, Robert D.
Tollison, Thomas D. Willett

THE THIRD WORLD: PREMISES OF U.S. POLICY
$7.95. 332 pages. Publication date: November 1978
ISBN 0—917616—30—8
Library of Congress No. 78—67593
Contributors: Dennis Austin, Peter T. Bauer, Max Beloff, Richard E. Bissell,
Daniel J. Elazar, S. E. Finer, Allan E. Goodman, Nathaniel H. Leff,
Seymour Martin Lipset, Edward N. Luttwak, Daniel Pipes, Wilson E.
Schmidt, Anthony Smith, W. Scott Thompson, Basil S. Yamey

UNION CONTROL OF PENSION FUNDS: WILL THE NORTH
RISE AGAIN?
$2.00. 41 pages. Publication date: July 1979
ISBN 0—917616—36—7
Library of Congress No. 78—66581
Author: George J. Borjas

WATER BANKING: HOW TO STOP WASTING
AGRICULTURAL WATER
$2.00. 56 pages. Publication date: January 1978
ISBN 0—917616—26—X
Library of Congress No. 78—50766
Authors: Sotirios Angelides, Eugene Bardach

WHAT'S NEWS: THE MEDIA IN AMERICAN SOCIETY
   $7.95 (paper). 300 pages. Publication date: June 1981
   ISBN 0—917616—41—3
   Library of Congress No. 81—81414
   $18.95 (cloth). 300 pages. Publication date: August 1981
   ISBN 0—87855—448—3. Available through Transaction Books,
   Rutgers—The State University, New Brunswick, NJ 08903
Contributors: Elie Abel, Robert L. Bartley, George Comstock, Edward Jay
   Epstein, William A. Henry III, John L. Hulteng, Theodore Peterson,
   Ithiel de Sola Pool, William E. Porter, Michael Jay Robinson, James
   N. Rosse, Benno C. Schmidt, Jr.

JOURNAL OF CONTEMPORARY STUDIES
   $15/one year, $25/two years, $4/single issue. For delivery outside the
   United States, add $2/year surface mail, $10/year airmail
A quarterly journal that is a forum for lively and readable studies on foreign
   and domestic public policy issues. Directed toward general readers as
   well as policymakers and academics, emphasizing debate and
   controversy, it publishes the highest quality articles without regard
   to political or ideological bent.